a-priori — 1) from cause to effect; from a
generalization to particular instances;
deductively
2) of such reasoning; deductive
3) based on theory instead of
experience a experiment
4) before examination a analysis

A higher form of intelligence is one which can step
out of its environment and manipulated and
make errors.

Kant says we can't know things in themselves.
Lewis doesn't seem to want to take this view.

Dictionary definitions are circular. There must be
a connection somewhere. It is via behavior

Lewis is interested in how to play the game not
how we came to do it the way we do.

A priori vs. the empirical.

MIND AND THE WORLD-ORDER

Outline of a Theory of Knowledge

Clarence Irving Lewis

Dover Publications, Inc.
New York

This Dover edition, first published in 1956, is an unabridged republication of the work originally published by
Charles Scribner's Sons in 1929. This edition incorporates
corrections by the author.

Library of Congress Catalog Card Number: 58-13364

Manufactured in the United States of America

DOVER PUBLICATIONS, INC.
180 Varick Street
New York, N. Y. 10014

TO
M. M. L.

PREFACE

The conceptions presented in this book have grown out of investigations which began in the field of exact logic and its application to mathematics. The historic connection which exists between mathematics and exact science on the one hand and conceptions of knowledge on the other, needs no emphasis: from Plato to the present day, all the major epistemological theories have been dominated by, or formulated in the light of, accompanying conceptions of mathematics. Nor is the reason for this connection far to seek; mathematics, of all human affairs, most clearly exhibits certitude and precision. If only one could come at the basis of this ideal character, the key-conceptions of epistemology might be disclosed. Thus every major discovery of theoretical mathematics, and every fundamental change in the manner in which this subject is conceived, is sure to find its sequel, sooner or later, in epistemology. Whoever has followed the developments in logistic and mathematical theory in the last quarter-century can hardly fail to be convinced that the consequences of these must be revolutionary. It has been demonstrated, with a degree of precision and finality seldom attained, that the certitude of mathematics results from its purely analytic character and its independence of any necessary connection with empirical fact. Its first premises are neither those self-evident truths of reason which inspired the continental rationalists to imitate the geometric method nor the principles of intuitive construction which, for Kant, assured a basis of application to all possible experience; they are not even empirical generalizations, as Mill and other empiricists have thought. Rather, they are definitions and postulates which exhibit abstract concepts more or less arbitrarily chosen for the purposes of the system in question. Intrinsic connection with experience is tenuous or lacking.

Concurrently, developments in physical science, such as the theory of relativity, have emphasized the fact that, here too, abstractness and systematic precision go together, and that exact deductive procedures may give rise to no corresponding certainty about empirical nature. Logical integrity and concrete applicability are quite separate matters. The empirical truth of geometry even is not assured by its absolute validity as a deductive system, nor by any intuition of space, but depends upon further considerations. The nature of these is not wholly clear, but it is evident that observation and the results of experiment must play some part in the determination of them. Thus the analytic character and abstractness of exact systems, which assure to them that kind of certainty which they have, tend to divorce them from that empirical truth which is the object of natural science and the content of our possible knowledge of nature.

We stand to-day so close to these developments that the far-reaching consequences of them may fail to impress us. It is not merely a change in one or two narrowly restricted disciplines at the farthest remove from direct study of natural phenomena: whatever affects the basic subjects, such as mathematics and physics, is bound to be reflected eventually throughout the whole of science. As a fact, this altered point of view is rapidly extending to other branches, and the independence of the conceptual and the empirical is coming to be accepted as a commonplace. It is not too much to say, I think, that it becomes a matter of doubt whether the structure science builds is solidly based upon the earth, or is a mansion in some Platonic heaven, or is only a kind of castle in the air. At least it appears that we must accept a kind of double-truth: there are the certainties, such as those of mathematics, which concern directly only what is abstract; and there are the presentations of our sense-experience to which we seek to apply them, but with a resultant empirical truth which may be no more than probable. The nature and validity of such empirical knowledge becomes the crucial issue. Traditional grounds of a priori truth have been, perforce, abandoned. What other grounds there may be; or whether without the a priori there can be any truth at all, must constitute our problem.

So far as this is the case, the outstanding questions concern the nature of our abstract concepts, such as those which figure in mathematics and theoretical physics, and the relation of them to concrete experience and to reality. Upon these points, the implications of current scientific developments are nothing like so clear. If I could hope that I read these aright, and that something is here done toward rendering them explicit and consistent, I should, of course, be more than satisfied.

The construction here attempted turns principally upon three theses: (1) A priori truth is definitive in nature and rises exclusively from the analysis of concepts. That *reality* may be delimited a priori, is due, not to forms of intuition or categories which confine the content of experience, but simply to the fact that whatever is denominated "real" must be something discriminated in experience by criteria which are antecedently determined. (2) While the delineation of concepts is a priori, the application of any particular concept to particular given experience is hypothetical; the choice of conceptual systems for such application is instrumental or pragmatic, and empirical truth is never more than probable. (3) That experience in general is such as to be capable of conceptual interpretation, requires no peculiar and metaphysical assumption about the conformity of experience to the mind or its categories; it could not conceivably be otherwise. If this last

needless repetition of an idea in different word

statement is a tautology, then at least it must be true, and the assertion of a tautology is significant if it is supposed that it can be significantly denied. The development of these three theses will be found principally in Chapters III, VIII, and XI.

Since this point of view will be likely to acquire some sort of label in any case, I shall venture to give it one myself and call it "conceptualistic pragmatism." Without the earlier conceptions of Peirce, James, and Dewey—especially Peirce—it would probably not have been developed. But these more orthodox pragmatists should not, of course, be made responsible for this view as a whole nor, particularly, for the doctrine of a priori truth which is included.

In writing the book, I encountered a considerable difficulty of exposition: with whatever one of its theses I should begin, the others would be more or less anticipated. In view of this difficulty, I have endeavored to keep the presentation as compact and swift as was compatible with clearness and proper emphasis. Controversial issues have been neglected except so far as discussion of them would contribute to the main development. And matters which lay to one side of the central theme but were still too important to be omitted altogether, have been covered briefly in appendices.

To the graduate students in my seminary in the theory of knowledge in the last six years, my thanks are due for their critical discussion of these views, which have served both to bring out crucial points and to clarify my own conceptions. Even more important help of this sort came from discussion with my colleagues of the Department of Philosophy in the University of California in the summer of 1926. To the officers of the Philosophical Union there and of the University of California Press, I am indebted for permission to use again in these pages the materials which entered into the Howison Lecture for 1926, "The Pragmatic Element in Knowledge." I am likewise indebted to the editors of the *Journal of Philosophy* for permission to reprint brief excerpts from two articles, "The Structure of Logic and Its Relation to Other Systems," and "A Pragmatic Conception of the A Priori." My friend and colleague, Professor E. G. Boring, has given me assistance of a kind most difficult to get by his critical appraisal of an earlier draft of the first four chapters and Appendix D. If these portions still leave much to be desired, at least they have been considerably improved as a result of his suggestions. Professor S. L. Quimby, of Columbia University, has assisted me with one of the illustrations in Chapter VI. As always, a principal stimulus and source of encouragement has been the association with my colleagues of the Harvard Department.

C. I. L.

CONTENTS

xiv CONTENTS

MIND AND
THE WORLD-ORDER

CHAPTER I

INTRODUCTION

ABOUT PHILOSOPHY IN GENERAL AND META-
PHYSICS IN PARTICULAR. THE PROPER
METHOD OF PHILOSOPHY

The general character of any philosophy is
likely to be determined by its initial assumptions
and its method. When Descartes proposed to
sweep the boards clean by doubting everything
which admitted of doubt and announced the initial
criterion of certainty to be the inner light of human reason, the distinguishing characteristics of
the philosophic movement which resulted were
thereby fixed. In similar fashion, the development
from Locke to Hume is, for the most part, the
logical consequence of the doctrine that the mind
is a blank tablet on which experience writes. And
when Kant proposed to inquire, not whether science is possible, but how it is possible, and identified the possibility of science with the validity of
synthetic judgments a priori, the successive attempts of the nineteenth century to deduce the
major philosophic truths as presuppositions of
experience was foreordained.

Because method has this peculiar importance
in philosophy, I believe that the reader of any

philosophic book is entitled to know in advance what are the underlying convictions of this sort with which the writer sets out. It is right and proper that one should begin with some statement of program and method.

It is—I take it—a distinguishing character of philosophy that it is everybody's business. The man who is his own lawyer or physician, will be poorly served; but everyone both can and must be his own philosopher. He must be, because philosophy deals with ends, not means. It includes the questions, What is good? What is right? What is valid? Since finally the responsibility for his own life must rest squarely upon the shoulders of each, no one can delegate the business of answering such questions to another. Concerning the means whereby the valid ends of life may be attained, we seek expert advice. The natural sciences and the techniques to which they give rise, though they may serve some other interests also, are primarily directed to the discovery of such means. But the question of the ultimately valuable ends which shall be served, remains at once the most personal, and the most general of all questions.

And everyone *can* be his own philosopher, because in philosophy we investigate what we already know. It is not the business of philosophy, as it is of the natural sciences, to add to the sum total of phenomena with which men are acquainted. Philosophy is concerned with what is already familiar. To know in the sense of familiarity and to comprehend in clear ideas are, of course, quite different matters. Action precedes reflection and even precision of behavior commonly outruns precision of thought—fortunately for us. If it were not for this, naïve common-sense and philosophy would coincide, and there would be no problem. Just this business of bringing to clear consciousness and expressing coherently the principles which are implicitly intended in our dealing with the familiar, is the distinctively philosophic enterprise.

For instance, everybody knows the difference between right and wrong; if we had no moral sense, philosophy would not give us one. But who can state, with complete satisfaction to himself, the adequate and consistent grounds of moral judgment? Likewise, everyone knows the distinction of cogent reasoning from fallacy. The study of logic appeals to no criterion not already present in the learner's mind. That logical error is, in the last analysis some sort of inadvertance, is an indispensable assumption of the study. Even if it should be in some part an unwarranted assumption, we could not escape it, for the very business of learning through reflection or discussion presumes our logical sense as a trustworthy guide.

That the knowledge sought in ethics and in logic is, thus, something already implicit in our commerce with the familiar, has usually been recognized. But that the same is true in metaphysics, has not been equally clear. Metaphysics studies the nature of reality in general. Reality is presumably independent of any principles of ours, in a sense in which the right and the valid may not be. At least initial presumption to the contrary might be hopelessly prejudicial. Moreover, reality forever runs beyond the restricted field of familiar experience. What hope that cosmic riddles can be solved by self-interrogation! The secret which we seek may be in some field which is not yet adequately explored or even opened to investigation. Or it may be forever beyond the reach of human senses.

But it is not the business of philosophy to go adventuring beyond space and time. And so far as a true knowledge of the nature of reality depends on determining questions of phenomenal fact which are not yet settled, the philosopher has no special insight which enables him to pose as a prophet. We can do nothing but wait upon the progress of the special sciences. Or if speculate we must, at least such speculation is in no special sense the philosopher's affair. It is true that metaphysics has always been the dumping ground for problems which are only partly philosophic. Questions of the nature of life and mind, for example, are of this mixed sort. In part such issues wait upon further data from the sciences, from biology and physical-chemistry and psychology;

in part they are truly philosophic, since they turn upon questions of the fundamental criteria of classification and principles of interpretation. No amassing of scientific data can determine these.

If, for example, the extreme behaviorists in psychology deny the existence of consciousness on the ground that analysis of the "mental" must always be eventually in terms of bodily behavior, then it is the business of philosophy to correct their error, because it consists simply in a fallacy of logical analysis. The analysis of any immediately presented X must always interpret this X in terms of its constant relations to other things —to Y and Z. Such end-terms of analysis—the Y and Z—will not in general be temporal or spatial constituents of X, but may be anything which bears a constant correlation with it. It is as if one should deny the existence of colors because, for purposes of exact investigation, the colors must be defined as frequencies of vibratory motion. In general terms, if such analysis concludes by stating "X is a certain kind of Y–Z complex, hence X does not exist as a distinct reality," the error lies in overlooking a general characteristic of logical analysis—that it does not discover the "substance" or cosmic constituents of the phenomenon whose nature is analyzed but only the constant context of experience in which it will be found.

So far, then, as the divergence of psychological

theories, from behaviorism which interprets mind
in terms of physical behavior to theories of the
subconscious which assimilate much of physiolog-
ical activity to mind, represents no dispute about
experimental fact but only disparity of definition
and methodological criteria, psychology and metaphysics have a common ground. The delineation
of the fundamental concepts "mind" and "mental" is a truly philosophic enterprise. A similar
thing might be discovered in the case of other
sciences.

   Newly discovered scientific data might make
such problems of fundamental concepts and classification easier—or more difficult—but of itself it
cannot solve them because, in the nature of the
case, they are antecedent to the investigation.
Such concepts are not simply dictated by the
findings of the laboratory, or by any sort of sense-
experience. Their origin is social and historical
and represents some enduring human interest. It
is the human mind itself which brings them to
experience, though the mind does not invent them
in a vacuum or cut them from whole cloth. The
tendency to forget that initial concepts are never
merely dictated by empirical findings is precisely
what accounts for the absurd prejudice—now hap-
pily obsolescent—that science is "just the report
of facts." And this likewise helps to explain the
common failure to distinguish between those cosmological speculations which are not philosophic

at all, because they are merely guesses at what future observation or experiment may reveal, from the legitimate and necessary philosophic question of a coherent set of fundamental categories, such as "life" and "mind" and "matter," in terms of which experience may consistently and helpfully be interpreted.

It would, of course, be captious to reserve this problem of initial concepts to philosophers, even though we should remember that, since everybody is to be his own philosopher, this merely means reserving them as *general* problems. The expert in the scientific field will have his special competence with respect to them; but they are not his exclusive property, because they are to be resolved as much by criticism and reflection as by empirical investigation. Conversely, it would be pedantic if we should forbid the philosophic student to speculate concerning undetermined scientific fact. It is even questionable to deny the caption "metaphysics" to those cosmological and ontological problems which have this partly speculative and partly critical or reflective character. Historically their title to the name is fairly good. All I wish to point out is that there is a real distinction here between the speculative and the reflective elements; that this distinction coincides with a difference in the method by which resolution of the problem is to be sought; and that it is only the reflective element in such "metaphysical" problems which coincides in its nature and in the method of its solution with the problems of ethics and logic.

With this explanation, I hope I shall cause no confusion if I say that it is only so far as they are thus critical and reflective that the problems of ontology and cosmology are truly philosophic; and that metaphysics as a philosophic discipline is concerned with the nature of the real only so far as that problem is amenable to the reflective method and does not trench upon the field where only scientific investigation can achieve success. There are such reflective problems within any special science, and these may be said to constitute the philosophy of that science. There are also those problems of initial principle and criteria which are common to all the sciences and to the general business of life. These last are the problems of philosophy proper.

There is another sense in which metaphysics has often been speculative and departed from its proper philosophic business and method; that is, not by seeking to anticipate the science of the future, but through attempting by sheer force of rational reflection to transcend experience altogether. Dogmatism is out of fashion since Kant.* But

---

*Perhaps I should say, "*has been* out of fashion," since just now we are being treated to various new forms of dogmatism. But this, I take it, comes partly as a counsel of despair, and partly it represents a reaction against the often exaggerated claims of "idealism" and post-Kantian "criticism" to be able to proceed a priori without reference to particular results of the empirical sciences.

that philosophic legerdemain which, with only experience for its datum, would condemn this experience to the status of appearance and disclose a reality more edifying, is still with us. The motives of this attitude are, indeed, ingrained in human nature, and I am reluctant to lay hands on that idealism which has played the rôle of Father Parmenides to all the present generation of philosophers. But at least we must observe that such metaphysics turns away from one type of problem which is real and soluble to another which may not be. Even if all experience be appearance, and all every-day thought and truth infected with contradiction, at least it must be admitted that some appearances are better than others. The mundane distinction of real and unreal *within* experience has its importance and calls for formulation of its criteria. It may be that Reality, with a capital *R*, the concrete-universal Reality which transcends all particular phenomena and underlies them, is a kind of philosophical *ignis fatuus*. Perhaps the idea of "whole" applies only *within* experience, and no whole can validly be conceived except such as stands in contrast with something else and has concrete bounds. Perhaps the whole of Reality is, as Kant thought, an inevitable idea but also a necessarily empty one, to remind us forever of the more which is to be learned and connected with our previous knowledge. But whether this be so or not, there is the less ambitious and more important problem of determining the criteria by which the adjective "real" is correctly applied—the problem of the *abstract* universal. And if any be inclined to think that this question is too simple or too meager for a philosophic discipline, I shall hope to indicate his error.

A metaphysics which takes this as its problem will remain strictly within the reflective method. It will seek to determine the nature of the real, as ethics seeks to determine the good, and logic, the valid, purely by critical consideration of what does not transcend ordinary experience. That is, it will seek to *define* "reality," not to triangulate the universe. It will be concerned with the formulation of principles, but of principles already immanent in intelligent practice. A person with no sense of reality (other-worldly philosophers, for example) will not acquire one by the study of metaphysics. And by no possibility can such investigation reveal reality as something esoteric and edifying and transcendent of ordinary experience. Any metaphysics which portrays reality as something strangely unfamiliar or beyond the ordinary grasp, stamps itself as thaumaturgy, and is false upon the face of it.

The problem of a correctly conceived metaphysics, like the problem of ethics and of logic, is one to be resolved by attaining to clear and cogent self-consciousness. As it turns out, the problem of metaphysics is "the problem of the cate-

The supposed working of a miracle

gories."* The reason for this lies in a curious complexity of the meaning of "reality." Logical validity is at bottom of one single type. And perhaps the good and the right are relatively simple in their ultimate nature. But the adjective "real" is systematically ambiguous and can have a single meaning only in a special sense. The ascription of reality to the content of any particular experience is always elliptical: some qualification — material reality, psychic reality, mathematical reality—is always understood. And whatever is real in one such sense will be unreal in others. Conversely, every given content of experience is a reality of some sort or other; so that the problem of distinguishing real from unreal, the principles of which metaphysics seeks to formulate, is always a problem of right understanding, of referring the given experience to its proper category. The mirage, for example, though not real trees and water, is a real state of atmosphere and light; to relegate it to the limbo of nothingness would be to obliterate a genuine item of the objective world. A dream is illusory because the dreamer takes its images for physical things; but to the psychologist, interested in the scientific study of the mental, just these experienced images, occurring in just this context of other circumstance, constitute a reality to be embraced

---

*A more logical terminology would qualify this as the "categories of reality," and would distinguish these from the "categories of of value."

under law and having its own indisputable place in the realm of fact. The content of every experience is real when it is correctly understood, and is that kind of reality which it is then interpreted to be. Metaphysics is concerned to reveal just that set of major classifications of phenomena, and just those precise criteria of valid understanding, by which the whole array of given experience may be set in order and each item (ideally) assigned its intelligible and unambiguous place.

So understood, the principles of the categories, which metaphysics seeks, stand, on the one side, in close relation to experience and can not meaningfully transcend it. But on the other side—or in a different sense—they stand above or before experience, and are definitive or prescriptive, and hence a priori.

Whatever principles apply to experience must be phrased in terms of experience. The clues to the categorial* interpretation—the correct understanding—of any presentation of sense must be empirical clues. If they are not contained within that segment of experience which constitutes the phenomenon itself, then they must be discoverable in its relation to other empirical fact. If the dream or illusion is not betrayed by internal evidence, then its true nature must be disclosed by the conjunction with what precedes or

---

* "Categorial" is used throughout with the meaning "pertaining to the categories." This avoids possible confusion wiih "categorical," meaning specifically "unconditional, not hypothetical."

follows. But while the distinguishing marks of reality of any particular sort are thus experimental, the principles by which the interpretation or classification is made are prior to the experience in question. It is only because the mind is prepared to judge it real or unreal according as it bears or fails to bear certain marks, that interpretation of the given is possible at all, and that experience can be understood.

It is through reflective examination of experience (more particularly of our own part in it or attitude toward it) that we may correctly formulate these principles of the categories, since they are implicit in our practical dealings with the empirically given. But they are not empirical generalizations in the sense that some later experience may prove an exception and thus invalidate them. They formulate an attitude of interpretation or discrimination by which what would be exceptional is at once thrown out of court. For example, no experience of the physical can fail to bear those marks the absence of which would bar the given content of experience from interpretation as physical reality. The formulation of our deliberately taken, and consistently adhered to, attitude of interpretation constitutes a categorial *definition* of "the physical." Such a categorial definitive principle forbids nothing in the way of experience; it prohibits neither illusion nor senseless dream. Thus such principles are not material truths: they can be a priori—knowable with certainty in advance of experience—precisely because they impose no limitation upon the given but, as principles of interpretation, nevertheless condition it as a constituent of *reality*. It will be the thesis of a later chapter that the a priori has in general this same character of definitive principle, which does not limit the content of the given. We shall find in this nature of the a priori the solution of many traditional problems of the theory of knowledge.

So conceived, the principles which formulate criteria of the real, in its various types, are a priori in precisely the same sense as are the canons of ethics and of logic. Experience does not itself determine what is good or bad, or the nature of goodness, nor does it determine what is valid or invalid, or the nature of logical validity. Equally it does not determine what is real or unreal (in any particular sense), or the nature of reality. Experience does not categorize itself. The criteria of interpretation are of the mind; they are imposed upon the given by our active attitude.

The main business of a sound metaphysics is, thus, with the problem of the categories; the formulation of the criteria of reality, in its various types. It is to the shame of philosophy that these problems, which by their nature must be capable of precise solution since they require only persistent regard for fact and self-conscious examination of our own grounds of judgment, have been so generally neglected. Just this common disregard of verifiable fact and mundane criteria of the real is largely responsible for that quagmire of incertitude and welter of the irrelevant and vague which at present bears the name of metaphysics. The problems of the categories admit of as much real progress as those of logic; in fact, they are problems of the same general type. We may congratulate ourselves, I think, that a growing interest in such study, in this reflective or phenomenalistic or critical spirit, is one of the characteristic of the present period in philosophy.*

The definition of the real in general, and the picturing of reality as a whole, are subordinate matters; and perhaps, as has been suggested, the second of these is not possible. The word "real" has a single meaning, of course, in the same sense that "useful" or any other such elliptical term has a single meaning. Nothing is useful for every purpose, and perhaps everything is useful for some purpose. A definition of "useful" *in general* would not divide things into two classes, the useful and the useless. Nor could we arrive at such a definition by attempting to collect all useful things into a class and remark their common characters, since we should probably have everything in the class

---

*I have in mind, as examples, Whitehead's "Concept of Nature" and "Principles of Natural Knowledge," Russell's "Analysis of Mind," and Broad's "Scientific Thought."

and nothing outside it to represent the useless. Instead, we should first have to consider the different types of usefulness or of useful things and then discover, if possible, what it is that characterizes the useful as contrasted with the useless in all these different cases. We should find, of course, that it was not some sense-quality but a relation to an end which was the universal mark of usefulness. Similarly, to arrive at a general definition of "the real" it would not do to lump together all sorts of realities in one class and seek directly for their common character. Everything in this class would be at once real, in some category, and unreal in others. And nothing would be left outside it. The subject of our generalization must be, instead, the distinction real-unreal in all the different categories. What definition of reality in general we might thus arrive at, we need not pause to inquire. Obviously it would be found to embrace some relation to empirical givenness in general or to our interpreting attitude, or to something involving both of these, rather than any particular and distinguishing empirical characteristics.

That in any case a successful definition of the real in general would not carry us far in any cosmological attempt to plumb the deeps of the universe, is evident from the fact that it would delimit reality in intension only, and would leave quite undetermined the particular content of reality *in extenso*. The total picture of reality can be drawn only when the last experience of the last man, and the final facts of science, are summed up. Why cosmology in this sense should be supposed to be the business of the philosopher—or of anyone else—I cannot see. In the nature of the case, it must be a coöperative enterprise, and presumably one that is always incomplete.

What we have here seen concerning the significance of "the real" will have its importance for certain topics discussed in later chapters. But our immediate interest in it lies in the fact that it brings metaphysics—which threatened to prove an exception—back into line with other branches of philosophy with respect to the method by which it should be pursued. It is only in and through the general course of human experience that we have a content for our philosophic thinking, and the significance of philosophic truth lies always in its application to experience. But it is experience from a certain point of view, or a certain aspect of it, with which we are concerned. Ethics cannot tell us how much of life is good, what particular sins are committed, or what proportion of men are moral; nor does metaphysics describe the course of the universe or determine the extent and the particulars of the real. It is the logical essence of goodness, the canons of validity, the criteria of the beautiful, and likewise, the principles of the distinction of real from unreal, that philosophy may hope to formulate. These criteria and principles, the mind itself brings to experience in its interpretation, its discriminations, and its evaluation of what is given. Thus philosophy is, so to speak, the mind's own study of itself in action; and the method of it is simply reflective. It seeks to formulate explicitly what from the beginning is our own creation and possession.

However, I should not like to appear to defend the notion that such analysis is a simple matter or that it requires only to express in precise terms the principles of common-sense. As has often enough been emphasized, common-sense is itself a naïve metaphysics and one which frequently breaks down on examination. Just as naïve morality may become confused before the dialectical attack, so common-sense categories of reality fail in crucial cases to meet the tests of consistency and accord with intelligent practice. It is true in metaphysics, as it is in ethics and in logic, that while valid principles must be supposed somehow implicit in the ordinary intercourse of mind with reality, they are not present in the sense of being fatally adhered to. If they were, the philosophic enterprise would have no practical value. Self-consciousness may be an end in itself, but if it did not have eventual influence upon human action it would be a luxury which humanity could not afford. That we coincide in our logical sense, does not make logic a work of supererogation. No more does coincidence in our ultimate sense of reality and in our categories render metaphysical discussion nugatory. Just as the study of logic may conduce to cogency of thought, and ethics contribute to greater clarity and consistency in moral judgment, so too the elucidation of metaphysical problems may contribute to the precision and adequacy of our interpretation of the real; it may even serve, on occasion, to work improvement in the concepts of the special sciences. Philosophy cannot be merely a verbally more precise rendering of common-sense, nor a direct generalization from actual practice. Though it rises from what is implicit in experience, its procedure must be critical, not descriptive. So far as it is to be of use, it must assume the function of sharpening and correcting an interpretation which has already entered into the fabric of that experience which is its datum. Logical principles aim to replace the uncritical moral sense, ethics, our naïve morality, and metaphysics, our unreflective ontological judgments. Such an enterprise is no simple matter of formulating the obvious.

The reflective method must, or course, be dialectical—in the Socratic-Platonic, not the Hegelian, sense. It accords with the Socratic presumption that the truth which is sought is already implicit in the mind which seeks it, and needs only to be elicited and brought to clear expression. It accords, further, in the recognition that it is definitions or "essences" which are the philosophic

goal. And it likewise recognizes that the hope of
agreement between minds, to be reached by philosophic discussion, must rest upon the presumption that this accord somehow exists already.

Historically, however, the dialectical method
has been overlaid with all sorts of addenda, and
perverted by extraneous assumptions which are
fallacious. So that I should choose the name "reflective" as less liably to unwarranted interpretation. It does not follow from the dialectical method
that the basis of the accord between minds represents some universal pattern of human reason,
apart from the world of sense in which we live;
nor that the mind has access to some realm of
transcendent concepts which it recovers, of its
own powers, at the instigation of experience; nor
that agreement of minds presumes initial principles which are self-evident. It does not even follow
that the agreement which we seek is already im-
plicity complete in all respects. To all such notions there is an alternative, to account for this
agreement between minds, which is simple and
even obvious. The coincidence of our fundamental
criteria and principles is the combined result of
the similarity of human animals, and of their primal interests, and the similarities of the experience
with which they have to deal. More explicitly, it
represents one result of the interplay between
these two; the coincidence of human modes of behavior, particularly when the interests which such
behavior serves involve coöperation.

Our categories are guides to action. Those attitudes which survive the test of practice will reflect not only the nature of the active creature but the general character of the experience he confronts. Thus, indirectly, even what is a priori may not be an exclusive product of "reason," or made in Plato's heaven in utter independence of the world we live in. Moreover, the fact that man survives and prospers by his social habits serves to accentuate and perfect agreement in our basic attitudes. Our common understanding and our common world may be, in part, created in response to our need to act together and to comprehend one another. Critical discussion is but a prolongation of that effort which we make to extend the bounds of successful human coöperation. It is no more necessary to suppose that agreement in fundamental principles is completely ready-made than it is to suppose that infants must already have precisely those ideas which later they find words to express. Indeed our categories are almost as much a social product as is language, and in something like the same sense. It is only the *possibility* of agreement which must be antecedently presumed. The "human mind" is a coincidence of individual minds which partly, no doubt, must be native, but partly is itself created by the social process. Even that likeness which is native would seem to consist in capacities and tendencies to action, not in mental content or explicit modes of thought. That the categories are fundamental in such wise that the social process can neither create nor alter them, is a rationalistic prejudice without foundation. There is much which is profound and true in traditional conceptions of the a priori. But equally it should be clear that there is much in such conceptions which smacks of magic and superstitious nonsense. Particularly it is implausible that what is a priori can be rooted in a "rational nature of man" which is something miraculous and beyond the bounds of psychological analysis and genetic explanation.

It may be pointed out also that if we recognize critical reflection or dialectic as the only method which holds promise in philosophy, we do not thereby commit ourselves to the assumption that coherence or internal consistency is the only test, or a sufficient test, of philosophic truth. In philosophy, as elsewhere, consistency is only a negative test of truth; it is possible, however unlikely, to be consistently in error. Consistency would be a sufficient test only if we should suppose that there is nothing external to our logic which we must be true to. The reflective method does not take it for granted that all fact follows, Hegelian-fashion, from the logical structure of thought itself. As has been suggested, it does not even presuppose that what is a priori and of the mind—our categorial attitude of interpretation—is completely independent of the general character of experience.

It is of the essence of the dialectical or reflective method that we should recognize that proof, in philosophy, can be nothing more at bottom than persuasion. It makes no difference what the manner of presentation should be, whether deductive from initial assumptions, or inductive from example, or merely following the order dictated by clarity of exposition. If it be deductive, then the initial assumptions cannot coerce the mind. There are no propositions which are self-evident in isolation. So far as the deductive presentation hopes to convince of what was not previously believed, it must either seek out initial agreements from which it may proceed, or—as is more frequently the case—the deductively first propositions must be rendered significant and acceptable by exhibiting the cogency and general consonance with experience of their consequences. If the method be inductive from example, then the principles to be proved are implicit in the assumption that cited examples are veridical and typical and genuinely fall under the category to be investigated. There can be no Archimedean point for the philosopher. Proof, he can offer only in the sense of so connecting his theses as to exhibit their mutual support, and only through appeal to other minds to reflect upon their experience and their own attitudes and perceive that he correctly portrays them. If there be those minds which find no alternatives save certainty, apart from all appeal to prior fact, or skepticism, then to skepticism they are self-condemned. And much good may it do them! As philosophers, we have something we must be faithful to, even if that something be ourselves. If we are perverse, it is possible that our philosophy will consist of lies.

Already this introductory analysis of method is too long. But the conception of the a priori here suggested is a novel one: a little further discussion may have its value by way of anticipating briefly what is to follow.

If Philosophy is the study of the a priori, and is thus the mind's formulation of its own active attitudes, still the attitude which is the object of such study is one taken toward the content of an experience in some sense independent of and bound to be reflected in the attitude itself. What is a priori—it will be maintained—is prior to experience in almost the same sense that purpose is. Purposes are not dictated by the content of the given; they are our own. Yet purposes must take their shape and have their realization in terms of experience; the content of the given is not irrelevant to them. And purposes which can find no application will disappear. In somewhat the same fashion what is a priori and of the mind is prior to the content of the given, yet in another sense not altogether independent of experience in general.

It is an error common to rationalism and to

pure empiricism that both attempt an impossible separation of something called the mind from something else called experience. Likewise both treat of knowledge as if it were a relation of the individual mind to external object in such wise that the existence of other minds is irrelevant; they do not sufficiently recognize the sense in which our truth is social. Traditional rationalism,* observing that any principles which should serve as ultimate criterion or determine categorial interpretation must be prior to and independent of the experience to which it applies, has supposed that such principles must be innate and so discoverable by some sort of direct inspection. If a canon of their truth is requisite, this must be supplied by something of a higher order than experience, such as self-evidence or the natural light of reason. The mistakes of this point of view are two. In the first place, it assumes that mind is immediate to itself in a sense in which the object of experience is not. But what other means have we of discovering the mind save that same experience in which also external objects are presented? And if the object transcends the experience of it, is not this equally true of the mind? The single experience exhausts the reality of neither. Any particular experience is a whole within which that part or aspect which represents the legislative or

---

*The rationalism (if that term is justified) of post-Kantian idealism rests upon different assumptions and proceeds by different methods. It is not here in point.

categorial activity of mind and that which is given content, independent of the mind's interpretation, are separable only by analysis. We have no higher faculty or more esoteric experience through which the mind discovers itself. And second, rationalism fallaciously assumes that what is prior to, or legislative for, the particular experience must be likewise independent of experience in general. Though categorial principle must, in the nature of the case, be prior to the particular experience, it nevertheless represents an attitude which the mind has taken in the light of past experience as a whole, and one which would even be susceptible of change if confronted with some pervasive alteration in the general character of what is presented. An example here may be of service: It is an a priori principle that physical things must have mass. By this criterion, they are distinguished from mirror-images and illusion. Since this is so, no particular experience could upset this principle, because any experience in which it should be violated would be repudiated as non-veridical or "not correctly understood." That is, by the principle itself, the phenomenon must be referred to some other category than the physical. In that sense, the truth of the principle is independent of the particular phenomenon. But a world in which we should experience phenomena having a persistence and independence not characteristic of imagination, and a coherence not characteristic of our dreams, but things which would still not be amenable to any gravitational generalizations, is entirely conceivable. In such a world our a priori principle would not be rendered false—since it is definitive of the physical; but the category "physical" might well be useless. (Incidentally it may be pointed out that this criterion of the physical is a historical and social product. Aristotle and the ancients knew it not.)

Though we bring the a priori principle, as criterion, to any particular experience, yet this legislative attitude of mind is clearly one which is taken because, our experience on the whole being what it is, this principle helps to render it intelligible, and behavior in accord with it is normally successful. The mind must bring to experience whatever serve as the criteria of interpretation— of the real, as of the right, the beautiful, and the valid. The content of experience cannot evaluate or interpret itself. Nevertheless the validity of such interpretation must reflect the character of experience in general, and meet the pragmatic test of value as a guide to action.

The fallacy of pure empiricism is the converse of that which rationalism commits. In seeking to identify the real with what is given in experience, apart from construction or interpretation by the mind, and to elicit general principles directly from the content of experience, empiricism condemns itself to a vicious circle. Experience as it comes to us contains not only the real but all the content of illusion, dream, hallucination, and misapprehension. When the empiricist supposes that laws or principles can be derived simply by generalization from experience, he *means* to refer only to *veridical* experience, forgetting that without the criterion of legislative principle experience cannot first be sorted into veridical and illusory.

It is this vicious circle which makes inevitable the historical dénouement of empiricism in Hume's skepticism. Berkeley pointed out that the real cannot be distinguished from the unreal by any relation between the idea in the mind and an independent object, but only by some relation within experience itself. In this, of course, he is right, whether we agree with his idealism or not: mind cannot transcend itself and discover a relation of what is in experience to what is not. Berkeley then seeks to indicate our actual empirical criteria: the real in experience is distinguished (1) by that independence of the will which is exhibited in the content of perception as contrasted with imagination, (2) by the greater liveliness of perception, (3) by the interconnection of veridical perceptions according to the "laws of nature." Obviously only the last of these is sufficient in critical cases such as hallucination and errors of observation. Hume wrecks the empiricist structure when he points out that such "laws of nature" cannot be derived by generalization from experience. For this, the distinction of necessary from contingent would be requisite. The basis of this distinction is not to be found in the content of experience; it is of the mind. Generalization from experience always presumes that the categorial interpretation already has been made. Laws which characterize all experience, of real and unreal both, are non-existent, and would in any case be worthless.

It is obvious that similar considerations hold for the other problems of philosophy. The nature of the good can be learned from experience only if the content of experience be first classified into good and bad, or grades of better and worse. Such classification or grading already involves the legislative application of the same principle which is sought. In logic, principles can be elicited by generalization from examples only if cases of valid reasoning have first been segregated by some criterion. It is this criterion which the generalization is required to disclose. In esthetics, the laws of the beautiful may be derived from experience only if the criteria of beauty have first been correctly applied.

The world of experience is not given in experience: it is constructed by thought from the data of sense. This reality which everybody knows reflects the structure of human intelligence as much as it does the nature of the independently given

sensory content. It is a whole in which mind and
what is given to mind already meet and are inter-
woven. The datum of our philosophic study is not
the "buzzing, blooming confusion" on which the
infant first opens his eyes, not the thin experience
of immediate sensation, but the thick experience
of every-day life.

This experience of *reality* exists only because
the mind of man takes attitudes and makes interpretations. The buzzing, blooming confusion
could not become reality for an oyster. A purely
passive consciousness, if such can be conceived,
would find no use for the concept of reality, because it would find none for the idea of the *un*real;
because it would take no attitude that could be
balked, and make no interpretation which conceivably could be mistaken.

On the other hand, we can discover mind and
its principles only by analysis in this experience
which we have. We cannot, unless dogmatically,
construct experience from a hypothetical and
transcendent mind working upon a material which
likewise is something beyond experience. We can
only discover mind and what is independently
given to it by an analysis within experience itself.
And it is only because mind has entered into the
structure of the real world which we know and the
experience of everyday, that analysis, or *any* attempted knowledge, may discover it.

In finding thus that the principles and criteria

which philosophy seeks to formulate must be significant at once of experience and of our active attitudes, the reflective method inevitably is pragmatic also. Concepts and principles reveal themselves as instruments of interpretation; their meaning lies in the empirical consequences of the active attitude. The categories are ways of dealing with what is given to the mind, and if they had no practical consequences, the mind would never use them. Since philosophy seeks to formulate what is implicit in mind's every-day interpretations, we may test the significance of any philosophic principle, and pave the way for determining its truth, if we ask: How would experience be different if this should be correct than if it should be false? or, How differently should we orient ourselves to experience and deal with it if this should be so than if it should be not so?

Metaphysical issues which supposedly concern what is transcendent of experience altogether, must inevitably turn out to be issues wrongly taken. For example, if one say—as Mr. Broad has recently said*—that scientific reality of perduring electrons or what not, is something which at best is probable only, since it does not enter our direct experience of "sensa," then I think we may justly challenge him as Berkeley challenged Locke: Why not a world of sensa with *nothing* behind them? What makes "scientific reality" even

---

*"Scientific Thought," see esp. pp. 268 *ff.*

probable if direct experience could be the same without its existence? Unless the modern physicist hopelessly deludes himself, does not the existence of electrons mean something verifiable in the laboratory? Otherwise, would he not be constrained to answer any question about electrons as Laplace is reputed to have answered Napoleon's question about God—that he had no need of this hypothesis? But if the existence or non-existence of "scientific reality" makes certain verifiable differences in experience, then these empirical criteria are the marks of the kind of reality which can be predicated of it. They are the "cash-value" of the category; they constitute what it means to be real in just the way that electrons can be real. "Scientific reality" is either an interpretation of certain parts and aspects of experience or it is a noise, signifying nothing.

The totality of the possible experiences in which any interpretation would be verified—the completest possible empirical verification which is conceivable—constitutes the entire meaning which that interpretation has. A predication of reality to what transcends experience completely and in every sense, is not problematic; it is nonsense.

Perhaps another illustration may make the point more clear. Occasionally philosophers amuse themselves by suggesting that the existences of things are intermittent; that they go out when we cease to notice them and come into being again at the moment of rediscovery. The answer is not given by any question-begging reference to the independent object or to the conservation of matter. What we need to inquire is why this notion of permanent objects was ever invented. If nothing in experience would be different whether the existence of things should be intermittent or continuous, what character of experience is predicated by their "permanence"? When we have answered to such questions, we have discovered the whole meaning of "permanent existence" and nothing further, unless paradox of language, remains to be discussed. Reflection upon experience and our attitude to what is given cannot discover what is not implicitly already there—and there is nothing else which philosophic reflection can hope to disclose.

To sum up, then: The reflective method is empirical and analytic in that it recognizes experience in general as the datum of philosophy. But it is not empirical in the sense of taking this experience to coincide with data of sense which are merely given to the mind. Nor is it analytic in the sense of supposing that experience is complete and ready-made.

Rather, it finds that philosophy is particularly concerned with that part or aspect of experience which the mind contributes by its attitude of interpretation. In thus recognizing that the principles which are sought are in some sense a priori, it is rationalistic.

It is not rationalistic, however, in the sense of presuming the mind as a Procrustean bed into which experience is forced, or as an initial datum which can be assumed or its findings known apart from sense-experience. Nor does it presume the "rational human mind" as something completely identical in and native to all human beings, or as a transcendent entity which, even if it lived in some other world of sense, would still possess precisely the same categories and pattern of intelligence.

The reflective method is pragmatic in the same sense that it is empirical and analytic. It supposes that the categories and principles which it seeks must already be implicit in human experience and human attitude. The significance of such fundamental conceptions must always be practical because thought and action are continuous, and because no other origin of them can be plausible than an origin which reflects their bearing on experience. Further, it claims for philosophy itself the pragmatic sanction that reflection is but a further stretch of that critical examination of our own constructions and interpretations by which we free them from inconsistency and render them more useful. Since experience is not just given but is in part a product of the mind, philosophy itself may work some alteration of the active attitude by which the given in experience is met and moulded. But the reflective method is not, or need not be, pragmatic in the sense of supposing, as current pragmatism sometimes seems to do, that the categories of biology and psychophysics have some peculiar advantage for the interpretation of the practical attitudes of thought.

The reflective method necessarily leads to the repudiation of any reality supposed to be transcendent of experience altogether. A true philosophic interpretation must always follow the clues of the practical reasons for our predications. A philosophy which relegates any object of human thought to the transcendent, is false to the human interests which have created that thought, and to the experience which gives it meaning. Philosophic truth, like knowledge in general, is about experience, and not about something strangely beyond the ken of man, open only to the seer and the prophet. We all know the nature of life and of the real, though only with exquisite care can we tell the truth about them.

Chapter II

THE GIVEN ELEMENT IN EXPERIENCE

The presumption from which we set out is that it is the business of philosophy to analyze and interpret our common experience, and by reflection, to bring to clear and cogent expression those principles which are implicit because they are brought to experience by the mind itself. Philosophy is the study of the a priori. It seeks to reveal those categorial criteria which the mind applies to what is given to it, and by correct delineation of those criteria to define the good, the right, the valid, and the real.

The attempt, however, so to approach the problems of philosophy leads at once to outstanding questions concerning the nature of knowledge, solution of which seems prerequisite. The distinction between what is a priori and what is not, is here presumed; as is also the correlative distinction between mind, or what mind brings to experience, and some other element, presumably independent of the mind's activity and responsible for other parts or aspects of experience. Have we a right to these distinctions? What are the grounds on which they can be drawn? How, in these terms,

are knowledge and experience constituted? It is
with such questions that the remainder of this book
is concerned.

Its principal theses are the following: (1) The
two elements to be distinguished in knowledge are
the concept, which is the product of the activity
of thought, and the sensuously given, which is independent of such activity. (2) The concept gives
rise to the a priori; all a priori truth is definitive,
or explicative of concepts. (3) The pure concept
and the content of the given are mutually independent; neither limits the other. (4) Empirical
truth, or knowledge of the objective, arises
through conceptual interpretation of the given.
(5) The empirical object, denoted by a concept,
is never a momentarily given as such, but is some
temporally-extended pattern of actual and possible experience. (6) Hence the assignment of any
concept to the momentarily given (which is characteristic of perceptual knowledge) is essentially
predictive and only partially verified. There is no
knowledge merely by direct awareness. (7) Actual
experience can never be exhaustive of that pattern, projected in the interpretation of the given,
which constitutes the real object. Hence all empirical knowledge is probable only. (8) The mutual independence of the concept and the given,
and the merely probable character of empirical
truth, are entirely compatible with the validity of
cognition. The problem of the "deduction of the

categories" can be met without any metaphysical assumption of a preëstablished amenability to categorial order in what is independent of the mind. (9) More explicitly, any conceivable experience will be such that it can be subsumed under concepts, and also such that predictive judgments which are genuinely probable will hold of it.

This chapter and the next are devoted to the distinction of the two elements in experience, and to the defense of this distinction from various common misinterpretations.

There are, in our cognitive experience, two elements; the immediate data, such as those of sense, which are presented or given to the mind, and a form, construction, or interpretation, which represents the activity of thought. Recognition of this fact is one of the oldest and most universal of philosophic insights. However, the manner in which these elements, and their relation to one another, are conceived, varies in the widest possible manner, and divergence on this point marks a principal distinction amongst theories of knowledge. As a result, even the most general attempt to designate these two elements—as by the terms used above—is likely to be objected to. Nevertheless this distinction, in some terms or other, is admitted to a place in almost every philosophy. To suppress it altogether, would be to betray obvious and fundamental characteristics of experience. If

there be no datum given to the mind, then knowledge must be contentless and arbitrary; there
would be nothing which it must be true to. And
if there be no interpretation or construction which
the mind itself imposes, then thought is rendered
superfluous, the possibility of error becomes inexplicable, and the distinction of true and false is
in danger of becoming meaningless. If the significance of knowledge should lie in the data of
sense alone, without interpretation, then this significance would be assured by the mere presence
of such data to the mind, and every cognitive experience must be veracious.

There are, to be sure, theories which emphasize
one of these two elements almost to the exclusion
of the other. Such theories are of both sorts—
those which emphasize what is given and those
which emphasize the active mind. Immediacy is
thus emphasized by the mystics generally, by
Bergson, and by the American new-realists—to
mention only those examples which will come at
once to the reader's mind. The idealists, on the
other hand (empirical idealists, like Berkeley, ex-
cepted), may seem to include the content as well
as the form of knowledge in what the activity of
thought creates. However, a closer examination of
such theories, of both sorts, will usually reveal that
the distinction is still recognized; it is merely ob-
scured by preoccupation with other issues.

In theories of the first type, which identify

knowledge with some state of pure immediacy, the description or analysis of the cognitive experience is subordinated to the attempt to establish the superior value of some one type of experience as compared with others. The mystic, for example, values preëminently that experience which he interprets as being the immediate presence to, and coalescence with, his own mind of the transcendent object which he seeks. But he will readily grant the presence and determining character of conceptual interpretation in ordinary non-mystical experience. Only he condemns the object of such experience as illusion or mere appearance. The world of every-day is not, for him, ultimately real; or at least its true nature is not revealed in ordinary experience. The moment of true insight is that in which the distinctions and relations which discursive thought creates are shorn away and reality stands forth, in luminous immediacy, as it truly is. Now all men restrict the word "knowledge" to the apprehension of the *real*. Hence the mystic's metaphysical conception, which leads him to use the word "real" differently than other men, likewise moves him to restrict the term "knowledge" to the peculiar experience in which this "reality" is apprehended. That in the ordinary experience which *other* men trust as truly cognitive, the element of interpretation is present, he fully recognizes and even insists upon. He recognizes also that this conceptual element represents something induced by the construction or attitude of the mind itself.*

The reason why Bergson identifies the truest knowledge with "intuition" is similarly rooted in metaphysical theory and not in any divergent reading of our ordinary experience. For him, the ultimate reality is life, or the inwardly grasped "real duration." For each mind, this is something which is immediate, in his own case, and is to be apprehended in its other manifestations only by empathy or *einfühlung*. The world of science and common sense Bergson recognizes to be construction or interpretation which the mind imposes upon the data of immediacy. Also, he is explicit that this construction is dominated by interests of action and of social coöperation. But the space-world which results from such interpretation, he regards as not an ultimate reality; hence the cognitive experience which includes this interpretive element is not a theoretically adequate knowledge. In short, with Bergson as with the mystics, identification of knowledge with intuitive apprehension

---

*Often the mystic, inheriting his terminology from Aristotle, interprets the attitude of mind in every-day experience as passivity rather than activity, reserving the latter term for his own kind of absorbed concentration. For him, the interpretation which characterizes ordinary thought is at the behest of enslaving "passions." That such construction is significant of ordinary and mundane interests, he fully understands. But such interests are, for him, to be avoided and quelled. Here again, his use of terms, reversing the usual one, is governed by metaphysical and ethical preoccupation which is irrelevant to the just analysis of mundane experience. He reserves the laudatory term "active" for the ethical attitude which he seeks to inculcate.

It is thus that in philosophy we give over the accurate report of fact to quarrel for exclusive possession of honorific terms.

of the immediate reflects no basic difference in the analysis of ordinary experience but rather a difference in the denotation given to the phrase "true knowledge" because of a metaphysical theory which denies ultimate reality to what is cognized by science and common sense.

Of all the current theories in which knowledge is portrayed in terms of receptivity alone, the new realism would seem to be the only one in which this predilection for the given does not reflect a metaphysical preoccupation. Here the activity of thought (or attention) is represented as selective only; it may determine what is included in or excluded from perception, but it does not supplement or modify the given data. Mind, so far as mind is just now a knowing of this object, and the object, so far as it is just now known by this mind, are represented as coinciding.*

Any such theory must reveal its inadequacy by failure to account satisfactorily for the possibility of error. So far as knowledge is pure receptivity, that with which the mind coincides in cognition must in all cases have the same objectivity. Or at least, no ground is here provided for the distinction between veridical and illusory apprehension. Thus we have the question whether mirror-images are truly located in the space to which they are

*It would seem that most, or all, of those who coöperated in the volume, "The New Realism," have since abandoned or considerably modified the positions there taken, so that what is here said may be a discussion of nobody's present conception. But the theory is of interest on its own account.

referred, the difficulty about the star seen now, though it may have ceased to send its light-rays from that point a thousand years ago, and a number of like problems. The new realist may go the whole length, as Mr. Holt did, and hold that contradictories and incompatibles can be objectively real.* But in that case he ceases, for most of us to be plausible. Or he may, as Mr. Montague did, introduce some theory of a plurality of causes which can produce the same brain-state, and explain error through the ambiguity thus introduced. But it would appear that, apart from any question about indentifying brain-states with perceptions, or any question about the propriety of the element of representationalism thus introduced into what is otherwise a purely "presentation" theory of knowledge, it will be impossible, on this account, to escape the admission of an element of interpretation in cognition. So long as the content of knowledge merely coincides with what is presented, knowledge must still be always veridical, because the brain-state (or perception) will contain only so much of the plurality of causes which may give rise to it as will in all cases coincide. The brain-state can be identical only with what is identical in the plurality of its causes —unless we wish to abandon the principle that things identical with the same thing are identical with each other. If a single brain-state, or modi-

* "The Concept of Consciousness," 1914.

fication of perceptive consciousness, is taken as meaning one thing when its veridical significance is of another, then some interpretation which goes beyond the content of this given state itself is the only conceivable basis of the error.

Furthermore, it is impossible to escape the fact that knowledge has, in some fashion and to some degree, the significance of *prediction*. As Berkeley put it, one idea or presentation is sign of another which is to be expected. So far as this is true, the cognitive significance may *attach to* the data of sense but cannot simply *coincide with* such given data. To know is to find what is presented significant of what is not, just now, so presented. It is because Berkeley failed to follow out the implications of his own theory and to examine the validity of this relation, by thought, of what is given to what is not thus immediate, that the way lay open to Hume's skepticism.

Failure to recognize and consider this element of construction or interpretation by the mind, will wreck any theory of knowledge. Failure to acknowledge its existence will make it impossible to account for error. And failure to find the ground of its validity will lead inevitably to skepticism; if not to skepticism ordinarily so-called, at least to that skepticism of every-day cognition which is involved in immediacy theories such as mysticism.

With theories of the opposite sort, which emphasize the constructive mind and seem to exclude any independent given such as sense-data, the explanation may similarly be found in a metaphysical preoccupation. This is obviously the case with Plato.* The data of sense are, for him, not relevant to true knowledge because only the transcendent ideas are fully real. In that mixed sort of apprehension by which the physical external world is grasped, the place of sense-data, on his account, is evident.

Post-Kantian idealism also may seem to contend for the identification of knowledge with what the activity of thought alone produces. But idealism can hardly mean to deny that the fact of my seeing at this moment a sheet of white paper instead of a green tree is a datum which it is beyond the power of my thought to alter. It can hardly mean to deny the given in every sense. As a fact, idealists of this school seldom speak directly to the question: "Does the activity of thinking create what would ordinarily be called the data of sense?" This question may not seem to them important because their metaphysical thesis does not turn upon it, but rather upon two somewhat different issues: "Can there be any apprehension of a *real object* without the active construction of the mind?" and, "Is the existence of sense-data, as such, evidence of a reality which is independent of mind?"†

*It is not clear that Plato is activist, rather than intuitionist, in his conception of noesis, but at least sense-data have no part in this highest kind of knowledge.
†See, for example, Green: "Prolegomena to Ethics," chap. I, secs. 12 and 13.

The first of these questions is answered to their satisfaction if it can be shown that the *objectivity* of the real requires always construction by the mind. This thesis does not imply any denial that the given is independent of the activity of thought in the sense explained above. It requires only the denial that the presentation of sense-data can by itself constitute valid knowledge. That I credit this presentation, or attribute to it objectivity, is a judgment, and as such an act of thought. (It would equally be an interpretation to discredit the presentation as merely subjective). This interpretive fiat is what Fichte stresses as the positing of the "not-me." The data of sense, apart from such positing, are neither external reality nor explicit self. In immediacy, there is no separation of subject and object. The givenness of immediate data is, thus, *not* the givenness of *reality*, and is not knowledge. Hence the idealist may insist that there is no (real) object without the creative activity of thought, without in the least meaning to deny that there is a datum prior to its being posited as real, a content judged which is given to the judgment. As a fact, however, he often slights this point in his anxiety to pass on and refute the implications, contrary to his metaphysical thesis, which are frequently drawn from it.

Also it may seem to the idealist more important to point out that given data are already *in mind*

than to inquire whether such data are created by
thought. If both the data interpreted and the interpretation put upon them belong to the mind,
then the real object, as cognized, may be represented as in both its aspects mind-dependent; and
no argument to an independent reality can be
drawn from the analysis of knowledge. Thus the
idealist may fail to admit, or even to recognize
explicitly, that there are given data of experience
which, merely as such and not as objective reality
or unreality, the activity of thought can neither
create nor alter.

It is also characteristic of idealism to point out
that the moment of pure givenness is a fiction, and
its data an "unreal abstraction." There is no apprehension—he will insist—without construction;
hence the distinction of subject and object, act
and given, must be *within* thought, not between
thought and an independent something thought
about. This consideration is of more importance
for us, and will be discussed in the next chapter.
But it implies no denial of the givenness of sense-
data. It contends only that the mental state which
should be purely receptive and coincide with the
given is a fiction—an observation which is unac-
ceptable only to the mystic and other protagonists
of pure intuition. Whether there is the beginning
of a fallacious train of reasoning in this stretch-
ing of the term "thought" to cover the cognitive
experience as a whole, we need not pause to in-

quire. At least, the denial of the given is not obviously necessary to any of the characteristic theses of idealism. Indeed, an unqualified denial of this element in ordinary cognition is sufficient to put any theory beyond the pale of plausibility.

We may, then, fairly take it for granted, as something generally recognized, that there are in experience these two elements, something given and the interpretation or construction put upon it. But the very fact that the recognition of this is so general and of such long standing enforces the necessity of considering the distinction with care. Different significances have been assigned to it, both historically and in contemporary thought. Moreover, various metaphysical issues gather about it: What is the relation between the given and the real? How does mind construct or interpret? What is this mind which can interpret: does it transcend experience? If so, how can it be known? If not, how can it condition experience in general by its interpretation? Confronted with such a tangle of problems, we shall do best, I think, if first we can catch our facts. If we can identify the thing to be discussed, a certain degree of clarity will accrue simply by telling the truth about it, if we can.

There is, in all experience, that element which we are aware that we do not create by thinking and cannot, in general, displace or alter. As a first

approximation, we may designate it as "the sensuous."

At the moment, I have a fountain pen in my
hand. When I so describe this item of my present
experience, I make use of terms whose meaning
I have learned. Correlatively I abstract this item
from the total field of my present consciousness
and relate it to what is not just now present in
ways which I have learned and which reflect modes
of action which I have acquired. It might happen
that I remember my first experience of such a
thing. If so, I should find that this sort of presentation did not then mean "fountain pen" to me.
I bring to the present moment something which I
did not then bring; a relation of this to other actual and possible experiences, and a classification
of what is here presented with things which I did
not then include in the same group. This present
classification depends on that learned relation of
this experience, to other possible experience and
to my action, which the shape, size, etc., of this
object was not then a sign of. A savage in New
Guinea, lacking certain interests and habits of
action which are mine, would not so classify it.
There is, to be sure, something in the character
of this thing as a merely presented colligation of
sense-qualities which is for me the clue to this
classification or meaning; but that just this complex of qualities should be due to a "pen" character of the object is something which has been

acquired. Yet what I refer to as "the given" in this experience is, in broad terms, qualitatively no different than it would be if I were an infant or an ignorant savage.

Again, suppose my present interest to be slightly altered. I might then describe this object which is in my hand as "a cylinder" or "hard rubber" or "a poor buy." In each case the thing is somewhat differently related in my mind, and the connoted modes of my possible behavior toward it, and my further experience of it, are different. Something called "given" remains constant, but its character as sign, its classification, and its relation to other things and to action are differently taken.

In whatever terms I describe this item of my experience, I shall not convey it *merely* as given, but shall supplement this by a meaning which has to do with relations, and particularly with relation to other experiences which I regard as possible but which are not just now actual. The manner of this supplementation reflects my habitual interests and modes of activity, the nature of my mind. The infant may see it much as I do, but still it will mean to him none of these things I have described it as being, but merely "plaything" or "smooth biteable." But for any mind whatever, it will be more than what is merely given if it be noted at all. Some meaning of it also will be contained in the experience. All that comes under this broad term "meaning" (unless immediate value or the specificity of sense-quality should be included) is brought to this experience by the mind, as is evidenced by the fact that in this respect the experience is alterable to my interest and my will.

This meaning or interpretation or construction which is attached to the given is significant in two directions, connected but different. The one is the relation of this which is immediately presented to further actual and possible experience; the other is its relation of my interest and action. The relation to other experience, is something which is brought to the present by a selective memory. As applied to this present given, however, it is significant, not of the past, but of an actual or possible future, continuous with this present moment. Thus this given is set in a relation with a to-be-given or could-be-given, and this setting is an interpretation of it which the temporal process of experience may verify or prove erroneous. The other relation—of the given to present interest or attitude—connotes an interplay between the temporal process of further possible experience and my own purposes and behavior. Since I not only think but physically act, I enter into the temporal process of the future as a factor which determines, in some part, what it shall present. Thus my interpretation is predictive of my own physical behavior as forecast by my present interested attitude, and of further experience as affected by that behavior. In all those ways in which my interpretation could be phrased as predictive not of future actual but only of *possible* experience, it very likely has reference to ways of acting which I know I might adopt at will and the future experience which I *should* then expect.

My designation of this thing as "pen" reflects my purpose to write; as "cylinder" my desire to explain a problem in geometry or mechanics; as "a poor buy" my resolution to be more careful hereafter in my expenditures. These divergent purposes are anticipatory of certain different future contingencies which are expected to accrue, in each case, partly as a result of my own action.

The distinction between this element of interpretation and the given is emphasized by the fact that the latter is what remains unaltered, no matter what our interests, no matter how we think or conceive. I can apprehend this thing as pen or rubber or cylinder, but I cannot, by taking thought, discover it as paper or soft or cubical.

While we can thus isolate the element of the given by these criteria of its unalterability and its character as sensuous feel or quality, we cannot describe any particular given *as such*, because in describing it, in whatever fashion, we qualify it by bringing it under some category or other, select from it, emphasize aspects of it, and relate it in particular and avoidable ways. If there be states of pure esthesis, in violent emotion or in the presence of great art, which are unqualified by thought, even these can be conveyed—and perhaps even retained in memory—only when they have been rendered articulate by thought. So that in a sense the given is ineffable, always. It is that which remains untouched and unaltered, however it is construed by thought. Yet no one but a philosopher could for a moment deny this immediate presence in consciousness of that which no activity of thought can create or alter.

If now we have fastened upon the fact of experience which we wish to discuss as the given element in it, it is time that we proceed to clarify this conception and guard against various possible misinterpretations.

An initial difficulty may arise from ambiguity of the word "given." This term has most frequently been used in philosophy in meanings at least close to the one here intended. But on occasion it has the widely different significance of denoting those data which philosophy in general finds or takes for granted at the beginning of its study. And occasionally those who use the term in this second meaning make it carry something of methodological polemic against any notion that "the immediate" or "sense-data" are allowable categories of explanation in epistemology.

What I should have to say on this point is, in part at least, already clear from the preceding chapter. It is indeed the thick experience of the world of things, not the thin given of immediacy, which constitutes the datum for philosophic reflection. We do not see patches of color, but trees and houses; we hear, not indescribable sound, but voices and violins. What we most certainly know are objects and full-bodied facts about them which could be stated in propositions. Such initial data of object and fact set the problem in philosophy and are, in a measure, the criteria of its solution, since any philosophic theory will rightfully be rejected as inaccurate or inadequate if it does not measure up to, or account for, experience in this broad sense.

But the acceptance of such preanalytic data* as an ultimate epistemological category would, if really adhered to, put an end to all worthwhile investigation of the nature of knowledge—or to any other intellectual enterprise. What lies on the surface can be taken as ultimate only so long as there is no problem to be solved, or else no solution to be hoped for. Without analysis, there can be no advance of understanding.

The given, as here conceived, is certainly an abstraction. Unless there be such a thing as pure esthesis (and I should join with the critic in doubting this), the given never exists in isolation in any experience or state of consciousness. Any

*I borrow this useful phrase from Professor Loewenberg; see his article, "Preanalytic and Postanalytic Data," *The Journal of Philosophy*, vol. 24 (1927), pp. 5 ff.

Kantian "manifold" as a psychic datum or moment of experience, is probably a fiction, and the assumption of it as such is a methodological error. The given is *in*, not before, experience. But the condemnation of abstractions is the condemnation of thought itself. Nothing that thought can ever comprise is other than some abstraction which cannot exist in isolation. Everything mentionable is an abstraction except the concrete universal; and the concrete universal is a myth. Thought can do just two things: it can separate, by analysis, entities which in their temporal or spatial existence are not separated, and it can conjoin, by synthesis, entities which in their existence are disjoined. Only the mystic or those who conceive that man would be better off without an upper-brain, have ground for objection to analysis and abstractions. The only important question is whether this abstracted element, the "given," is genuinely to be discovered in experience. On this point I can, of course, only appeal to the reader. I shall hope that he has already identified provisionally what the word intends, and proceed upon that basis.

Assuming, however, such provisional identification, there are still ambiguities of language to be avoided. I have so far spoken of "the given" and "data of sense" as roughly synonymous, but the latter phrase has connotations which are slightly inappropriate. In the first place, "sense-data," as a psychological category, may be distinguished from other mental content by their correlation with the processes in the afferent nerves. A distinction made by the criterion of such correlation with nervous processes is open to two objections in epistemology. In the first place, the thing or mental state itself must first be accurately identifiable before such correlation can be established. If it is thus identifiable, the correlation is not essential and is, in fact, superfluous in discussions of epistemology by the method of reflection and analysis. Second, there is the more general objection that the theory of knowledge is a subject too fundamental to rest upon distinctions drawn from the particular sciences. Basic problems of category and of the general nature of knowledge are antecedent to the special sciences and cannot, therefore, legitimately depend upon their particular findings. Especially is this important as regards psychology, a valid method for which is, at the present moment, a serious problem. The manner in which my own body is known to me, the subjectivity or objectivity of pleasantness or emotional tone, the validity of the correlation between mental states which I inspect directly only in my own case (if such is the fact) and nervous processes which I can observe only in another organism; these are themselves problems which have at least an epistemological side.

Also, the particular purposes which the psychologist has in mind in making his analysis of mental states may be out of place in epistemology. "Sense-datum" may connote relation to particular sense-organs (as in the distinction between taste and odor), and hence mark a division where none can be drawn by direct inspection. Also other qualities than the strictly sensory may be as truly given; the pleasantness or fearfulness of a thing may be as un-get-overable as its brightness or loudness—that question, at least, must not be prejudiced. Hence "sense-data," defined by correlation with nervous processes, should have no place in our program. It is the brute-fact element in perception, illusion and dream (without antecedent distinction) which is intended.

However, if it be understood that the methodological connotation of psychological categories is not here in point, it will cause no confusion if I continue to refer to the "sensuous" or the "feeling" character of the given: the element in experience which is intended is difficult to designate in any terms which are not thus preëmpted to slightly different uses. It seems better to use language which is familiar, even at some risk of ambiguity, than to invent a technical jargon which would, after all, be no less ambiguous until its precise connotation could be discovered from its use.

There is also another and different kind of ambiguity which must be avoided. Obviously, we must distinguish the given from the *object which* is given. The given is presentation of something real, in the normal case at least; *what* is given (given in part) is this real object. But the whatness of this object involves its categorial interpretation; the real object, as known, is a construction put upon this experience of it, and includes much which is not, at the moment, given in the presentation.

Still further comment is required in view of contemporary theories which deal with the content of immediacy in a different fashion.*

When we remember that even the delimitation of that in which we are interested, the singling out of the presentation of our object from other accompanying consciousness is, in some part at least, a work of excision or abstraction wrought by the mind, we may be led to remark that there is, in all strictness, only one given, the Bergsonian real duration or the stream of consciousness. This, I take it, is at least approximately correct. The absolutely given is a specious present, fading into the past and growing into the future with no genuine boundaries. The breaking of this up into the presentation of things marks already the activity of an interested mind. On the other hand, we should beware of conceiving the given as a smooth undifferentiated flux; that would be wholly

---

*Extended discussion of such theories cannot be included here; the object of the discussion is merely that of clarifying, by contrast, the terminology and procedure here adopted. Though criticisms will be ventured, it is recognized that the discussion is not sufficient fully to substantiate these.

fictitious. Experience, when it comes, contains within it just those disjunctions which, when they are made explicit by our attention, mark the boundaries of events, "experiences" and things. The manner in which a field of vision or a duration breaks into parts reflects our interested attitudes, but attention cannot mark disjunctions in an undifferentiated field.

The interruptions and differences which form the boundaries of events and things are both given *and* constituted by interpretation. That the rug is on the floor or the thunder follows the flash, is as much given as the color of the rug or the loudness of the crash. But that I find this disjunction of rug and floor possessed of a meaning which the wrinkles in the rug do not have, reflects my past experience to taking up and putting down rugs. The cognitively significant on-the-floorness of the rug requires both the given break in the field of vision and the interpretation of it as the boundary between manipulable object and unyielding support.

Even in that sense in which the given is always one whole, it is not important for our purpose of analyzing knowledge that we should dwell upon this integrality of it. Our interest is, rather, in the *element* of givenness in what we may, for usual and commonplace reasons, mark off as "an experience" or "an object." This given element in a single experience of an object is what will be meant by "a presentation." Such a presentation is, obviously, an event and historically unique. But for most of the purposes of analyzing knowledge one presentation of a half-dollar held at right angles to the line of vision, etc., will be as good as another. If, then, I speak of "*the* presentation" of this or that, it will be on the supposition that the reader can provide his own illustration. No identification of the event itself with the repeatable content of it is intended.

In any presentation, this content is either a specific quale (such as the immediacy of redness or loudness) or something analyzable into a complex of such. The presentation as an event is, of course, unique, but the qualia which make it up are not. They are recognizable from one to another experience. Such specific qualia and repeatable complexes of them are nowadays sometimes designated as "essences." This term, with such a meaning, will here be avoided ; the liability to confuse such qualia with universal concepts makes this imperative.

It is at once the plausibility and the fatal error of "critical realism" that it commits this confusion of the logical universal with given qualia of sense by denominating both of these "essences." As will be pointed out later, what any concept denotes— or any adjective such as "red" or "round"—is something more complex than an identifiable sense-quale. In particular, the object of the concept must always have a time-span which extends beyond the specious present; this is essential to the cognitive significance of concepts. The qualia of sense as something given do not, in the nature of the case, have such temporal spread. Moreover, such qualia, though repeatable in experience and intrinsically recognizable, have no names. They are fundamentally different from the "universals" of logic and of traditional problems concerning these. Elucidation of this point must wait upon the sequel.

The somewhat similar use of the terms "sensa" and "sense-data" is also likely to prove prejudicial. Mr. Broad in particular has used these terms in a fashion which gives what is denoted by them a dubious metaphysical status. He says, for example:* "We agreed that, if they (sensa) are states of mind at all, they must be presentations. But we find no reason *for* thinking that they are states of mind, and much the same reasons *against* that view as led us to hold that sensations are analyzable into act and sensum. . . . We saw no intrinsic reason why coloured patches or noises should not be capable of existing unsensed." And elsewhere:† "A sense-datum with which I am acquainted may perfectly well have parts with which I am not acquainted. If therefore I say that a given sense-datum has no parts except those which I have noticed and mentioned I may quite well be wrong. Similarly there may well be differences of

*"Scientific Thought," p. 265.
†"Proceedings of the Aristotelian Society," supp. vol. II, p. 218.

quality which I cannot detect. If I say: This sense-datum with which I am acquainted is coloured all over with a uniform shade of red, this statement may be false."

Now it is indeed obvious that I may make erroneous report of the given, because I can make no report at all except by the use of language, which imports concepts which are *not* given. The sensum-theory, like the essence-theory, fails to go deep enough and to distinguish what is really given from what is imported by interpretation. There is interpretation involved in calling the *sensum "elliptical"* as much as in calling the *penny "round."* It means, for example, to assert something about the motion one must make with one's finger in order to hide successively the different portions of the periphery. Also it is true, of course, that if I report the given as "red," I may convey an erroneous impression because I am heedless of color-meanings, and another observer who should have an experience qualitatively the same might report "orange" or "violet." Similarly I may report "round" when an artist would report "elliptical," because I am not used to projecting things on a plane. All those difficulties which the psychologist encounters in dealing with reports of introspection may be sources of error in any report of the given. It may require careful self-questioning, or questioning by another, to elicit the full and correct account of a given experience. But Mr. Broad seems here to assert an entirely different ground of possible mistake. He seems to mean that with the same sensum before me I may at one moment see it red and at a later moment somewhat mottled or more deeply shaded at the center, and so forth.

Now if I look fixedly at a card and see it first uniform and then mottled, I shall very likely and quite properly report that the color of the surface has a quality which I did not at first see. But the subject of this statement is the *real* color of the *real* card, and the statement itself is not a report of the content of sense but *an interpretation* put upon my succession of sensory experience. It imports a distinction between the subjective and the objective which is irrelevant to *givenness* as such. There certainly is such a thing as the shape of a penny or the color of a card which can exist unnoticed while I am looking at it—or when I am not. This is because the shape of the penny has the same *kind* of enduring reality as the penny, and a quite different kind of reality from the intermittent presentation of the penny in my consciousness. But I thought it was the initial point of the sensum-theory to provide a name—if not a local habitation—for what I *see* as opposed to *what* I see, the elliplicity of the appearance as against the real roundness of the penny. As such, it should be of the essence of the sensum to be sensed; the sensum which is neither the real shape of the real penny nor the appearance of it in a mind is neither fish, flesh nor good red herring. A sensum which is not sensed, or a sense-datum which continues unaltered while consciousness of it changes, is merely a new kind of *ding an sich*, which is none the better for being inappropriately named so as to suggest its phenomenological character.

What is given may exist outside the mind— that question should not be prejudiced. But in order that we may meaningfully assert such existence, it is essential that there be an answer to the questions: What would it mean if that which is given has such independent existence? In what respect would experience in general be different if it had no such independent reality? For a sensum which is not sensed, it is difficult to see what answer there can be to such questions.* The main objection to the sensum-theory is that it leaves at

*I am never quite sure that I may not be misunderstanding Mr. Broad on this point. (I might say the same thing about Mr. Russell's "perspectives.") It may be that he means only that when no eye is situated at a certain angle from the penny, it is still true that if there were a normal observer there, he would observe this elliptical appearance, and that the appearance is there whether the observer is or not. To this I can give real meaning: the last part of the statement means the first part—that the appearance is there when *not* observed, means that *if* any observer *were* there he *would* observe it. Or it means that other effects of the penny are there, such as an image registered on a camera-plate, and that these may be verified by the same methods as the existence of physical objects when not observed. But if what Mr. Broad means to call to our attention is the fact that the truth of the statement, "If an observer were there, he would observe so and so," can not be tested when no observer *is* there; and if its being thus true when not verified is what is meant by the existence of unsensed sensa; then I am compelled to say that the hypothesis is merely verbal nonsense. A hypothesis which in the nature of the case is incapable of any conceivable test is the hypothe-

once the ground of the analysis of experience and plunges into metaphysics. It would explain the immediate and indubitable by something intrinsically unverifiable and highly dubious.

It is of the essence of what will here be meant by "the given" that it should be *given*. We need not say that what is given is a "mental state" or even "in the mind" in any more explicit sense than is itself implied in such givenness. Nor should it be presumed that what is thus in mind is *exclusively* mental. The nature of that interpretation or construction by which we come to know objects suggests that the given must be, in some sense or other, a constituent of objective reality as well. All such questions are simply *later questions*. If there should be metaphysical problems concerning the kind of reality which what is "in mind" may have, it is not necessary to anticipate the solution of these beyond what may be verified in the discovery that certain items or aspects of

sis of nothing. What is *normally* meant by saying, "If an observer were there he would observe so and so," is verifiable by the fact that, other conditions being altered at will, whenever an observer *is* there he *does* see this. As will be pointed out later, the attribution of properties to objects and of existence to objects, consists, from the point of view of cognition, precisely in the truth of such hypothetical propositions. And these are held to be true *when* the hypothesis is contrary to fact. But what we *mean* by the truth of such propositions is precisely the sort of thing set forth above: the hypothetical, "If X were, then Y would be," means, "However other conditions be varied, and condition X being similarly supplied at will, whenever X is, Y is." If the existence of an appearance or sensum when it is not sensed means its observability at will, then it means its existence *whenever* it *is* sensed. So far as I can see, there is nothing else which such existence reasonably could mean. In this, of course, I am merely arguing for the indispensability to meaning of the "pragmatic test" of Peirce and James.

the content of experience satisfy the criteria of givenness. These are, first, its specific sensuous or feeling-character, and second, that the mode of thought can neither create nor alter it—that it remains unaffected by any change of mental attitude or interest. It is the second of these criteria which is definitive; the first alone is not sufficient, for reasons which will appear.

This given element is never, presumably, to be discovered in isolation. If the content of perception is first given and then, in a later moment, interpreted, we have no consciousness of such a first state of intuition unqualified by thought, though we *do* observe *alteration* and *extension* of interpretation of given content as a psychological temporal process. A state of intuition utterly unqualified by thought is a figment of the metaphysical imagination, satisfactory only to those who are willing to substitute a dubious hypothesis for the analysis of knowledge as we find it. The given is admittedly an excised element or abstraction; all that is here claimed is that it is not an "unreal" abstraction, but an identifiable constituent in experience.

Chapter III

THE PURE CONCEPT

We have so far been concerned mainly with the distinction between the two elements in knowledge, the given and the construction or interpretation put upon it, and particularly with the criteria of the given. We turn now to consideration of the conceptual or interpretational element.

The word "concept" is used, in philosophic discussion, in many different senses, three of which it is particularly important to distinguish. It may signify (1) the psychological state of mind when one uses a word or phrase to designate some individual thing or some class of objects. Or (2) it may refer to the meaning of a word or phrase throughout some period of the development of the individual's thought, or some period of the development of a science, of a given culture, or even of humanity altogether. Or, (3) it may signify the logical intension or connotation of a term. This third meaning is exemplified by dictionary definitions where these are satisfactory—and is the usual signification of "concept" in the study of logic.

The use of any substantive phrase or term ordinarily undergoes a process of development, both in the history of society and in the history of any individual who uses it. Usually, though not always, the denotation of the term remains unchanged throughout this process; we apply it to the same class of objects, but our realization of what is essential to these things reflects a process of learning. Such learning may consist in an enlargement of our experience of the class of things in question, or it may occasionally represent simply our more accurate apprehension of what are the universal properties and relations of the familiar objects thus classified. But if the meaning of a word or phrase undergo evolution, then, however normal or inevitable or commendable this process may be, we must, for the sake of clarity, recognize that this meaning is one unitary entity only in some generic and genetic sense, and that logically what we have is a succession of different meanings, related in ways which may be important. The recognition of their historical continuity must not obscure the fact of their logical distinctness.

The problem of the developing adequacy of thought is an interesting and important one; it requires as one of its fundamental categories the notion of just such historical and psychological continuities; and the selection of the word "concept" to designate this category is natural. No criticism of such genetic study or of this use of the term is intended. But this psychological and educational category must not be confused with "meaning" in the sense in which logic, for instance, requires that term. Here a meaning must be precise and clear, or be capable of being made so, and must remain unaltered throughout any discussion in which it occurs. No psychological or historical process is legislated out of existence by this restriction in the use of the word, but if there should be development or learning which affects the connotation of a term, then, from this point of view, we have *another* meaning; that is all.

Again, the psychological state is not the object in which we are here primarily interested. If a psychologist, thinking in terms of a context-theory of meaning, says, "Infinity means to me the image of the blue-black, dense, arched sky,"* then we must observe that such a psychologist blurs over the distinction between what is essential and what is non-essential in meaning. He is in no danger of misunderstanding one who talks about what the symbol ∞ denotes to be referring to the heavens, nor does he, even in his own thinking, suppose that infinity is blue-black. To use "concept" to designate such a psychological state or association-complex, is to fail to mark the distinction between what is objective in meaning and what is adventitious or purely personal. Indeed, the question how meaning *can* be objective and shared, when the psychological states which are bearers of this meaning are separate existences

*The reference is, of course, to Titchener.

and not even identical in their qualitative content, is one of the important problems of meaning.

Because it is our main interest here to isolate that element in knowledge which we can with certainty maintain to be objective and impersonal, we shall define the pure concept as "that meaning which must be common to two minds when they understand each other by the use of a substantive or its equivalent." (For brevity, the qualification "pure" will be omitted throughout the remainder of this chapter.) However, this designation of community of meaning as the distinguishing mark of the concept is, in part, merely an expository device for singling out that element in knowledge which, for reasons which will appear, I wish here to discuss.

That meanings may have this sort of objectivity, is a fundamental assumption of science or of any other intellectual enterprise. If there is nothing objective about propositions and concepts, then there is no such thing as truth and there can be no serious purpose in reflection or discussion. There must be meanings which are common to minds when they coöperate in scientific or even in merely practical endeavors. Otherwise the coöperation is illusory; and one cannot escape the question how such common meaning stands related to different minds or psychological states which mean. One may follow Plato and cut the Gordian knot by removing these precise and logically meanings beyond our earthly sphere and establishing them as transcendent ideas or eternal objects. This reflects a judgment of their value but leaves our commerce with them a miracle; it substitutes adoration of a mystery for explanation of a fact. A similar remark would apply to any doctrine like that of the new realism, so far as this doctrine hypostatizes conceptual realities, such as those of mathematics, setting them up as objective realities without further ado and then explaining our apprehension of them as coincidence of mind and object. One does not answer the numerous objections which the nominalists and conceptualists in logic have urged—and very plausibly urged—by first setting up what they claim can exist only in a mind as something outside it and then offering coincidence of mind and object as explanation of the fact that these conceptual objects are also *in* minds. The new realist here follows the obvious analogy of the common-sense view concerning knowledge of the physical. There is the brick out there; we both see the brick, hence we have an idea in common. So—the new realist seems to say —there is the mathematical entity out there; we both apprehend this mathematical entity, hence we have an abstract mathematical concept in common. Even in the case of the physical object there are all sorts of difficulties to be met before community of knowledge can be understood. And in the case of the purely abstract or conceptual (if there be any purely conceptual entities) we have the added difficulty that such an object cannot arouse sensation. Undoubtedly the conceptual has its own appropriate kind of reality; but what that kind of reality is, is precisely the problem. It is not to be resolved by a phrase such as "neutral entity," or "eternal object," or "essence." We must assume the objectivity of conceptual meaning. But if in order to philosophize sensibly we must assume something to be true when we do not understand how it can be true, then our philosophy is, so far, a failure.

On the other hand, I see no necessity for resigning the problem of common meanings to the psychologist as his exclusive affair, especially since he, like the rest of us, must begin by assuming their existence. The meaning must be somehow identified before it can be correlated with behavior or motor-set or context or anything else. And it must be identified as somehow common to two minds before individual psychological differences will be pertinent to it; if what they are pertinent to is not somehow identical, but A's state is pertinent of x and B's to y, then there is no basis for comparison by which individual differences could be discovered as such.

Psychological differences of individuals are indeed impressive. Long before scientific psychology was thought of, the skeptic appealed to them to prove the impossibility of knowledge or the com-

munication of ideas. For imagery and feeling, and
even to some extent for sensation, idiosyncrasy is
the rule. Furthermore, as the ancient skeptic was
fond of pointing out, there can be no final verification of any community in these respects. The
sense-quality of green cannot be conveyed to the
congenitally blind; and if I suppose some idiosyncrasy of sense which makes my perception of
green unique, I shall never discover that peculiarity provided it does not impair my powers to discriminate and relate as others do. In brief, there
can be no verification of community between minds
so far as it is a question of the feeling side of experience, though the assumption that there is no
community here seems fantastic.

However, it is obvious that common meanings
do transcend such individual differences of perception and imagery. We use language to convey
thought. If language really conveys anything,
then there must be something which is identical in
your mind and in mine when we understand each
other. And if our thought is objective and not
merely a report of introspection, then what is
identical in our two minds must also be somehow
germane to that objective reality as we know it.

Suppose we talk of physical things in physical
terms, and our discussion involves physical measurement. Presumably we have the same ideas of
feet and pounds and seconds. If not, the thing is
hopeless. But in psychological terms, my notion of

a foot goes back to some immediate image of visual so-long-ness, or the movements which I make when I put my hands so far apart, or a relation between these two. Distances in general mean quite complex relationships between such visual images, muscle and contact-sensations, the feeling of fatigue, and so on. Weight goes back to muscle-sensations, the "heft" of the thing. And our direct apprehension of time is that feeling of duration which is so familiar but so difficult to describe.

Now in such terms, will your sensory image of a foot or a pound coincide with mine? I am near-sighted; your eyes are good. My arms are long; yours are short. If we lift a weight, there is the difference in strength between us to take into account. So it is with everything. In acuity of perception and power to discriminate, there is almost always some small difference between the senses of two individuals, and frequently these discrepancies are marked. It is only in rough and ready terms that we can reasonably suppose that our direct intuitions and images are alike. That so often theories of knowledge have ignored such differences, which are the rule and not the exception, or have proceeded as if our common and supposedly veridical knowledge depended on coincidence of such sensory content, is really a frightful scandal.

Even for the large and crude distinctions, what assurance is there that our impressions coincide? Suppose it should be a fact that I get the sensation you signalize by saying "red" whenever I look at what you call "green" and vice versa. Suppose that in the matter of immediate sense-qualities my whole spectrum should be exactly the reverse of yours. Suppose even that what are for you sensations of pitch, mediated by the ear, were identical with my feelings of color-quality, mediated by the eye. Since no one can look directly into another's mind, and the immediate feeling of red or of the middle C can never be conveyed, how should we find it out if such personal peculiarities should exist? We could never discover them so long as they did not impair the power to discriminate and relate as others do.

Furthermore, what difference to our common knowledge would it make? That is precisely the first point which needs to be emphasized: idiosyncrasy of intuition need not make any difference, except in the esthetic quality of the experience of one as compared with that of another. Let us take it for granted (it seems fairly sensible) that the sense-data of one are seldom precisely those of the other when we address ourselves to the same object. That, by itself, will in no way impede our common knowledge or the conveying of ideas. Why? Because we shall still agree that there are three feet to the yard; that yellow is lighter than blue; and that middle C means a vibration of 256 per second. In other words, if we *define* any one of the unit-ideas or concepts which enter into the expression of our thought, we shall define it in the same or equivalent fashion, and we shall apply the same substantives and adjectives to the same objects. So far as we fail in *these* two things, our knowledge will be really different and the attempt to convey our thought will break down. These, then, are the only practical and applicable criteria of common knowledge; that we should share common definitions of the terms we use, and that we should apply these terms identically to what is presented.

I am not, of course, trying to argue that individual feelings *are* thus unique. *Some* differences of subjective experience are attested by the inability of one person to discriminate where another can. For the rest, the question of such identity is, in the end, mere idle speculation because we have no possible means of investigating it. What I would point out is, rather, that in the determination of common concepts, the conveying of ideas, such possible idiosyncrasy in the correlated sense-feelings is entirely negligible. You and I mean the same by "red" if we both define it as the first band in the sun's spectrum, and if we both pronounce the same presented objects to be red. It does not matter if neither the red rug nor the first band of the spectrum give to the two of us identical sensations so long as we individually discover that same sense-quality in each thing which we agree in describing as "red."

Moreover, it is obvious that unless one have some peculiarity which both he and others will learn to recognize as a defect of his sense-perceptions, the very manner in which we learn the names of things will secure such unanimity in the ascription of terms, regardless of any idiosyncrasy of purely inner sense feelings.

Even those individual peculiarities which become recognized as inability to discriminate, limitation of the range of sensation, and so on, do not prevent us from sharing and conveying ideas, though they may impede the process of learning. We talk together and coöperate successfully about the vibration of 19,000 per second in the vacuum-tube, though for one of us this vibration is evidenced by a note and for the other it never can be. We both have a perfectly good concept of ultra-violet, though neither of us will ever see it, just as we know well enough what we mean by the other side of the moon. To be sure, no such concept would have a meaning if we could not, through the terms in which that meaning is explicated, get back eventually to concepts which are correlated for us with specific and identifiable qualities of sense. It is thus that we surmount our individual limitations. The pitch which is beyond my auditory range, I understand through the notion "vibration of 19,000," which is definitive both for me and for those who hear it as a note. This process of leading back, by which we understand what we can not directly perceive, may be quite complex and prolonged without defeating the purpose of sharing ideas and conveying thought. It is the same sort of process by which we must all of us understand what we mean by "ultra-violet" or "electron," and its objectivity is not affected by the fact that such indirection of understanding is, in this case of limitations of perception, necessary for some of us only.

The methods of verifying community of meaning are principally two, neither of which depends on any supposed community of feeling or imagery. Either we define our terms or, by our behavior, we exhibit their denotation. The second procedure is less conclusive for reasons which are fairly obvious. No collection of cases, or examples pointed to, is ever sufficient to determine uniquely the denotation of a term—to determine what other cases, not so far examined, would be included and what excluded. The meaning of the term will be what is common to the various examples pointed out as meant by it. In general, the larger the number of things so indicated, the smaller the chance that these will have in common other properties than those which are essential or comprehended within the conceptual meaning of the term. But that possibility can never be ruled out. Moreover, the exhibition of meaning in this way depends for success upon the ability of the person to whom the meaning is conveyed to make the analysis which will isolate correctly just that totality of properties which is common to the things indicated, not omitting to remark any which are essential. This is an important consideration, because concepts which stand in any need of being learned will represent analyses which are matters of some difficulty. On account of these shortcomings of it, the actual use of this method—of indicating a meaning by exemplifying its denotation—is confined almost exclusively to conveying the meaning of a *word* where the *concept* itself is already something shared; as, for instance, where teacher and taught have no language in common.

The method of definition specifies a meaning directly. In defining, we refer one concept to others; the typical definition equates the term defined with a complex of other terms in definite relations. To be sure, it may not be sufficient that you and I both define A in terms of B and C, since B and C may have for us different significations. But if B also is defined by both in the same or equivalent fashion, and C, and so on, that *is* sufficient to assure common meaning, regardless of all differences of imagery or any idiosyncrasy of sense. Such verification of community of meaning by comparison of definitions is obviously a process which must be incomplete, but it makes clear precisely what is essential to a genuine identity of meaning in two minds.

Speaking in terms of logic, these facts may be

expressed by saying that sensation and imagery
are essentially individual, and do not possess
meaning in the sense in which meanings are common and shareable and expressible. The concept,
which is the common, shareable and expressible
meaning, must be distinguished from such feelings; it is constituted by that pattern which is set
up by the expression of one concept in terms of
others. These patterns must be identical and
shared by all who really possess ideas in common
and are capable of conveying them to one another.

Psychologically, this conceptual pattern of relations is, of course, an abstraction; no such concept ever existed, apart from imagery and sensory
material, in any human mind. *For each individual*
there must be a correlation of concept with specific sense-quality. But this correlation of concept and sense is intrinsically individual; if it,
too, should be shared, we could not verify that
fact, and it is not in the least essential to common understanding that it should be. The concept, so defined, is precisely that abstraction which
it is *necessary* to make if we are to discover the
basis of our common understanding of that reality
which we all know. On a day which is terribly long
to me and abominably short to you, we meet, by
agreement, at three o'clock, and thus demonstrate
that we have a world in common. An "hour" is not
a feeling of tedium or vivacity, but sixty minutes,
one round of the clock, a pattern of relations

which we have established between chronometers
and distances and rates of movement, and so on.

Defining, like logical analysis in general, sets
up a pattern of relationships. We are all of us
fond of what Bosanquet called the "linear" mode
of thinking in such matters, and we might easily
suppose that definition chases a conceptual meaning back into other such concepts, and these into
still others, until finally it is brought to bay in
some first (or last) identity of meaning which is
identity of sensation or imagery. So far as meaning within the individual mind is concerned, I
should suppose this is precisely what takes place;
we analyze the meaning back until we come to rest
in familiar imagery. But the end-terms, which for
us are thus understood directly by reference to
sense and feeling, have still a conceptual meaning;
they are not indefinable. This conceptual meaning is shareable; our imagery essentially not.
Thus the end-terms of such analysis are no different than the beginning terms; they have meaning in two senses—the logical, shareable meaning
of further conceptual relations, and the direct,
non-shareable meaning of reference to some complex of sense-qualities.

The notion that the analysis of meaning must,
in linear fashion, go back eventually to ultimate
constituents whose meaning *cannot* in turn be
thus relational, is a prejudice which is very largely
due to a false metaphor. Logical analysis is con-

ceived after the fashion of the physical dissection of a whole into parts, or the chemical analysis of a compound into elements. But it will not escape the thoughtful reader that all definition is eventually circular. It is often the case that A can be defined in terms of B and C, B in terms of A and C, or C in terms of A and B. Where the circle is so small, and the defined meaning so promptly returns upon itself, the analysis is likely to be inadequate. But this circularity would never be possible at all, if the relation of defining to defined were that of part to whole. Moreover, the difference between a good and a bad definition, on this point, is only, so to speak, in the diameter of the circle. All the terms in the dictionary, however ideal its definitions, will be themselves defined.

Logical analysis is not dissection but relation; the analysis of A into B and C does not divide A into constituents B and C but merely traces a pattern of relations connecting A with B and C. As regards their conceptual meaning, terms are very closely analogous to points in space. A point is nothing whatever apart from its relation to other points; its very essence is relational. Likewise the conceptual meaning of a term is nothing whatever apart from other such meanings. Also it is true that if point A is located by reference to B and C, B and C in turn, and the other points in any spatial array, have their position eventually, in circularwise, in their relation to A and to one another. The positional relationships of any point are internal to its nature and constitute that nature. Likewise, the definitive relations of a term, signifying a concept, are internal to the meaning of that term and constitute it. The nature of a concept as such is its internal (essential or definitive) relationships with other concepts. All points have their positions eventually in terms of the array of all space: no point or set of points has any primal position in any other fashion; we merely choose as an arbitary basis of reference some set which is convenient or marks the place where we happen to be. All terms or concepts similarly have their meaning eventually in the array of all meanings, and no member of this array is intrinsically primal or privileged.

Concerning this interpretation of the concept as consisting in relational structures of meaning, there can be two doubts. We seldom "have in mind" any such conceptual pattern of definition. When we reflect upon the manner in which coincidence in the meaning of one term involves coincidence in the meaning of others, we see that such an ideal pattern of meaning goes far beyond what anyone could consciously have in mind at any one time. Again, we often coincide in our use of terms, and thus seem to possess meanings in common, when the definition of our terms would be a matter of some doubt and one holding possibility of disagreement.

Three points are here pertinent: First, that over and above the ambiguities of language commonly recognized, the same word may convey different concepts on different occasions; in particular, that it may convey a meaning which is more or less restricted. Second, when the denotation of a word rules, there are degrees of clearness about its meaning. Third, identity of meaning consists practically in implicit modes of behavior, and what is involved in these always runs beyond what can be explicit in consciousness at any one time.

If I talk with a chemist about helium or with a biologist about cells, we may understand each other perfectly. But without recourse to some reference book, I could not define "helium" or "cell" in a fashion which the specialist would accept as adequate. To me "helium" means "a non-inflammable gas a little lighter than hydrogen (or a little heavier—I forget which), produced in the disintegration of alpha-particles and found in the sun." I could not specify either atomic-weight or spectrum characteristics, one or other of which the chemist will regard as essential to a sufficiently guarded definition. But as long as we converse together without misunderstanding, the *common* meaning of "helium" is just what is set down above. This is a less specific meaning than the chemist's, but included in it, and sufficient for our present purposes. If our discussion should touch upon more recondite matters, he might need to instruct me about helium, and thus establish a more specific common concept, before we could go on. I recognize his authority to do so, and should accept his definition (which I cannot now give) as the "true" meaning of the word "helium." But this does not alter the fact that, for the time being, the common concept which serves our purposes is my looser understanding of the term. Such is quite commonly the case. Our actual meanings, the concepts we are concerned to convey, are more restricted than the true or full or dictionary meanings of the terms we use. Most words may convey any one of a whole range of more or less full and accurate meanings. It is, thus, quite possible that we may understand each other perfectly even when we should disagree about the definition of our terms, because only some restricted meaning, covered in both our definitions, is required by our discussion.

Second, it is obvious that in some sense or other we may have a meaning in mind when we could not state it without further thought. Any true account of thought and speech must recognize this. The ruling interest in knowledge is the practical interest of action. A meaning may be implicitly present in the consistency of behavior when confronted with experience of a certain type without the explicit recognition of what this behavior implies having come into consciousness or even been brought in question. Such we must suppose to be the child's early use of language. And in this sense, we may perhaps say that meanings must be implicit in the mind before they can become conscious. In fact, we may doubt whether any meaning would ever become conscious if it were not for the practical difficulties which arise when meanings are not thus explicit—the difficulties of hesitant or inconsistent behavior in border-line cases, and the social difficulty of misunderstanding, that is, of incongruous behavior when the same term has been used with apparently the same meaning.

Josiah Royce used to speak to his classes of the three grades of clearness about the meanings of terms.* We have the first grade of clearness when we are able appropriately to accept or reject any object of our acquaintance as belonging or not belonging to the class in question. The second grade of clearness involves, further, the preparedness to classify correctly objects not precisely like those with which we have previously been acquainted; that is, to make the dichotomy, X or not-X, not only for familiar but also for unfamiliar things, not only for all actual but also for all conceivable objects. The third grade of clearness consists in the ability to specify the criteria by which such classification is determined. This last, of course, is equivalent to definition, the explicit possession of the concept. That the mind

---

*He used to attribute this to Charles Peirce, but Peirce's discussion in "How to Make Our Ideas Clear," does not so precisely cover the point.

may have the first or second grade of clearness
without the third, is obvious. It is also evident
without discussion, that even when we have, in the
ordinary sense, this highest grade of clearness, we
do not have this definition explicitly in mind whenever we use a term with understanding.

Any controversy as to whether a mind possesses
a meaning whenever a term is used intelligently,
would be useless because it would be verbal. The
pertinent facts are sufficiently clear; that it may
possess meaning in the sense of determining a consistent mode of behavior (such as the consistent
use of a term) without our being able out of hand
to specify the ground of our own discrimination,
we can all of us testify. The psychology of this is
doubtless a difficult and important topic; but with
that we are not concerned. It would be an anomalous use of language to deny meaning to terms
which are used without this explicit consciousness
of what is essential, especially since the use of
terms, like other modes of deliberate behavior, is
most frequently a matter of habit, reflecting previous experience in which the mode of action was
determined by clearer consciousness. It would also
be anomalous to deny meaning where there is consistency of behavior or of consciously determined
attitude which does not directly concern the use of
language. In such cases the meaning is possessed
by the mind both in the sense of this consistently
determined attitude and in the further sense that

how this meaning should become explicit and *what* would be recognized as essential, when the attitude became self-conscious, is already implicit in the attitude itself. There is such a thing as confusion of attitude, reflected in hesitation of behavior and self-frustration, just as there may be inconsistency in the use of terms and in our explicit concepts. It is such hesitation and dubiety which provides the spur to that self-consciousness and self-criticism which renders meanings explicit. If meanings could not be present and determined in the attitude and behavior itself, there would be nothing to become conscious of. Objects do not classify themselves and come into experience with their tickets on them. The classifying attitude or mode of behavior which the mind brings to the given experience and which represents its meaning, dictates the explicit concept and implicitly possesses it already.

If, however, in the light of this, it should be charged that I have used the phrase "common to two minds" in a figurative and Pickwickian sense in the definition of "the concept," I shall plead guilty. I shall urge in extenuation that to begin the discussion by introducing all the qualification and explanation required for strict accuracy would have been confusing and impossible. I have but followed the custom to attributing to mind what is ideally determined by conscious attitude even though it is not explicitly present in consciousness. Whatever is merely convenient fiction in this can now be withdrawn in favor of an accurate equivalent. The concept is a definitive structure of meanings, which is what *would verify* completely the coincidence of two minds when they understand each other by the use of language. Such ideal community requires coincidence of a pattern of interrelated connotations, projected by and necessary to coöperative, purposeful behavior. It does *not* require coincidence of imagery or sensory apprehension. The concept is, thus, psychologically both an abstraction and an ideality, though in no greater degree or different sense than are most of things which are commonly attributed to mind. Both community of meaning and genuine understanding of reality are projected ideals more truly than realized actualities. We study them as what our purposes intend and as that the approximation to which gives value to our practice. It is concepts, as precisely such ideal abstractions, which must be implicitly present in our practice, which constitute the element of interpretation which underlies our common understanding of our common world. To that topic, we may now proceed.

CHAPTER IV

COMMON CONCEPTS AND OUR COMMON
WORLD*

The significance of conception is for knowledge.
The significance of all knowledge is for possible
action. And the significance of common conception
is for community of action. Congruity of behavior
is the ultimate practical test of common under-
taking. Speech is only that part of behavior which
is most significant of meanings and most useful
for securing human coöperation.

Common meaning may override all idiosyncrasy
of feeling or sense, so far as such idiosyncrasy
does not prevent congruous distinction and relations. It may even override differences which are
reflected in failure of discrimination and relation,
in ways which have already been commented on.
In fact, I think we may fairly be impressed with
the tremendous achievement which our common
meanings and our intellectual coöperation represent in the life of the race. Community of meaning
may also override much idiosyncrasy of behavior.

*This chapter consists mainly of an elaboration and defense of con-
ceptions put forward in the preceding one. It may be omitted, by any
reader who chooses to do so, without prejudice to the understanding
of later chapters.

But eventually the very purposes for which communication exists insure a certain congruity of behavior when meanings are the same.

Berkeley pointed out that we can never test the validity of knowledge by comparing an idea in the mind with an object outside the mind. We can only compare ideas among themselves. This is a pertinent consideration about the *criteria* of knowledge, whether one agrees with Berkeley's idealism or not. What I would here point out about the concept has a certain similarity. We cannot test community of meaning, even eventually, by comparing the immediate experience in our own mind with the immediate experience in another mind, nor by comparing another's concepts, conveyed to us, with his immediate feelings and sensations. We can only compare meanings among themselves, as purely conceptual and abstracted from the character of any experience beyond our own. We can only grasp another's meanings by observing the relation of his meanings to one another and to his behavior.

In the end it can hardly fail to be the case that the possibility of our having concepts in common is conditioned by two things; first, by the fact that we are creatures fundamentally alike, having in the large the same needs and interests and powers of discrimination and relation; and second, that we are confronted by a common reality, mediated to us in sense-experience which is comparable.

Seeing that, in the large, such conclusions are indicated, there is a tendency to jump to them at the start—on the part of rationalists to assume an ideal and complete agreement in an iron-clad and immutable set of categories, hypostatizing these as "human reason"; on the part of empiricists to presume that our common world is exhibited to all of us (that is, to all "normal" persons, the others being simply left out of account) in a common sensory experience. Theories of both these types are based on nothing more nor less than a beautiful myth.

With the topic of the categories we are not just now concerned except for one point. Coincidence of categories may be interpreted to mean a necessary psychological coincidence of a certain aspect of experience, the formal or relational. Now I feel quite sure that something of this sort is true. My conviction is that one kind of likeness which is essential to our common understanding consists in certain very fundamental tendencies to action, growing out of basic similarity of needs and of physical structure; these tendencies to action will, of course, be reflected in some aspect of experience. But it is of some importance to see that even such fundamental tendencies in which we coincide need not necessarily be mediated by any direct psychological identity of experience. There seems to be the same possibility of systematic difference here that there is among our intuitions of length

or of weight if one of us is tall and strong and the
other short and weak. I should not stress this
otherwise trivial point if it were not that a theory
which, admitting divergence of experience at the
level of ordinary perception, still bases itself upon
a psychological identity of an esoteric and recondite "human reason," seems to me just the reverse of what a sensible account of the common
aspects of our common experience should be. Psychologically "human reason" is a very remote abstraction; if the conception is to be retained, its
aura of the transcendental needs to be removed.

As for that other presumption, that our common understanding is based upon the presence to
us of a common world, it too is unduly simple. Our
common world is very largely a social achievement
—an achievement in which we triumph over a
good deal of diversity in sense-experience. Common understanding would become progressively
more difficult as community in what is given in experience should become more meager; so much,
the example of intelligent persons with defects of
sense makes evident. But if we inquire at what
point the limit may be set, or just what items of
sense are absolutely requisite, we shall see, I think,
that there is nothing of which we can say absolutely, "Unless *this* much were common in what is
given to us, we could not understand each other
at all."

For these reasons, the problem of the genesis

of common concepts will bear a little further consideration.

In the first place, it may be pointed out that an initial community between "likeminded" individuals is capable of enormous expansion, and that the manner of such expansion is familiar.

Suppose two men speaking different languages but having a few words in common to be chained to the opposite walls of a dark cell, so that the possibility of establishing common meanings by such methods as pointing and naming would be at a minimum. With good luck in the initial common concepts, and with a high enough order of intelligence, they might eventually establish a very large range of common notions by methods which the reader can imagine for himself.

The actual case of Miss Helen Keller, in which a normal range of understanding has been developed from original coincidence in kinesthetic and contact-sensation (*absolute* coincidence even in these being somewhat doubtful) need only be mentioned.

Or suppose there should be creatures on Mars of a high order of mentality. They might be psychologically rather different from ourselves and have senses and experience largely incomparable with our own. Yet if we could establish some initial common understanding (say if we should signal to them in light-flashes -, - -, - - -, and they should eventually respond with - - - -, - - - - -,

- - - - - -), then in spite of our differences from them, it would be hard to set a limit beyond which it could be said with certainty that our common understanding could not go.

In fact, it is just this indefinite extensibility of conceptual understanding which is exhibited by abstract mathematical systems. To take the best illustration; by a miracle of patience and insight, Mr. Russell and Mr. Whitehead have achieved, in "Principia Mathematica," such an analysis of various branches that the whole field of this subject (excepting the geometrical, so far omitted) can be developed from seven initial concepts. These undefined ideas are of such a sort that they must almost inevitably belong to any creature which should be conscious of its own ways of acting and should possess the habit of communication—ideas such as "proposition" and "either-or." Supposing these notions to be common to two minds—in any terms you please—these two minds could, if their patience and intelligence should be sufficient, arrive eventually at a common understanding of the whole of mathematics.

So far, I am only concerned to point out that an initial community could extend itself extraordinarily. The exigencies of common life, the need of coöperation, the tendency to imitation in behavior, and the enormously developed institution of human education—using the term in its widest meaning—all go to enforce just this sort of elaboration and extension of any initial mutuality of human understanding. Idiosyncrasy is pretty systematically suppressed. And what cannot be suppressed (abnormalities and deficiencies) we go about it most earnestly and ingeniously to get around. A relatively meager mutuality of concepts, given human powers of discrimination, abstraction and relation, and our human social habits, would be sufficient as the initial foundation for our actual and most elaborate mutual understanding. I am not trying to argue that it *is* from such a meager basis of initial mutuality that the community of understanding actually develops, though obviously one could make out a pretty good case from the manner in which the infant acquires his social inheritance of ideas. I wish only to point out the fact that, given such a meager mutuality, elaborate common understanding could develop; and that to argue straight from our elaborate common understanding to an equally extended coincidence of felt qualities or given experience, is unnecessary and fallacious.

The same considerations are pertinent as against those who would hold that an initial community of categories, as a psychologically identical and miraculous endowment, is necessarily presumed. Any who hold this doctrine are likely to argue against the view here presented something as follows:*

*I am not imagining what such critics might say but reporting what, in substance, some of them *have* said.

It is possible that you can escape postulating psychological identity of sensuous content at the first stage, in the analysis of meaning, by resolving the content of the concept into relations, but you will be forced to come back to it in the second, or some later stage, because the apprehension of *relations* must be common. It may be true that "red" or "an hour" is conceptually the same for A and B, not because felt red or felt duration is sensuously identical in the two minds but because both define red as the first band of the spectrum and an hour as sixty minutes. But— the critic continues—relations themselves must be discoverable in experience in a manner not essentially different from that in which substantive terms are given. That X is bigger than Y, or is to the left of, or better than, or stands in any other relation to Y, is something which must be disclosed by *some* sort of felt, empirical quale of the X–Y complex. Otherwise experience could never determine for us whether X *is* better than Y or stands in any other relation to Y; and experience would in fact be irrelevant to the truth of judgments of relation—which means, of course, all judgments.

So far, the critic's point is well taken. As was indicated in Chapter II, relations in general are given in very much the same sense that other properties of objects are given. However, it is equally true that relations, as cognized, are the result of conceptual abstraction and of a setting in connection with what is *not* given, just as properties in general are. That is, I should wish only to file an exception, or a caution, that just as the predication of—let us say—roundness is not merely a direct report of sense-content, so the predication of "greater than" or "predecessor of" involves something more than the given. Though relations in general are given in experience like other properties, and though the applicability to experience of the predication of any particular relation depends, for any individual, upon the possibility of that relation's being given to him in *some* experience, still exactly those relations which constitute the *interpretation* of what is given are such as are *not*, just now, given in the experience which is the subject of such conceptual interpretation.

The critic continues: If, however, the presence or absence of certain relations between X and Y is revealed to the mind by the presence or absence of some identifiable characteristic of experience, and if identical concepts in two minds means the coincidence of a certain pattern of relationships, then the assumption that two minds have a concept in common is an assumption of *some* identity of the order of psychological content. Relations are, of course, definable in general. So it is conceivable that if substantive concepts are analyzable into relations, relations may be analyzable into relations of relations—as we see in mathematics sometimes. But—and now the critic reaches the point of his argument—unless you are to have an infinite regress, somewhere you must come to an end in a psychological identity which is absolute, in what I should think of as the categories. These will have to be at once the underlying pattern of all human experience and the elemental structure of human reason.

Now I am not specially anxious to controvert anything which such a critic has to urge. I should wish merely to make two points against him which must greatly qualify the force of his argument. If conceptual analysis discovers the meaning of substantive terms in definitive relations, and consonantly, the meaning of relations in relations of relations, it does not in the least follow that there is a regress here which must either be infinite or come to some absolute end-terms. And second, the kind of psychological identity which most plausibly belongs to common concepts of the basic sort meant by "categories" is not at all of the type most frequently contemplated by those who talk, in capitals, about "Human Reason."

To take the last point first; whether we take our examples of "the categories" supposed to represent the structure of human reason, from the traditional historical sources, or take them—with much better reason—from those scientific analyses which reveal basic concepts of mathematics, phys-

ics, and so on, in either case our categorial concepts, "substance and accident," "cause and effect," "different from," "either—or," are certain
to be such as are exemplified in experience by a
very wide range of heterogeneous sensory content. If, for example, the category "different
from" must be common to two minds before they
could even begin to create a common understanding, then it must at once suggest itself that what
empirically exemplifies this category will be itself
most markedly divergent in particular cases. If
we must seek some psychological identity which is
the vehicle of the category "different from," then
about the only plausible place to look for it will
be in our own activity of distinguishing. Any
reasonably conceived set of categories will exhibit
these as a very high order of abstractions, and
abstractions most unlikely to be identifiable by
any simple coincidence of empirical quale in what
is brought under them. Psychologically they will
reflect much more directly our ways of acting than
they will the character of that upon which these
acts are directed.

Apart from a prepossession in favor of some
transcendental and miraculous status for "the
categories," I suspect that the point which such a
critic seeks to make against the view here presented, is that human experience, at the lowest
level at which it can be discerned—the level here
indicated by "givenness"—already possesses a

structure which reflects the nature of "human reason." This, I take it, is entirely erroneous. Though doubtless the general character of sensory content reflects the nature of the animal, it is not such differences which are attributable to human reason or categories; it is precisely such divergence which community of thought and concept may triumph over. If, for example, one examines such a list of basic concepts as the primitive ideas of "Principia Mathematica," one may see, I think, that the reason I cannot teach my dog the calculus is not because empirical exemplifications of these primitive concepts are not possible, or even familiar, to him, but because he is not capable of making an abstraction which is not dictated directly by instinctive interest and because a structure of relations must be either very simple or strongly enforced by repetition without exception in order for him to hold it in his mind. There is no reason to think that the absence of human categories affects the content of his given experience in the least.

Other considerations, pertinent to this topic, will be set forth in Chapter VII and VIII. But already it may be clear that the sense in which the categories "inform" experience is not any sense in which different sets of categories (for different kinds of creatures) would presume any corresponding difference in experience as given. As Royce was fond of insisting, the categories are our ways of acting. What we can distinguish as attributable to our own acts are not, and can not be, limitations in the content of the immediate experience which is acted on.

If, then, what the critic means to urge is that we must have identical *feelings* of the relation of substance and accident or of "if—then," etc., I can only say that I still do not see the necessity of this; that I regard the point as rather tenuous for argument; and that in any case I do not see its importance for the theory of concepts in general which is here presented. It has been admitted that within the individual mind *every* concept must have its correlation, directly or eventually, with specific sensory content. If it should be the case that this specific sense-content, in different minds, is, for all our basic concepts, identical, it would still be true that this sense-content can never be conveyed. We are concerned with two things in our practical understanding of each other—with communication and with behavior. My concepts are, from the outside view of me which you have, revealed as modes of my behavior, including speech. My words must maintain a certain relation to other words which I use and to the things I do. It is necessary that we should act alike, in fundamental and important ways, if we are to have a possible basis for understanding one another. But it is *not* necessary that when we act alike we should *feel* alike, however large the presumption that actually we do.

The eventual aim of communication is the co-
ördination of behavior; it is essential that we
should have purposes in common. But I can understand the purposes of another without presuming that he feels just as I do when he has
them. The psychology of purpose is an especially
difficult topic, but it would seem that what is most
essential is a certain relation between anticipation
and realization. If, in another mind, both what is
anticipated and what is realized should be, in
terms of immediacy, different than for me, I could
still attribute this relation between the two to him
when I observe him to behave as I do. In other
words, I correctly attribute a certain purpose, like
mine, to another if I observe that he performs an
act like mine and suppose correctly that it is the
result of an intention involving the same congru-
ence between anticipation and result which I find
in my own case. I do not need to suppose that
either purposes in general or the content of this
act in particular are, as items of immediate experience, identical in his case and in mine, in
order to "understand his purposes."

Let us return now to the second point which
we have supposed to be urged by our critic—that
the notion of the concept as a relational pattern
of meanings among themselves must eventually
break down because the analysis of substantive
terms into relations presumes a similar analysis of
relational terms into relations of relations, and so
on; that hence we shall be confronted either with

an infinite regress of a hopeless sort or with the necessity that there should be some end-terms of such analysis which are absolute and have their meaning exclusively in some different fashion, such as imagery, which must therefore be identical in two minds which understand each other.

One might indulge in a great deal of loose talk about such an issue without reaching any real clarity. But as it happens there are excellent examples to which the discussion can be tied, and these examples show that our critic is entirely wrong. I refer to the systems of pure mathematics, in their modern form. Such a system is generated deductively from certain primitive ideas which are taken for granted. All other concepts in the system are defined in terms of these. Unless these primitive ideas possess meaning—it may be said —the whole system would be meaningless; they are the end-terms of that particular analysis of the field in question which the system represents. Now let us imagine for a moment that this branch of mathematics should be a closed field; that if, for example, it is arithmetic which we are considering, then no concept which occurs in arithmetic has any meaning outside arithmetic or other than an arithmetical application. This is not, of course, true; and it is for this reason that the ordinary "linear" method of developing mathematical systems can work so well. These initial notions really would be—and usually are—clear before one un-

derstands just what the system is to develop, because these concepts have an application and a
meaning outside arithmetic. But suppose this were
not the case; would it then be true that all the
concepts of the system must remain forever meaningless? I think we can see that this would not
be so.

In the first place, we may remark that there
are entirely different sets of undefined concepts
which would serve equally well as a basis. It is
quite generally true that the same deductive system can be developed in a number of different
ways, the only limit to this number of alternative
developments being the practical difficulty of finding alternative sets of initial notions which are
sufficiently clear and are economical as to the
number of required postulates. If we take two
different sets of undefined ideas (and of correspondingly different assumptions in terms of
them) from which the same system may be developed, then all the undefined ideas of the one set
may be defined in the other; they are defined in
terms of ideas which, in the other case, they themselves serve to define. In other words, we can enter
into the complex network of mathematical meanings in a number of different ways, from different
points of departure.

Since this is so, it is quite obvious that there is
no inherent simplicity in either set of undefined
ideas, and that the comparison of terms to points

in a spatial pattern, and of definitions to the tracing out of such patterns of relationship, is much more apt than that other metaphor which represents logical analysis as physical dissection. If the undefined idea is "simple" and the predicate which defines it "a complex," then what is to be taken as simple and what as complex, is merely a matter of convenience and in no wise a logical necessity.

Furthermore, some of the undefined notions in any deductive development of a mathematical system are pretty sure to be relations or "operations." There is the same possibility of choice here that there is for the "substantive" notions. That is to say, relations are *not* necessarily defined by relations *of relations* but in a manner essentially the same as substantive terms. The supposition on which our critic charges our conception with requiring either an infinite regress or some absolute end-terms, is a natural one but quite erroneous. It is based upon the false analogy of logical to physical analysis. To discuss the logic of relations and of substantives so as to disclose general principles in precise language, would take us too far afield. Briefly, we may observe that it is as easy to define relations by the terms they connect as to define substantive terms by other substantives related to them. There is a certain analogy here to the fact that lines may be defined by the points they connect or points defined by the intersection of lines.

If it should be said that this range of choice amongst the concepts of mathematics is due to the fact that *all* mathematical concepts are complex, and that *every* mathematical system presumes notions of a more fundamental sort which are used in it without explicit mention, then we may point out that in "Principia Mathematica," where *all* the concepts of mathematics are defined or analyzed, they are generated from the basis of concepts of logic; and that the deductive development of logic itself presents exactly the same picture as here outlined. There is here the same range of choice as to undefined notions and postulates. In fact, the most economical development of logic yet discovered—requiring only three symbolic postulates—is in terms of an undefined idea so *un*obvious that most people misinterpret it until they see precisely how it is related to other notions in the development based upon it.

Now mathematical systems are by far the most extended and exact examples of logical analysis that we have. All such examples illustrate the fact that there is no such thing as intrinsic simplicity or indefinability. *All* meaning is relational. Deductive order is, to a considerable extent, a matter of choice and is, in fact, usually determined by practical considerations of economy of assumption and the like. The mathematician does not choose his undefined ideas with any thought that they must be better understood than those which he intends to define, any more than he chooses his initial postulates in terms of them on the ground that these assumptions will be readily agreed to while the theorems he intends to prove might not. Often, in fact, the mathematician does not tell us explicitly what things he is talking about but assumes "A class K of terms a, b, c, . . . and a relation R or an operation such that . . . ," and leaves it to the postulated relations and the development of the system itself to identify his meanings. In general the theorems are no more "proved true" by the postulates than the postulates are by the fact that they lead to the theorems, and the terms defined are no more made clear by their definitions than the undefined terms are by the definitions into which they enter. What is, in fact, essentially demonstrated in a deductive system is the total fact of the order and connectedness which is exhibited by the system as a whole. Even if the undefined ideas do happen to be clear initially, while those defined are not, nevertheless the development of the system serves to enrich and explicate those original meanings. The significance of the original notions is made clear by the relationships into which they enter, much as the significance of an hypothesis is increasingly obvious in any considerable survey of its consequences.

To bring this discussion back to its connection with the earlier point: If the mathematical sys-

tem were a closed field, then the originally undefined concepts would of necessity possess the *whole*
of their meaning in the extended order and inter-
relationships of the system itself. The concepts of
a particular mathematical system do not, of
course, represent such a closed field. But the field
of our concepts altogether is, and must be, closed
in this sense. It is this fact which has been referred to as the inevitable eventual circularity of
definition and illustrated by the example of the
ideal dictionary. Relations, we may further note,
would be defined in such a dictionary as well as
substantives. The conceptual meaning of terms is
to be found in the array of their definitive or deductive relations to one another. That the relations themselves are definable, does not lead to any
regress.

Very likely it will be urged that, so far, I have
ignored the large and important part which is
played in the identification of meanings by the
common reality which is presented. I have so far
ignored it for the reason—obvious to the reader, I
hope—that this "common reality" is precisely one
of the things which needs to be accounted for, in
the face of the fact that we cannot reasonably
suppose that presented or immediate experience is
actually common to the degree that reality is.

Meanings are identified by the relational patterns which speech and behavior in general are
capable of conveying. The sensuous content of

experience in one mind cannot be conveyed to another, but the characteristic order of some set of items in the experience of A can be identified by B as belonging exclusively to some set of things in his own experience. The presence of like interests, if such may be presumed, will narrow the field within which search for such conceptual identity of order is to be made, and assist identification. Most such identifications of meaning will, of course, be based upon previous identification of *other* and related meanings. But the higher the order of intelligence, the greater the capacity to identify concepts simply and directly by their logical structure. A mathematician, for example, confronted by a system in entirely novel notation or in a language strange to him, might identify it in just this way. The complex numbers—he might say—are the only things in mathematics which have just that type of order. It is thus that we may imagine that intelligent Martians might catch our meaning in sending successively larger numbers of light-flashes. It is in such fashion that the meaning concealed in a cipher is finally disclosed by finding that rule which turns it into something which makes sense.

In general, we are able to understand one another because—for one reason—a common reality is presented to us. But so to put it is to reverse the order of knowledge. We have a common reality because—or in so far as—we are able to identify, each in his own experience, those systems of orderly relation indicated by behavior, and particularly by that part of behavior which serves the ends of coöperation. What this primarily requires is that, in general, we be able to discriminate and relate as others do, when confronted by the same situation.

Although different individuals may, and to a certain extent verifiably do, intuite things differently, still the basic discriminations which one can make can also be made by another. Especially those distinctions and relations which concern our major purposes and hence are such as it is practically most important for us to discern in our adjustment of behavior to environment, will be made by different individuals in comparable ways. Or to put it the other way about, we are "like creatures" and capable of understanding one another if, regardless of the sense-quality of what we intuite, we make the major discriminations and relations concerned by the adjustment of behavior to environment in comparable ways.

The "common reality" projected by such understanding of each other is, to an extent not usually remarked, a social achievement. It triumphs over a good deal of verifiable difference in the power of individuals to discriminate and relate in the presence of the same situation. The need to coöperate is always there. This being so, the importance of those concepts which are framed in terms of distinctions and relations which *are* common, is enhanced, and of those which should be in terms of what some only can discriminate, is diminished. If these distinctions which only some can make directly in the content of their experience, do not concern what is important for behavior adjustment, then very likely no socially current concept will be framed in terms of them. There will be no language to describe these personal and peculiar phases of experience. And—remembering how largely our thought is informed by social relationships—it is likely that these phases of experience will largely pass unnoticed by the individual himself. Again, even if they are noted, their significance will be regarded as "subjective" rather than of objective reality.*

However, if, or in so far as, those distinctions and relations which can be made by some only are

---

*In the end, the supposition of a difference in immediate experience which is *not* to be detected through divergence in discrimination and relation, is a notion very difficult to handle. Because such difference would, *ex hypothesi*, be ineffable. We can have no language for discussing what no language or behavior could discriminate. And a difference which no language or behavior could convey is, for purposes of communication, as good as non-existent. But this consideration only serves to enforce the fact that the assumption of qualitatively identical immediate experience is unnecessary for community of knowledge—that it is germane at all only so far as it affects that pattern of relationships here called the concept.

The only reason that the possibility of such ineffable individual difference of immediacy is not altogether meaningless, is that we have interests which pass beyond those of cognition. Interests such as those of appreciation, sympathy, love, concern the absolute identity and quality as immediate of other experience than our own. Esthetics, ethics, and religion are concerned with such interests, which transcend those of action and of knowledge, as that term has here been used.

important for survival or for the behavior-ad-
justment required for the satisfaction of important needs, then—like the blind man following his
companion who sees—we shall interpret "reality"
in terms of the more differentiated experience of
the better discriminator. Others will attach to concepts so framed some indirect meaning in terms
of other aspects of their own experience; if in no
other way, then in terms of the observed behavior
of other persons.

That we like-minded creatures have presented
to us a common reality might seem to be, like the
preëstablished harmony of Leibnitz, simply a major miracle which must be accepted as a fact,
whether we forthwith hypostatize that fact as "independent reality" or not. But this miracle is in
some part only the result of looking at the situation wrong way to. We do not expect to have a
common reality with an insect or an imbecile.
"Like-mindedness" consists primarily of three
things; the possession of like needs and of like
modes of behavior in satisfying them, second, the
possession of common concepts, represented in behavior by discrimination and relation, and third,
the capacity (evoked particularly when community in the other two respects threatens to fail)
of transcending our individual limitations of discrimination by indirect methods. This last is a
considerable item in what is meant by "intelligence." In short, the power to attain, directly or

indirectly, to common concepts, applicable in common ways, is itself the criterion of like-mindedness. Such like-mindedness requires *either* a considerable community of order directly identifiable in experience *or* a considerable degree of intelligence by which disparity in the first respect may be compensated for. A Martian might be like-minded with ourselves in spite of quite different immediate experience. But, if so, he must be very intelligent. And such like-mindedness is prerequisite to having a reality in common.

When we remember that amongst "normal" individuals there is very considerable variation in the acuity of perception, revealed in individual differences of discrimination, and when we remember how plausible it is that other individual differences in presented experience exist but escape notice because of their small importance to our major needs, or because we *learn* our conceptual interpretations largely through imitation and cooperation, it becomes evident that the significance of the above considerations is by no means confined to the situation as between "normal" and "defective" perceivers.

The eliciting of "reality" from that presented experience in which the subjective and the objective are jumbled up together, is an achievement of intelligence expressed in our categorial distinctions. Our common reality reflects our common categories. But it is both unnecessary and implausible to assume this fundamental community to be simply ready-made and miraculous. It seems much more reasonable to allow that this major outline of common reality reflects, in some degree, our common needs, our social organization for fulfilling them, and our learning from social example. Thus even our common categories may be, in part, a social achievement of like-mindedness. The sharing of a common "reality" is, in some part, the aim and the result of social coöperation, not an initial social datum, prerequisite to common knowledge.

To sum up, then: The purely conceptual element in knowledge is, psychologically, an abstraction. It is a pattern of relation which, in the individual mind, is conjoined with some definite complex of sense qualia which is the referent or denotation of this concept and the clue to its application in presented experience. These two together, the concept and its sensory correlate, constitute some total meaning or idea for the individual mind. As between different minds, the assumption that a concept which is common is correlated with sensory contents which are qualitatively identical, is to an extent verifiably false, is implausible to a further extent, and in the nature of the case can never be verified as holding even when it may reasonably be presumed. Nevertheless, community of meaning is secured if each discover, within his own experience, that complex of content which this common concept will fit. When the behavior of each, guided by this common concept, is comparable or congruous, we have, so far, a reality in common. The traditional argument of the skeptic, that knowledge or the communication of ideas is dubious or impossible in the light of the subjectivity of sense, is without valid foundation. That our possession of any considerable array of common concepts depends upon the presence to our minds of a common reality is—or should be—a commonplace. But both our common concepts and our common reality are in part a social achievement, directed by the community of needs and interests and fostered in the interest of coöperation. Even our categories may be, to a degree, such social products; and so far as the dichotomy of subjective and objective is governed by consideration of community, reality itself reflects criteria which are social in their nature.

As he goes further on in the book he gets more concerned with reality

Chapter V

THE KNOWLEDGE OF OBJECTS

We have so far taken the clue of common meaning—of what can be conveyed from one mind to another—as the criterion of the concept. But, as has been noted, this was in part merely an expository device. However much our concepts are shaped by social intercourse and borrowed ready-made by the individual, a human being without fellows (if such can be imagined) would still frame concepts in terms of the relation between his own behavior and his environment. Knowledge must always concern principally the relations which obtain between one experience and another, particularly those relations into which the knower himself may enter as an active factor. It is the given as thus conceptually interpreted which is envisaged as the real object.

It is also true that exclusive emphasis upon the social, or the taking of language as a point of departure, might easily lead to an oversimplification of our notions of conceptual interpretation. Words represent rather large and ready-made wholes—relatively stable and relatively simple concepts which are a somewhat loose fit for the precise and complex knowledge of perceived objects. In a glance of the eye, so to speak, we apprehend what whole paragraphs will do no more than suggest. Language is primarily useful for conveying *generalizations* or else very specific abstracted items of experience. Not only is that knowledge of an object which is mediated by perception something which is usually difficult to convey precisely in words but usually it is not important to convey it in more than very partial fashion, since those who are required to act directly toward what is presented to us are usually those who are also present to it themselves.

In fact, this difference between what words convey and what perception mediates is so marked that it may suggest a distinction of two kinds of knowledge; direct knowledge of objects (acquaintance with), gained by the presentation of them in experience and immediately verifiable, and propositional knowledge or generalization (knowledge about) which concerns more than can be given at one time and thus requires some mental synthesis of what is temporally disjoined.

Such a dichotomy, however, would be falsely taken. It is the first thesis of this chapter that there is no knowledge merely by acquaintance; that knowledge *always* transcends the immediately given. The merely contemplated or enjoyed may possess esthetic significance, but if it is to have cognitive meaning this immediacy must become the subject of an interpretation which transcends it; we must take toward the given some attitude which serves practical action and relates it to what is not given. Let us first briefly illustrate the nature of such conceptual interpretation. We may then turn to the special problems which are involved.

At the moment, a certain "that" which I can only describe (in terms of concepts) as a round, ruddy, tangy-smelling somewhat, means to me "edible apple." Now my ultimate purpose toward it may be the enjoyment of an ineffable taste. But that taste not being given, I need a conceptual go-cart to get me over the interval between this round, ruddy presentation and the end projected by my purpose. Life is full of such undesirable interstices; in fact just so far as it needs to be earnest and active, it is made up of them. It is the function of mind to bridge these by assigning to the present given an interpretation through which it becomes related to, or a sign of, a correlation between certain behavior of my own and the realization of my purpose. This interpretation has the character of a generalization which has been learned. I phrase it by saying "That (denoting the given presentation) is a sweet apple (connoting among other things the possible taste)." If I should be completely absorbed in the first given, as an infant might, then I should frame no concept, it would have no meaning, and no action, unless a merely instinctive one, would be evoked.

An object such as an apple is never given; between the real apple in all its complexity and this fragmentary presentation, lies that interval which only interpretation can bridge. The "objectivity" of this experience means *the verifiability of a further possible experience which is attributed by this interpretation.*

The notion that there is a simple sort of knowledge, gained by direct apprehension alone, has two major sources. In the first place it is falsely supposed that there are some concepts at least which denote "simple qualities"—something which can be directly exhibited in a single experience. And second, the word "knowledge" is sometimes used for that enjoyment or contemplation which projects no purposes but is completely absorbed in the given as an esthetic object. (Whether there are any experiences which have exclusively this character is open to doubt, but at least experience may have this ingredient or this aspect.) Putting these two together, it is easy to arrive at the erroneous conclusion that there is a kind of cognitive apprehension—of simple qualities or essences—which terminates directly in the given; it may even be supposed that other knowledge rises out of this by some kind of complication and thus that direct awareness is the simplest and the basic type of knowledge.

That there is direct apprehension of the immediate, it would be absurd to deny; but confusion is likely to arise if we call it "knowledge." There are no "simple qualities" which are named by any name; there is no concept the denotation of which does not extend beyond the immediately given, and beyond what *could be* immediately given. And without concepts, there is no knowledge.

There *are* recognizable qualitative characters of the given, which may be repeated in different experiences, and are thus a sort of universals; I call these "qualia." But although such qualia are universals, in the sense of being recognized from one to another experience, they must be distinguished from the properties of objects. Confusion of these two is characteristic of many historical conceptions, as well as of current essence-theories. The quale is directly intuited, given, and is not the subject of any possible error because it is purely subjective. The property of an object is objective; the ascription of it is a judgment which may be mistaken; and what the predication of it asserts is something which transcends what could be given in any single experience.

Consider such a property as "round" or "blue." The real roundness of the real penny is seen as all degrees of elliptical appearance; the blueness of the blotter may be seen as any one of a whole range of color-qualia, depending on the illumination. The judgment that the penny is round may be made because it "looks round" or it may be made because, under given conditions which are

understood, it "looks elliptical." But the givenness of the appearance is not the givenness of objective roundness. Given the elliptical appearance,
the judgment "That is round," may be in error.
Indeed, given the *round* appearance, the judgment may still be in error, as measurement with
precision instruments might reveal. A thing which
looks blue under a certain light may *be* blue or it
may be green, and a thing that looks green or
purple may be blue. A penny run over by a railroad train will look round when held at a certain
angle, while one which looks elliptical may be
round. In other words, the same quale may be, for
a correct interpretation, the sign of different objective properties and different qualia may be the
sign of the *same* objective property.

The confusion of the quale and the objective
property has doubtless come about through a
short-cut in the use of language which is characteristic of common-sense. A thing is said to "look
round" when it presents the quale which a really
round object does when held at right angles to the
line of vision; and a thing is said to "look blue"
when it looks the way a really blue thing does under usual or standard illumination. In general,
the name of the property is also assigned to the
appearance of it under certain optimum conditions. The round penny *looks* round when held
at that angle at which judgment of actual shape
from visual appearance is safest. And an object

looks the color that it is under that illumination
which is conducive to accurate color discrimination. A thing looks as big as it is at about that
distance (for objects of its size) at which human
beings make fewest mistakes in judgments of
magnitude. This use of language has its obvious
practical motives, but it would be an extraordinarily poor observer who should suppose that
what the name means in ordinary parlance is the
appearance as such and not the objective property.

It is not, of course, a philosophic problem to determine how such language should properly be
used. But it is worth remarking that those philosophers who suppose that the names of properties
are first the names of certain given qualia and
therefore of the properties of objects which, under optimum conditions, present them, have
missed something significant which determine the
common-sense use of language.

Qualia are universals, and they are universals
such that without the recognition of them by the
individual nothing presented in experience could
be named or understood or known at all. At this
point it would be very easy to fall into controversy about the use of language which above
all things I wish to avoid. Whether one should say
that there must be concepts of qualia because they
are recognized, or no concepts of qualia because
they are ineffable; whether the immediate appre-

hension of qualia should be called "knowledge" because of its function in the cognition of objects, or should not be called "knowledge" because it neither needs nor can have any verification; whether this direct awareness should be merely so designated or should be termed a "judgment"—all this has to do only with the meaning of the terms "concept," "knowledge," "judgment." What I wish to point out is the real and important distinction between qualia and the immediate awareness of them on the one hand and the properties of objects and our knowledge of them on the other.

Qualia are subjective; they have no names in ordinary discourse but are indicated by some circumlocution such as "looks like"; they are ineffable, since they might be different in two minds with no possibility of discovering that fact and no necessary inconvenience to our knowledge of objects or their properties. All that can be done to designate a quale is, so to speak, to locate it in experience, that is, to designate the conditions of its recurrence or other relations of it. Such location does not touch the quale itself; if one such could be lifted out of the network of its relations, in the total experience of the individual, and replaced by another, no social interest or interest of action would be affected by such substitution. What is essential for understanding and for communication is not the quale as such but that pattern of its stable relations in experience which is what is implicitly predicated when it is taken as the sign of an objective property.

Apprehension of the presented quale, being immediate, stands in no need of verification; it is impossible to be mistaken about it. Awareness of it is not judgment in any sense in which judgment may be verified; it is not knowledge in any sense in which "knowledge" connotes the opposite of error. It may be said that the recognition of the quale is a judgment of the type, "This is the same ineffable 'yellow' that I saw yesterday." At the risk of being boresome, I must point out that there is room for subtle confusion in interpreting the meaning of such a statement. If what is meant by predicating sameness of the quale today and yesterday should be the immediate comparison of the given with a memory image, then certainly there is such comparison and it may be called "judgment" if one choose; all I would point out is that, like the awareness of a single presented quale, such comparison is immediate and indubitable; verification would have no meaning with respect to it. If anyone should suppose that such direct comparison is what is generally meant by judgments of qualitative identity between something experienced yesterday and something presented now, then obviously he would have a very poor notion of the complexity of memory as a means of knowledge. He might be advised to try buying a spool of thread to match something left at home. The usual statement, "This is the same yellow I saw yesterday," truly represents a judgment because at least one of the things compared is an objective reality—a temporally continuing entity which retains its identity and character. This meaning is something which could be verified, under conditions which are conducive to the permanence of color, by going back to the *object* seen yesterday, or in some other, and perhaps indirect, fashion. The judgment is about an objective property of a thing. To suppose that a quale itself is such an enduring entity is to work confusion between what is immediate and something else which, from the point of view of knowledge, is an intellectual construction of a highly complex sort.*

An immediate quale apart from some relational context which "locates" it in experience is intrin-

---

*Immediate comparisons are presumably very important in determinations of value. Such determinations of better and worse, as between immediately presented qualia such as two pleasures or pains, conjointly experienced, are often called "value-judgments." Such comparison is doubtless indispensable to determination of value, but, here as elsewhere, judgment, in the ordinary sense, does not concern the immediately presented as such or for its own sake, but the *enduring* value of something *objective* to which this immediate comparison may be a clue. Here as elsewhere, the immediate comparison is indubitable and verification has no meaning for it; what needs to be verified and is worth *judging* is the permanent quality of some object, or type of objects, or some permanent possibility of value-experience.

It may be further noted that it is this confusion of subjective and objective, referred to in the text above, which almost inevitably results from the interpolation of a "sensum" between the subject and the object. If a sensum has character which endures and can be wrongly apprehended or "not noticed," then a large part of the problem of knowledge concerns our *veridical* apprehension of sensa; the supposition that they simply are in mind or identical with the

sically and absolutely inarticulate. It is inarticulate not only in the sense that it cannot be expressed to another; it would be impossible for it to be abstracted and envisaged as an object of our own thought. Imagine a man to suffer all his life from toothache, but in such wise that no pressure on the jaw, no change of temperature or of the heart-beat, no behavior of himself or difference of surroundings would ever alter it. Not only would a person so afflicted be unaware that he suffered toothache—it would not in fact *be a toothache;* he could not even become conscious of the *ache* as a distinct fact of his experience. He would be aware of it as the cow is aware of hunger, perhaps, but it would never become for him an explicit object of thought. Such an all-pervasive

---

content of awareness is incompatible with the possibility of erroneous judgment of their enduring and objective character.

Also, it may be said that the statement "This is the same yellow that I saw yesterday" has meaning in a sense which does *not* have to do with the objective quality of a physical thing. I believe this is correct; it may intend the assertion of the qualitative identity of two *psychological states.* But the statement with this meaning is significant only in the same sense in which it is verifiable; that is, on the assumption that psychological states are events which modify a substantive thing, the mind, and that this enduring mind is an organized reality in which, as in physical things, events are later verifiable by the effects which they produce. What is not a "thing" or objective, in terms of our knowledge of the physical, may be something objective in the categories of psychology. Qualia as presentations of external reality and qualia as states of a mind are quite different matters. In both cases, they are presentations of objects—quite different objects because the *relational context* into which the presentation is brought in being understood is quite different in the two cases. In the one case, they are presentations of an external reality, a physical thing or property; in the other, they are presentations of a psychic reality, a mind. In no case are they objective or the object of knowledge apart from a relational context of conceptual interpretation. And in all cases, the judgment or knowledge is about what is objective.

ingredient of experience could never become articulate, because it would lack the ground of any possible discrimination and relation. No language could express it; there would be no thinking to be done about it; there would be no possibility of bounding it or eliciting it as a separate fact. For the person in question, it would be a part of his life or a coloring of reality but no part of his knowledge. The concept of a toothache does not consist of the ache but—broadly speaking—in the apprehension of what brought it on and the formula for getting rid of it. All that is intelligible about it is the set of relations in which it stands.

There are no concepts of immediate qualia as such—not because the word "concept" as here used has any unnecessary connotation of the verbal, but because articulation is the setting of bounds and establishing of connections; because what does not affect discrimination and relation has no handle by which the mind can take hold of it. It would be erroneous to take this fact to mean some positive bafflement in the presence of the immediate, because there is here no question we can ask which fails to find an answer; there is no interest which is baffled. The interest of knowledge is for action, and action proceeds by way of relation.

If, then, we take "simple ideas" such as "blue" and "round" as, so to speak, the least concepts that there are, we find that what such concepts embrace is not an immediate quale as such but some stable pattern of relations. We have concepts of objective properties—these are indicated by the manner in which we should proceed to verify the blueness of the blue blotter or the roundness of the penny. The manner in which such verification must take place is obvious. To verify a shape, we walk around the object or manipulate it. Its successive perspectives and their relation to our behavior meanwhile, must present a certain order of temporal relationships. If it is a small object, we may corroborate the visual by tactile and kinesthetic impressions. If a large one, we may measure it. Feeling the roundness of a marble as we roll it between thumb and fingers, or measuring a house, is again a temporally extended and ordered relation of apprehended qualia. To verify a color, we change the conditions of illumination or alter the angle so as to get rid of the sheen, or we bring the thing into juxtaposition with some object whose color has previously been tested or is accepted as a standard of comparison. When we thus manipulate the object or behave toward it, we must know what we expect if it really is round or blue, or what not. If what is thus predicted does not supervene, then our first ascription of the objective property will be withdrawn as proven false. The objective reality of the property consists, of course, from the point of view of knowledge, of what would verify it, and includes everything the failure of which would lead to the withdrawal of the judgment as mistaken. The concept of the blueness or round-ness of an object which is presented includes all that is essential to the truth of the predication of the property. Thus what constitutes the existence of an objective property and the applicability of a concept—even of the simplest sort—is not a given quale alone but an ordered relation of dif-ferent qualia, relative to different conditions or behavior. This pattern or order, which is what the adjective names, will always be *temporally ex-tended* (which is the same as to say that the predi-cation of the property is something *verifiable*), and always it will have relation to our own possible ways of acting toward the presented object.

If then, one approach the problem of our knowledge of objects—as many have done and do —with the notion that the object is "known as" some complex of presented or presentable quali-ties, and is thus analyzable into "simple" quali-ties which are capable of being presented and identified in a momentary experience and are es-sences or the denotation of certain simple con-cepts, I hope the nature of his error will be clear. If concepts are to be articulate and meaningful, then the application of them must be something verifiable; which means that what they denote must have a temporal spread. Not a momentary

presented quale but an ordered relationship of
such, is the least that can be meaningfully named.
The predication of a property on the basis of
momentarily presented experience, is in the nature of an hypothesis, which predicts something
definitely specifiable in further possible experience, and something which such experience may
corroborate or falsify. The identifiable character
of presented qualia is *necessary to* the predication
of objective properties and to the recognition of
objects, but it is not *sufficient for* the verification
of what such predication and recognition implicitly assert, both because what is thus asserted
transcends the given and has the significance of
the prediction of further possible experience, and
because the *same* property may be validly predicated on the basis of *different* presented qualia,
and *different* properties may be signalized by the
same presented quale. If the denotation of any
concept were an immediately apprehensible quale
or complex of such, then the ascription of this
concept when such qualia were presented could
not conceivably be in error. That the predication
of a property may be mistaken, or the perception
of it illusory, corroborates the fact that what is
involved in the cognition of the property transcends the given. One cannot be mistaken about
the content of an immediate awareness. If I have
bitten an apple, I cannot be mistaken about the
taste in my mouth. But I may conceivably fall

into error in predicating sweetness of the apple or expecting a similar taste from another bite. The only sense in which apprehension could be illusory or erroneous is just this sense of including a meaning which is not given but is added to the given and must be verified, if at all, in some other experience.

It is evident that the considerations here brought forward with reference to the knowledge of objective properties will hold for the knowledge of objects in general. Knowledge *always* transcends the immediately given. It begins with the recognition of a qualitatively specific presentation, but even that minimum of cognition which consists in naming is an interpretation which implicitly asserts certain relations between the given and further experience. The ascription of a substantive or an adjective is the hypothesis of some sequence in possible experience or a multiplicity of such sequences. The verifiability of such is essential to the nature ascribed to the object in recognition, or even to the acceptance of this experience of it as presentation of the real. The criterion of the objectivity of what is presented is always such a relation to further experience. In the nature of the case, the difference between veridical perception and an experience which is genuinely illusory (really deceptive to the individual in question) is never to be discovered within what is strictly given in the presentation. When we distinguish one experience as illusory, another as presentation of the real, we can intend nothing even conceivably verifiable except that, starting from the given experience and proceeding in certain ways, we reach other experience which is predictable in the one case and not in the other. *Thus "acquaintance with," the recognition of what is presented as a real object of a certain kind, has already the significance of prediction and asserts the same general type of temporal connection as our knowledge of law, the "knowledge about" which is stated in generalizations.* This is merely to reiterate Berkeley's doctrine of the "idea" as a sign, with the added thought that what is contained within any one idea or presentation is never more than a fragment of the nature of the real object. The ascription of this objectivity to the presentation is *the conceptual interpretation of what is presented.*

On the other hand, that kind of knowledge which may strike us as more truly conceptual must always—if it be knowledge of reality—come down to just such interconnectedness of experience and must be verifiable in the pattern of presented experiences. It is this which is affirmed in the dictum of Charles Peirce: "Consider what effects that might conceivably have practical bearings you conceive the objects of your conception to have. Then, your conception of those effects is the whole of your conception of the object." "Effects" which are *verifiable* can, in the end, mean nothing more than actual or possible presentations.

The perceptual knowledge of an object is neither the coincidence of mind and object in the momentary experience nor any duplication of the object in the mind. A presentation bespeaks the activity of the mind, first, in that it means an abstraction and a setting of bounds within the total field of the given. And second, the manner of this abstraction already reflects a classification which is the implicit prediction of further experience. This excision of the presentation is its recognition as the appearance of a thing—its classification with other such presentations (of the same kind of thing). Such classification reflects a generalization from experience which predicts certain orderly and lawful connections of this presentation with further experience. In the absence of such implicit prediction, the presentation would be meaningless. Thus the classification of what is presented and the predicted relationship of it with further experience are *one and the same thing*. This implicit prediction is at once a general principle and our concept of the object.

The concept, to be sure, is substantive or adjectival, not propositional, but the application of the concept to the presentation is an interpretation of the same fundamental sort that propositions express. The validity of such application de-

pends on the subsistence of those relations to other
experience which are implicit in the concept. It is
such propositions which we implicitly assert in
naming and recognizing, and do not think to express. They are the knowledge upon which all
other knowledge of reâlity is built.

We have knowledge of objects, then, not
through any coincidence of mind and object in
awareness but precisely so far as this is transcended. The merely contemplated or enjoyed
may possess esthetic significance but it has no
cognitive meaning. The dictum of the new realists, that mind and object coincide so far as the
object is just now known by this mind and so far
as the mind is just now a knowing of this object, is as wrong as possible. So far as mind and
presentation coincide, the state of mind is not cognition and the presented object is not known.
Presentative theories of knowledge in general—as
well as representative theories—commit a similar
error.

For the object presented to be real, there must
be more to it than *could* be given in any single
experience. The objectivity of the experience implies this "more." And this cognitively signified
"more," which is the meaning of the presentation,
must be verifiable. But what does it signify that
there should be verifiably more to any object than
is given in the single experience of it? It can mean
nothing else than the possibility of *other* experi-

ences, of a predictable sort, related to this experience in predictable ways. Any other kind of
"more" attached to the presentation would be unverifiable. If some will contend that there can be
any other kind of "more" to the object, they must
tell us how the existence of the unverifiable is to be
known.

To be sure, that "more" which is the verifiable
meaning of the presentation, and our concept of
the object, is normally not verified in any but the
most fragmentary fashion. When I interpret a
certain round ruddy presentation as "sweet apple," I implicitly predict that if I should bite,
then I should get a certain taste. But perhaps I
am not hungry now, so I merely file away this
possibility for future reference. The "if" clause of
my prediction is allowed to remain contrary to
fact. Precisely here, in this apparently commonplace fact that the meanings ascribed in our recognition of objects and predications of properties
must be *verifiable*, yet are commonly not *verified*
or only verified in part, is something of great importance both for understanding the relation of
knowledge to our ways of acting and for the nature of objectivity or thinghood.

A mind for which, whatever happened, nothing
could be done about it, could possess no knowledge, either of generalizations or of objects. Not
only would knowledge in such a mind serve no purpose, and thus be a genetic puzzle; it would not

exist at all. For the merely receptive and passive mind, there could be no objects and no world.

A thing—we may say as a first approximation —is a complex of properties or qualities, recognizable by some uniformity of appearance; a generalization or law designates some uniformity of behavior. But, as we have seen, appearance and behavior are not wholly separable. An appearance, if it be that of a recognizable and nameable thing, and not merely some meaningless and indescribable cross-section of the flux of experience, must recur in predictable ways. It must be a subject about which we can generalize. My desk-chair is not a universal entity but a unique object; in my experience, however, and in that of the household, it is a reliable uniformity. Every morning I find it there before my desk. It is this recurrence, and a hundred other trivial uniformities of its behavior as a part of my experience, which constitute it a thing. If we consider some even more stable object —say the vase on the mantel which stands always in one place and exhibits no alteration whatever that can be detected—then there would be *no* behavior which is ascribable to the object itself; *it* does not change. But it is still because of its recurrence, in a certain context, in my experience that I recognize this presentation as a thing. That change which constitutes the background within which it persists as an identity, is a charge which I ascribe to my own behavior, my comings and goings. But it is still true that if this recurrence in experience did not conform to certain generalizations about the process or eventuation of experience, it would not be a thing but an illusion, like the quite different object which I saw there last night in my dream.

There may seem to be a fundamental categorial distinction between what is thing, designatable by a substantive, and what is transition, relation, some connection of things which is designatable only by a proposition and, when predictable, is known as generalization or law. It is this dichotomy which, by being misunderstood, leads to the false division of knowledge into immediate "acquaintance with" and "knowledge about." We might suppose that this dichotomy correlates with the division of experience into what James called "flights and perches." An appearance of a thing is a kind of arrest; relation or the propositional signifies the flux. But this, I think we may see, is false. Experience may be as full of flux as a trip in a roller-coaster, but if it is a flight which is repeatable under conditions which can be specified, it is the appearance of a thing. It is true that thinghood connotes some stability and persistence, while "law" designates some uniformity of change or process. But the true basis of this dichotomy is not the division into flights and perches in experience; *it is the division between that part of the flux of experience which I ascribe to myself*

and my own activity, and that change which can-
not be so predicated of myself and is objective.

Both thing and the change described by law belong to the objective world. The objective reality
of things is that uniformity I reach by a reorder-
ing of the actual process of experience so as to
subtract, or integrate out, "my own activity"; objective change is that part of the process which
remains after such subtraction. That a thing is
always there in the objective world, does not mean
that it is always there in experience; it means that
it is always there when I look for it in the right
place or in the right way. It means that its recurrence in experience in uniform ways *relative to*
my own action is predictable. "Looking for it"
may, of course, mean a quite complex process and,
in certain types of cases, may reach the object
only indirectly; also the kind of "stability" or
"persistence" to be expected varies with the type
of object and may be highly complex. But at bottom, when complications and qualifications have
been dealt with, thinghood means a stability or
uniformity of appearance which can be recovered
by certain actions of my own.

This distinction between objective change and
those transitions of experience which are not objective because attributable to myself, was first
pointed out by Kant. The order of positions of the
boat going down the stream is objective because
by nothing I can do is this order in experience to

be reversed. But the sides of the house are simultaneous and are merely partial presentations of one stable and unchanging thing because the order of their succession in experience is due to my own action. It is obvious that we here confront a fundamental consideration of the utmost importance for the analysis of the categories, for the distinction of self and external world and for the division of the flux of experience into time and space. Into these most difficult matters, we cannot go, but it may be in point to observe the basic character of the conception of "activity."

To ascribe an objective quality to a thing means implicitly the prediction that if I act in certain ways, specifiable experience will eventuate: if I should bite this, it would taste sweet; if I should pinch it, it would feel moderately soft; if I should eat it, it would digest and not poison me; if I should turn it over, I should perceive another rounded surface much like this; if I should put it on the scales, they would register about three ounces. These and a hundred other such hypothetical propositions constitute my knowledge of the apple in my hand. These are *the meaning which this presentation has to me now,* but it may be that neither now nor in the immediate future do I actually verify these possibilities.

It is only because we are active beings that our world is bigger than the content of our actual experience. For the active being, reality is as much bigger than the content of given experience as is measured by the totality of all that is related to what is presented by those propositions of the type "If I should . . . then . . ." which he takes to be true. All that "more" which belongs to the objects presented to him, over and above what is immediately given, and all the rest of reality, as it stands related to his object but not presented with it, resides in this potency of possible experience. For the passive being, the *only possible* passage of experience is the actual one: the only continuities of reality—the only relations with any given—would be the actual flux of experience. No object would be thicker than its presentation. And since all motive to that analysis which delimits the presentation would be lost in the lapsing of any manner of relating it except to the actually antecedent and consequent items of the given, the distinction of the given field into presentation and background would serve no purpose and would presumably fail to be made. Thus for the passive being the whole of reality would collapse into the actual procession of the given; indeed it must collapse into the specious present, since the objectivity of memory and anticipation is a complex interpretation put upon presented imagery. Even the "stream of consciousness" itself is a highly conceptual construction, requiring, amongst other items, the category of objective time as the order of that change which is irreversible by the "if" of any altered mode of action. For the passive being, there would be no distinction of subjective and objective; the given would be both subject and object, and the whole of both. Nothing would be verifiable save what was presently verified, and hence nothing would mean anything. There could be no distinction between real and illusory. Since nothing given would transcend its givenness and there would be no distinction of real from unreal, there would be no reality.

The whole content of our knowledge of reality is the truth of such "If—then" propositions, in which the hypothesis is something we conceive could be made true by our mode of acting and the consequent presents a content of experience which, though not actual now and perhaps not to become actual, is a possible experience connected with the present. For the active being such hypothetical propositions can be meaningful and true when the hypothesis is false.* The attribution to what is given of connection with such a content of further possible experience is the conceptual interpreta-

---

*The significance of knowledge depends upon the significance of possibility that is not actual. Possibility and impossibility—hence necessity and contingency, consistency and inconsistency, and various other fundamental notions—require that there should be "If —— then—" propositions whose truth or falsity is independent of the truth or falsity of the condition stated in their antecedent clauses. Those readers who happen to be familiar with my doctrine of "strict implication" will find here a motive for the distinction of "strict" from "material" implication and for other basic conceptions of the system of "strict implication." A "material" implication represents an "If —— then—" proposition the truth of which is *not* independent of the *truth* of its antecedent clause.

tion of the presentation and our knowledge of the object.

Furthermore, when we distinguish one experience as illusory, another as presentation of the real, what we intend can be nothing other than that those sequences of possible experience which are implicitly predicted in the concept of the object would fail to eventuate in the one case but would be realized in the other. The difference between illusion and veridical perception is not in the given experience (even though its failure to be found there is due to our own inattentiveness or other neglect to behave suitably to our interests), else there is not really any illusion. Hence the real-ity of any object is known, not by its being presented simply, but by judgment or interpretation which is predictive.

Knowledge of objects, then, knowledge of the real, involves always two elements, the element of given and ineffable presentation, and the element of conceptual interpretation which represents the mind's response. We might say that the conceptual is the formal element, of order or relation, and the given is the material or content element. But there are here two misunderstandings to be guarded against.

First, the given is not formless in the sense of being indefinite. One kind of definiteness which the given has—its qualitative specificity—is too obvious to need pointing out. Further, it is not formless in the sense that this qualitative and ineffable character of it is indifferent for knowledge. If there were no correlation in the individual mind between the concept and particular qualia, then no experience could be the signal of any particular meaning. It is also to the point that the implicitly predicted relationships, comprised in the conceptual interpretation of what is presented, must be such that further possible experience could verify or fail to verify them. Without the correlation of concept and qualia, no experience could verify or fail to verify anything. My presently given experience leads me to say that if I should move ten feet to the left I should reach the wall. If the visual presentation interpreted as "wall" were not identifiable by its sensory qualities, or if stepping and contact did not have this identifiable qualitative specificity, then my statement could have no meaning. For another person, the sensory qualia which would be in point when he saw the wall from this chair might be different from mine. But for each of us, within his individual experience, if we did not correlate certain concepts with certain identifiable feelings, there could be no knowledge of objects at all.

The intelligibility of experience consists precisely in this; that between the specific quality of what is given and the pattern of its context in possible experience there is some degree of stable correlation. So that the quality is due to the relations and the relational pattern is due to the quality. Such stable correlation is *not* a universally discovered fact, all-pervasive in experience. (We shall return to this topic in a later chapter.*) Experience is completely intelligible only in the sense that every experience will exhibit *some* discoverable correlation between presented quality and relational context. So far as such correlation is a fact, it is simply the miracle that an intelligible world exists.

In saying that knowledge consists of the conceptual element and only points or refers to the given, there is no intent to deny that the eventual significance of knowledge may be in the quality of immediate experience. It is quite possible and plausible that the direction of our action and the ultimate significance of our attempts to know are determined by the value-aspect of experience, which is a dimension of, or derivative from, felt quality. Knowledge may be, in general, a means to some more valuable end which is not knowledge. Indeed, so far as the nature of the goods of life admits of any ultimate separation of means and end, I should suppose this view to be correct. Knowledge is pragmatic, utilitarian, and its value, like that of the activity it immediately subserves, is extrinsic. It has value as an end in itself only so far as, in life, the activity is the goal, or at least the two cannot be separated.

*See pp. 348–358.

Nor do I mean to assert that *consciousness* is essentially relational, though I suspect this to be the case. I assert only that it is relation which constitutes that *intelligibility* which is essential to *knowledge*. Whether consciousness of pure immediacy without conceptual interpretation would be below the level of awareness altogether, I hesitate to judge. But if complete absorption in the immediate is not equivalent to unconsciousness, at least it is the bourne from which no traveller can bring back any intelligible report.

As was suggested in Chapter II, the mystic and the protagonist of "pure perception" will probably differ with the account here given primarily by their insistence that such absorption in the inexpressible immediate is the valuable *end*. They tend to reserve the word "knowledge" for this relation of the mind to the given which they thus esteem it desirable to take. I reserve the word for that which is articulate and verifiable, and has a significant opposite, "error." So far, the difference will be purely verbal. They would agree that absorption in the immediate transcends conceptual thinking altogether. The further point, that conceptual thinking, articulation, and the interests of action go together, they would also admit. To the mystic, negation of conceptual distinctions and absorption in the immediate represent the desirable attitude because this solves of problems of action, for his world-weariness, by negating them.

To say, "The identification of mind with the ineffable object is the valid end," is the same as to say, "The interests of action are *nil*."

The motive from which Bergson, who does not thus extol the mystic experience, restricts theoretically true knowledge to "pure perception" in which practical interests are transcended, is a matter which his writings do not make wholly clear. Indeed I am minded to ask: What difference would it make if his "scientific constructions" and "interpretations in the interest of action" were renamed "knowledge" and the object of them "reality"; if his "intuition" and "pure perception" were labelled "esthetic experience" and their object "subjective immediacy"? Apart from some moral or religious interest in setting intuition and its object higher than science and the scientific (and social) object, what point in this ascription of "knowledge" and "reality" to pure intuition and its object? For Bergson, the scientific (the social and the common-sense) interpretation is, theoretically considered, a misinterpretation made in the interests of practice. But in what sense can it be misinterpretation if, follow it however far, one never reaches any undesirable dénouement which could be avoided by refraining? Since conceptual interpretation serves the interests of action, why this invidious denial to it of the term "knowledge" unless action is essentially undesirable and its interests are a low sort?

He also thinks that conceptual interpretation reveals its inadequacy in the end by disclosing its internal inconsistency as well as its untruth to the given. This is the significance of his resuscitation of Zeno's paradoxes and of much else in "Time and Free Will." If he should mean by this that prevailing scientific conceptions—of time, space, motion, etc.—are defective and need to be replaced, many will agree with him. But if he means —as seems to be the case—that *no* scientific construction in the interests of action and social coöperation can escape eventual inconsistency, then it would appear to be implied that the interests of action are themselves self-frustrating. If the significance of conceptual interpretation lies in action, then the significance of inconsistent interpretation must be in self-defeating action. But if Bergson should commit himself to the thesis that practical action is essentially self-defeating, he will indeed agree with the mystic. So far as his objection is that scientific conception turns the flight of pure duration into objects which are static, it may be suggested that the mistake lies in supposing that the object denoted by common-sense and scientific concepts *is* thus static, instead of something temporally extended and identified as a certain predictable flux of experience.

It is a frequent criticism of the type of theory here outlined that it cannot account for our knowledge of the past. Knowledge, it is said, is here identified with verification, and verification comes about by some proceeding from the present into the future. Thus the past, so far as it can be known, is transformed into something present and future, and we are presented with the alternatives, equally impossible, that the past cannot be known or that it really is not past.

Without a metaphysical analysis of temporal categories it would be difficult to answer this criticism completely. But I should like to present certain considerations which may be put forward briefly.

The first of these is of a general sort which has much wider application. The philosophic analysis of any object or content of knowledge is not completely achieved by even an ideal epistemology. The theory of knowledge, to be successful, must disclose, for every major type of object, the *ratio cognoscendi*. But the achievement of an account which should accomplish this would still not abolish nor make superfluous analyses of other sorts, directed to some different problem. In some one of the innumerable meanings of the word "is" it must be true that a thing is what it is "known as," identifiable with its *ratio cognoscendi;* but it is also the effect of its causes, the cause of its effects, the organized whole of its physical or other constituents, and a hundred other significant things besides. There has been some tendency in philosophy since Kant, and perhaps particularly amongst idealists, to attach to epistemological analyses a kind of *exclusive* truth, but to do this is to commit what Professor Perry has called "the fallacy of initial predication." If, then, we assert that, from the point of view of knowledge, the past is so and so, this is not to deny to the past various types of significance not included in such an epistemological account.

It may also be legitimate to observe that the criticism in question would have greater weight if in general those who urge it were prepared to tell us how the past, which is really dead and gone, can be known. Epistemological analyses of the past, consistent with theories maintained, are conspicuous mainly by their absence. Those who do not speak in the interest of such an alternative account should not too hastily reject a theory which at least begins with an obvious fact (the verifiability of the past) because it affects them with a feeling of paradox. Paradox is indeed a danger-signal, but the trouble it signalizes may be in the theory which appears paradoxical or it may be in the relatively inchoate character of common notions.

In general, the past is verifiable. We are probably safe in assuming that any satisfactory metaphysics will hold that there could not be any item of the past which is *intrinsically* unverifiable. Knowledge of the past, like knowledge of anything else, may be verified only in the present and future. But if one suppose this to mean that a past event, verifiable as being so and so by certain present and future possible experiences, is thereby transformed into something present or future, the error he commits is in a failure to understand what is involved, from the point of view of knowledge, in assigning temporal locus to an object known. We may remind ourselves of the example, borrowed from Kant, of the permanent house and the impermanent position of the boat in the stream, both "known as" certain types of sequence in experience, fundamentally alike in their merely temporal aspects. That a thing endures through a given period is more or less completely verifiable. But if permanence of the thing were justifiably predicated only of what is permanently experienced, there would be nothing permanent.

The assumption that the past is intrinsically verifiable means that at any date after the happening of an event, there is always something, which at least is conceivably possible of experience, by means of which it can be known. Let us call these items its "effects." The totality of such effects quite obviously constitute all of the object that is knowable. To separate the effects from the object is, thus, to transform it into some incognizable *ding an sich*. We may then say, from a certain point of view, that the event is spread throughout all after time,* much as modern phys-

---

*We may neglect the question whether all events are intrinsically predictable and, hence, extend through all preceding time as well.

ics may say that the field of an electronic charge is spread through all space and that this field *is* the electron. That the field of a charge *is* the charge and is throughout all space, does not abolish the difference between a charge at one point and a different charge at another; these are different *ways* of being throughout space, a different totality of effects. Just so, the conception that an event is spread throughout the time "after its occurence" will not abolish the difference between different events occurring at different times; these will be identifiable through a different totality of effects. We must avoid the fallacy of simple location* with respect to temporal as well as spatial attributes. In so far as an event, or the existence of a thing at a certain date, is intrinsically verifiable, and is thus spread through all after time in its effects, what cognition of it apprehends as its presentation and what historical knowledge proceeds to verify, is a part of its nature. Or it is the "appearance" of the event at the time of this verification, much as a presented surface may be the appearance of a solid object. Events are knowable "after they occur" because their appearances or effects are "there" at the later date to be experienced.

For a satisfactory account, it would be essential to reveal, by analysis of experience, those peculiar characteristics by which the pastness of a

---

*I borrow this phrase, of course, from Professor Whitehead.

thing is presently identified; as would also a similar account of the categories "permanent" and "future." But for present purposes it will be sufficient to remark that obviously *some* kind of identifiable marks in presented experience must mean the pastness of the thing presented, since otherwise the past event could not be distinguished from the present. Doubtless one item would be a certain kind of unalterability and unresponsiveness to desire and purpose in which respect what is present or future would not be thus unalterable. This character, like unalterability in general, would be verified by proceeding from the present into the future in certain ways. In any case the past can be known—if not completely, at least so far as it can come in question for a theory of knowledge—and it can be known to *be* past. Whatever it is by means of which past fact is verified, it is something which is capable of present and future experience. The past is known through a correct interpretation of something given, including certain given characters which are the marks of pastness. If this be paradox, then so much the worse for common-sense.

Chapter VI

THE RELATIVITY OF KNOWLEDGE
AND THE INDEPENDENCE OF
THE REAL

The history of philosophy since Descartes has been largely shaped by acceptance of the alternatives; either (1) knowledge is not relative to the mind, or (2) the content of knowledge is not the real, or (3) the real is dependent on mind.

Kant, and phenomenalism in general, recognizes the relativity of knowledge, the dependence of the phenomenal object on the mind, and hence the impossibility of knowing the real as it is in itself. Idealism, taking the relativity of knowledge as its main premise, argues to the unqualified dependence of reality upon mind by holding the alternative—that there is no valid knowledge of the real—to be logically impossible. Realists in general seek to reconcile the possibility of knowing reality with its independence of the mind by one or another attempt to escape the relativity of knowledge.

However, the alternatives accepted are false alternatives. This whole historical development, so far as it turns upon them, is a mistake. There is no contradiction between the relativity of knowledge and the independence of its object. If the real object can be known at all, it can be known only in its relation to a mind; and if the mind were different the nature of the object as known might well be different. Nevertheless the description of the object as known is true description of an independent reality.

This sounds at first like unintelligible paradox. But, as I shall hope to convince the reader, relativity of this sort, which is entirely compatible with independence, is a commonplace, capable of illustration for all sorts of relations which have nothing directly to do with knowledge.

If this position can be successfully maintained, then the fundamental premises of phenomenalism and idealism fall to the ground, some of the main difficulties posed by skepticism are met, and the general attitude of common-sense realism can be reinstated without attempting to do the impossible and avoid the relativity of knowledge.

The question whether we know reality truly, is often made to turn upon the relation between presentation, or appearance, and the real object. The assumption upon which Descartes set out— the assumption of the copy-theory—is that knowledge of the external world requires that the sense-quale we apprehend should be identically present in the object perceived and in the mind when we perceive it. Perhaps, remembering the subtleties of the critical realists, we ought to phrase this more sharply: The validity of sense-perception does not depend upon the, *numerical* identity of, *e. g.*, blue in the perceiving mind and blue in the object; state of mind and property of the object may be separate existences. But it is required that they be identical in quality; that the quality perceived as blue be in the object just as it is perceived. Failing this, the real object is a *ding an sich*, a "something, I know not what."

That the sense-qualities as perceived are relative to the perceiver, and hence subjective only, is an old thought. It goes back to Empedocles and the Sophists, in the earliest theory of sense-perception as something produced by the mingled motions of the object and of the sense-organ. It is the main root of ancient skepticism. The reasons for it are pretty obvious and historically have been well exploited. In the first place, there are individual differences of perception, and differences between our own perceptions under different circumstances. Second, there is the correlation between differences of behavior—power to discriminate and compare — and differences of the receptor organs; from which we conclude a dependence of sensory qualities upon the senses and the nervous system. And third, there is the discovery of physical phenomena, such as certain wave-motions, closely analogous to the stimuli of perception but not affecting human senses at all.

We have, then, good reasons to believe in the

relativity of the quality of what is given, and the limits of what can be given, to the nature and capacity of the perceiving subject. This being so, can reality be given to us as it is in itself? Is this relativity compatible with the truth of immediate experience to its object?

Whether the character of the given is untrue to reality in any other sense, it should first be admitted that certainly it can be, at times, practically misleading. It can be the occasion of errors of judgment. And the nature and limits of the mind or sense-organs may be what gives rise to such errors. If I cannot discriminate what you discriminate, I may mistake one thing for another in ways which you do not. In general, for every discoverable peculiarity of the subject which is reflected in the character of the presented as such, there is some imaginable or actual misleading which can result from it. The qualia of the given are the clue to the applicability or inapplicability of concepts, and set the limits of conceptual interpretation. Wrong understanding may be due to stupidity; that fact does not here concern us. But also it may be due to the nature of the given. All illusory experience is thus misleading. If my poor vision does not enable me to detect that one wall of the room is a mirror, or if I merely fail to notice this, then I may walk into the wall. Even if I do not thus put it to the test, my perception leads me to predicate a possibility of experience which does not in fact obtain. The given, because of its character as given, means for me an object which does not in fact exist. With greater acuity of vision, I should have avoided this error. The reason for it lies in the character of presented experience, which is conditioned by the limitations of my senses.

Entirely similar considerations apply in most cases of illusion and in all cases of errors of perception due to limitation or peculiarities of sense. But we have so far told only half the story. Such errors, we have said, are due to the character of the given in the particular case. They are also due to the conceptual interpretation which has been put upon what is given. In fact they are due *directly* to the conceptual interpretation and only indirectly to the given experience.

The difference between veridical perception on the one hand, and illusion and error on the other, is not in the nature of what is given except so far as this leads to the likelihood of an interpretation which is invalid. Such interpretation has to do with the relation between the presentation and that further possible experience which our classifying or recognizing or understanding of what is presented implicitly predicts. When this predicted relation actually obtains, the presented object is recognized for what it truly is. When it does not, our understanding of the object is erroneous. Sometimes such mistake amounts to illusion; sometimes not. But this is a comment on our use of the term "illusion" rather than upon the relation between presentation and the real. It depends upon the degree and importance of our failure to apprehend this relation to further experience, which in turn depends on the breadth of our knowledge and various other circumstances affecting our judgment.

Whether a mirror-image is illusory or veridical depends on our previous experience of mirrors, or upon the degree of attention which determines whether we notice the frame, and so forth. A mirror-image recognized as such, is veridical perception. When I take it for a thing which can be grasped by moving in the direction of the mirror, it is illusion. If I recognize it as a mirror-image but take it as the image of another person when it is my own reflection, then we have a perfectly definite and commonplace experience which is partly correct and partly erroneous—what is usually called a "mistake." In these three cases, what is given might be identical. Similarly if I judge an object ten feet off to be a mile away, it is illusion; but if I judge it to be fifteen feet off, it is a "slight error." All sorts and degrees of mistake in the implicit prediction of further experience are possible, and readily illustrated; the flat dichotomy into illusion and veridical perception ill accords with the facts. In part, this classification reflects the importance of certain interests of action which the perception serves. When such interests are completely thwarted, we have illusion; when they are only partly or momentarily thwarted, the perception is usually classed as inaccurate, more or less mistaken. And in part, our use of such terms reflects the fact that the implicit prediction of further possible experience would often, if explicitly stated, be quite detailed and circumstantial, and that such prediction may be verifiable in part and in part not. The question of veracity is the question how much and how important a part of the prediction is valid. There is no distinct type of cases, classifiable as "illusion," which are the seeing or feeling what is "not true to reality" as contrasted with normal perception which is "seeing things as they are."

Furthermore, is illusion ever intrinsic to the given? Are there cases in which what is presented is *inevitably* mistaken? Obviously the answer is that there is no presentation which it is totally impossible to mistake and none with reference to which it is impossible to avoid mistake. Whether one is deceived depends always on the previous experience, the breadth of understanding, and the wit of the perceiver. The classic "illusions," such as the psychologist uses for illustration, are such as are pretty sure to deceive us the first time we experience them—unless we are on our guard. Sometimes the so-called "illusory perception" persists after experience has dispelled our "belief" in it. But it is then no more truly illusory than the clear and normal visual images which I receive since I put on spectacles, but never had in all the years before. Whoever has had such experience knows that a new correlation of image and distance has to be learned. Such an example well illustrates the fact that no appearance is intrinsically illusory, because the correlation with appropriate action and further experience is *always* something which has to be learned. When the presentation arouses anticipation or leads to action which is instinctive or habitual, but nevertheless in this instance proves to be ill-judged, the perception is classified as illusory or erroneous. But it is no more intrinsically so than that of the near-sighted man with his first spectacles, who misjudges the height of curbings and the distances of door-knobs.

Not all presentations, of course, are presentations of real physical objects. There is, however, something a little arbitrary in this statement, since it is fairly clear that there is never any presentation which is not, in one way or another, conditioned by the existence and nature of certain physical things; and there is thus never any presentation which is not, for intelligent understanding, a clue to some physical reality. But there are appearances so closely like normal presentations of physical things, and so different in their correct interpretation, that they may seem to be a special class. However, there is no important difference, for the theory of knowledge, between such cases and those previously mentioned. Only children and savages are deceived by dreams, and few are incapable of intelligent discrimination of the merely imagined.

The error which is responsible for this persistent notion that some presentations are intrinsically illusory, is the prejudice of the copy-theory that knowledge of objects means qualitative coincidence of the idea and the real. Such a conception is meaningless. Knowledge does not copy anything presented; it proceeds from something given toward something else. When it finds that something else, the perception is verified. When it fails, or to the extent that it fails, we have error or illusion. My visual image of the doorknob is my perception of its distance, among other things. With my spectacles on or off, two somewhat different images are signal for the same successful grasping motion. If I should try on and become habituated to various other kinds of lenses, I should find a great variety of such images, any one of which would, with experience, signalize the distance to the doorknob. That man makes glasses and nature makes eyes, does not mean that images seen without artificial aid are peculiarly different in their cognitive significance. If one could try on, as one tries on spectacles, all the different kinds of eyes that nature has produced, one would find a similar variety of visual images, every one of which would be, for the owner of those eyes who was accustomed to them, veridical perception. If one could similarly try on all the different kinds of musculature and length of arm that nature makes, one would acquire a whole museum of sensory "distances of the door-knob." Any one of them would be perception of reality, and *none of them would copy anything.*

However, this may not touch the question supposed to be at issue. Are there not presentations such that within them, merely as given, there is no clue to a veridical anticipation? As presented, there is no clue that this is X and not Y. To class it as X is to be wrong; as Y to be right; but even the most astute and experienced perceiver could not find within this momentary experience any reliable clue that it is X and not Y. To admit this unqualifiedly might be to exaggerate; we are all of us capable of being Sherlock Holmeses about familiar imagery. But within limits there certainly are such experiences; in fact, all presentations have this indecisiveness to a degree. That, however, has nothing to do with any supposed intrinsic illusion. At the present moment, nothing in my perception will enable me to decide whether yonder tree is fifty or seventy feet away, whether that bird I hear singing is an oriole or a grosbeak, whether that weather vane I see is brass or copper, whether the breeze that has just sprung up is decidedly cooler or only a little so. There is nothing illusory in these indecisive aspects of my present experience, because I have learned not to jump to conclusions in such matters. Both veridical perception and error are judgmental. An infant who should see the sights and hear the sounds which I do could not possibly be deceived. He does not know enough to be wrong. Where there is no interpretation or anticipation, there can be no error. Between such commonplace experiences and those which are illusory, there is no intrinsic difference. Present experience is a *certain* clue to very little. It enables me to anticipate other experience only within limits (the tree is between forty and eighty feet away) or with a certain degree of probability (the grosbeak's song, as I remember it, is less interrupted; this is probably an oriole).

All presentation is valid perception when it is correctly understood. Understanding is not a matter of the qualitative character of the given but of the anticipatory attitudes which it arouses. What these are, in any particular case, depends partly on the characteristics of the presentation but equally upon the perceiver, his past experience, and his judgment. Since there is no experience which is intrinsically incapable of being correctly understood and interpreted, there can be no presentation which is intrinsically illusory. So to speak, any reality does and must appear in the way it "*ought*" to appear to the kind of subject who perceives it under the conditions in which he perceives it. Between those given experiences which are most flagrantly likely to mislead and veridical perception, there are all degrees and kinds of intermediaries. *No* experience can be guaranteed to be either veridical or illusory unless the mind of the perceiver can be guaranteed.

In other words, knowledge as valid interpretation is independent of the question whether presentation and real object coincide in quality (if that means anything), because the validity of understanding does not concern the relation between experience and what is usually meant by "the independent object"; it concerns the relation between this experience and *other experiences* which we seek to anticipate with this as a clue. In Berkeley's language, this experience is "sign of" other experience; it may be such quite without reference to its "copying reality" or even if there be no "independent reality" to copy. As the history of phenomenalism serves to illustrate, conceptual knowledge may be valid provided only there is *order* in experience—if experience is lawful—quite without reference to any further question.

This disposes of the first point; that the given may be untrue to reality in that it may give rise to illusion and mistake. Such error consists in misunderstanding or practical misleading; this is always a matter of conceptual interpretation, and always it is avoidable. However, this does not dispose of the question of the relation between the phenomenal and the real. Descartes took this same position that the content of given experience is always veridical, and error is always due to inference which outruns the percept. But for Descartes this meant that, when interpretation is shorn away, the percept matches the independent reality, concerning which God in His goodness would not deceive us.

We may note in passing the total impossibility of this representationalist position. We cannot both of us see reality as it is when we do not see it alike; and differences of discrimination indubitably prove divergence of the given in different minds. The combination of representationalism with realism of the Cartesian type inevitably falls before the attack of the skeptic. Indeed, this combination of doctrines could only survive in an age when it was possible to believe that there was some normal content of veridical perception, exactly shared by the great majority of persons—the others to be somehow dealt with in a foot-note.

The relativity of presentation to the perceiver can hardly be denied. That this does not affect the validity of knowledge, can be established, since all knowledge is conceptual or interpretive. But this only renders more acute the problem posed by phenomenalism: How can a knowledge which is relative to the knower's mind and senses be true to a reality which is independent? How can the object of knowledge be identified with the real? This question resolves itself into two parts; (1) the bearing of a knowledge which is relative upon an object which has an independent nature, and (2) the valid significance of that "independence" which may be ascribed to reality. It is the first of these which is particularly in point in the dicussion of phenomenalism; the second has mainly to do with certain arguments of idealism.

We turn to the thesis with which the chapter opened. Reality, so far as it can be given in experience or known, is relative to the knower. It can be apprehended only as it does or would appear to some perceiver in some actual or possible experience. But that the only character which can be attributed to anything real is a character described in relative terms—relative to some experience—does not deny to it an independent nature, and does not deny that this nature can be known. On the contrary, true knowledge is absolute because it conveys an absolute truth, though it can convey such truth only in relative terms.

There is much here that is in no wise peculiar to knowledge but has to do with the logic of relativity in general. It is equally true of weight, for example, that it can only be described in relative terms, but that the property of the object, so described, is independent of the particular standard in terms of which the description is given. The situation in which truth can be told only in relative terms, is obviously a common one, if not universal. But this relational truth may nevertheless be absolute. To put the matter in general terms: If relative to R, A is X, and relative to S, A is Y, neither X nor Y is an absolute predicate of A. But "A is X relative to R" and "A is Y relative to S," are absolute truths. Moreover they may be truths about the independent nature of A. Generally speaking, if A had no independent character, it would not be X relative to R or Y relative to S. These relative (or relational) characters, X and Y, are partial but absolutely valid revelations of the nature of A. If we should add, "There is no truth about A which can be told without reference to its relation to R or S, or some other such," we should then have a very good paradigm to the relativity of knowledge.

To make this clear, let us turn to a few simple examples of relativity, some of which have nothing specially to do with knowledge.

The size of Cæsar's toga is relative to the yardstick.* But if we say, "The number of square yards in the toga is determined by the yardstick," the statement is over-simple. Given the toga, its size in yards is determined by the yardstick; given the yardstick, the number of yards in the toga is determined by the toga itself. If the toga had not a determinate sizableness independent of the yard-

---

*I choose this example partly because no yardstick ever was or will be laid on Cæsar's toga. I hope the parallel will be drawn in terms of human minds and past geologic ages.

stick, or if the yardstick had no size independent of the toga, then there would be no such fact as the number of yards in the toga; the relation would be utterly indeterminate. This independent character of the toga, or of the yardstick, is what we should be likely to call its "absolute" size. This can only be described in terms of *some* measure, though the description will vary according to what this measure is. The size of the toga in yards is relative to the yardstick, but it is nevertheless an independent property of the toga, a true report of which is given by its correct measurement in yards. Thus what is relative is also independent; if it had no "absolute" character, it would have no character in relative terms.

This example leads naturally to another—another sense in which size is relative. One might be moved to observe that this conceptual relativity of size is something which goes round in a circle. The toga is of so many yards; a yard, so many feet. But how big is a yard or a foot? Eventually this goes back to something like the king's foot, which is a fact of the same order as the toga. A size is relative to *other* sizes; but *some* size must be an absolute so-bigness, immediately apprehended, or there is no size at all. This would be to maintain the eventual reference of the concept to something immediate. But it is well to note in passing that, except in precisely such relative terms, the absolute so-bigness of the king's foot is also an absolute inexpressible.

Size as an absolute and immediately given so-
bigness is quite similarly relative when this size
is attributed to the object. As Berkeley put it:
How big is a mite's foot? As big as it looks to the
mite or as big as it looks to us? We here confront
a relativity of sense-experience which concerns its
supposed truth to the real object. Size, as perceived, varies with distance from the perceiver.
And there is no possibility of perceiving size at
all except at *some* distance. Perceived size is a
function of two terms, distance and X. The distance being fixed, differences of perceived size are
attributable to differences in X. The perceived
size is, so to speak, the value of the function. This
is a function of two variables; its value, perceived
size, is not determined by distance alone; it depends also on X. Distance being specified, and the
value of the function, perceived size, being given,
X is thereby determined. Distance being known,
the perceived size is a true revelation of X, which
we may call the independent size of the object.

If it be asked, "But what precisely is this independent size in any intelligible terms," we can
carry our mathematical analogy one step further.
(It is, in fact, a little more than an analogy, for
the logic of functions is not confined to mathematics.) The independent size, X, of the perceived object is the integration of the function, its
perceived size or perceived sizes, over the whole
range of the other variable, distance. That is, all

the perceived sizes, at different distances, belong to
or are parts of the objectively real size of the thing
perceived. The analogy holds good, further, in
that from the value of the function, perceived size,
for any given distance, its value for other distances are predictable. If, now, we remember that
the conceptual interpretation of the immediately
presented as the size of an objectively real thing,
is precisely such implicit prediction, from its perceived size at this distance, of perceived sizes at
other distances (among other things), we shall
observe that the "independent size of the object"
is precisely the content of a correct concept by
which its size as presented is understood. For such
a correct conceptual interpretation, *any one* of its
perceived sizes is a true revelation of this independent property.

If any one ask for an absolute size which perception or knowledge could copy or be true to in
any fundamentally different sense, I can only say
that the meaning of his inquiry escapes me, and
I believe it escapes him also.

It is obvious that what is here pointed out for
size, holds for properties in general. Just as size
may be in terms of the king's foot or the platinum
bar in the Bureau of Standards, so color, for example, may be determined by reference to the
sun's spectrum or the color-pyramid. This is conceptual relativity. Thus, in turn, we may seem to
be thrown back on color as perceived, the visual

quality just as we perceive it. But this, as a property of the real thing, is something which can hardly be supposed to represent simple coincidence of mind and object, because color, as perceived, varies with illumination. Except in light of *some* candle-power color cannot be seen at all, but the perceptual content itself varies with variation of the candle-power. Does this mean that we never see color as it is? Or that we see it as it is only at some standard illumination, arbitrarily determined? Or that we always see it as it is, when we see it at all, if what we see enables us to predict our altered visual experience of the object under other conditions?

Similarly for shape. Conceptually a shape is relative to other shapes. It can be described only in relation to standard shapes, such as square and round or by analysis into elements of shape, such as angles (measured by reference to a standard) and linear measure (obviously again relative). And shape as immediately presented configuration, if referred to the object, is relative to perspective.

The logic is the same throughout. Relativity is not incompatible with, but *requires*, an independent character in what is thus relative. And second, though what is thus relative cannot be known apart from such relation, still the other term or terms of the relation being given, all such relative knowledge is true knowledge of that independent character which, together with the other term or terms of this relationship, determines this content of our relative knowledge. The concept, or conceptual interpretation, *transcends* this relativity precisely because what the concept comprises is this relational pattern in which the independent nature of what is apprehended is exhibited in experience.

This being so, the nature of the fallacy committed by phenomenalism becomes apparent. From the relativity of knowledge to the mind, it argues to the impossibility of knowing the independent real. This is as if the question about the size of Cæsar's toga were to be answered: "Its size in our yards is so and so; in terms of some other measure which other creatures might apply, it would be different. Apart from yards or some other measure, size has no meaning. So you see that the real toga in itself is something outside the category of size. Whether it can have size at all or, if so, what that size would be, we can never know." The premise is correct. The conclusion *non sequitur*.

It may seem that our illustrations are not precisely to the point since neither distance nor degree of illumination nor angle of perspective, etc., is a property of the perceiving mind or of the sense-organs. But such illustrations have the advantage of making it clear that the logic of relativity is unaltered whether the object in question is an independent real, supposedly beyond or behind its appearances altogether, or is recognized to be the merely phenomenal object. The penny whose apparent size and configuration are relative to distance and perspective is recognized to be phenomenal and wholly knowable whether it is admitted to be independently real or not. If the relativity of its various appearances to perspective, distance and so on, does not defeat the possibility of our knowing the *phenomenal* object, how can relativity to mind, the logic of which is point for point identical, defeat the possibility of knowing the *independently real object?*

The one ground on which it might be urged with some show of reason that the relativity of the content of knowledge to the mind prevents true knowledge of the real, is that the nature of one term in this relation—the mind itself—is not known. That is, it might be said that we cannot stand outside ourselves and critically bound our own limitations. The elliptical appearance of the penny—it may be urged—conveys true knowledge because I know my angle of vision, and know how this appearance would vary as my perspective was altered. If all objects were seen from one angle only—as all objects are perpetually viewed from within the limitations of the human mind—then the relativity of perceived shape to perspective would lead to a confusion of configuration as (always) perceived with an absolute shape, which it is not.

There is much here that is worthy of careful attention, though the point is not sufficient to establish the phenomenalist's conclusion.

In the first place, it needs to be remarked that the criticism, as put, overlooks the fact that I can not know my own angles of vision except through *those same given configurations,* and the alterations of them, by which I know the shapes of things. I learn to understand both objective shape in general and the phenomenon of perspective in general when I learn how to introduce order into the given phenomena of perceived shape by treating them as functions of two variables, different perspectives and different objective shapes. And the analogue holds: I can know my own mind through its commerce with objects—and only so —just as I know objects through their commerce with mind. I learn to understand both objective reality in general and the general character of my own human mind when I learn how to introduce order into the procession of given presentation by treating this experience as a function of two variables, the subject and the object. To revert to the mathematical terms, the data of appearance are the values of the function, cognition. This is a function of two variables, mind and object. I know the object by an integration of its appearance over the range of the other variable, mind or "the subjective conditions." (For example, as has been pointed out, objective change is divided from permanence of the thing by integrating with respect to those changes, in experience as given, which are due to "my own activity.") And I know mind by an integration of this function over its whole range (or the widest possible range) of variation in the objective. That the phenomenalist treats mind as transcendent is a fallacy which is correlative to his treatment of the independent object as beyond knowledge.

We must, further, distinguish between the notion that unrecognized limitations of the human mind would mean any *deceitfulness* or *erroneousness* of knowledge—a failure to accord with the true nature of the real—and the quite different notion that such limitations would mean a corresponding degree of *ignorance* of reality. When this distinction is drawn, the whole point of phenomenalism, as regards the relation of mind to independent reality, will be found to be lost; because when we grant to his arguments the utmost which can be granted, the conclusion to which they point is that our knowledge of the independent object is veridical but partial, not that it is untrue to absolute reality.

Our analogy may be of further assistance here. It is true that if we were restricted to one angle of perspective, one distance, etc., this would lead to *limitation* of knowledge. If we were restricted to perception at five feet, whether we knew it or not, that would mean a real limitation of our knowledge, because we could not understand or predict the systematic variation of perceived size with distance, which is an *additional* insight into the nature of that independent X, the size of the object, which is one term of the relation which determines size as perceived. Because we are able to see things at a wide range of distances, we learn to predict from our image at any one distance the appearance of the thing at other distances. Though the momentary perception is limited to a single distance, the breadth of previous experience, and knowledge of this momentary condition, enable us to transcend the momentary limitation. A *permanent* limitation could *not* be thus transcended.

However, we must not confuse limitation of knowledge with misrepresentation or mistake. Any sort of limitation of sense-organs or mind which should be reflected in perception, so far from meaning that we do not perceive things as they are, means that in certain respects we are freed from all possibility of error and are fatally certain to perceive things as they are, though to perceive and understand only part of what we otherwise might. The penny which looks elliptical may deceive us into thinking that it *is* elliptical, precisely because we are capable of viewing things from other angles than the present one. If we were limited to just one angle of vision, we should be restricted in our knowledge but we should thereby be freed from all possible mistakes of perspective. Similarly, if the image I have of a mite's foot should register on the retina of an intelligent mite, it would lead to error. But the limitation which prevents him from seeing his foot as it looks to me, at the same time prevents him from suffering certain illusions about his feet which would otherwise be possible.

That we humans do not have senses which register directly the whole known range of harmonic motions, means that there is much of reality which, until we learned to call upon various indirect modes of observation, was beyond our knowledge. And our inability to imagine how certain ranges of vibration might register upon sense-organs which should be sensitive to them, is as much a limitation as the blind man's inability to imagine color. But just as blindness does not condemn a man to false perception or even false interpretation (although it does make it practically necessary to run more risks and hazard judgment in the absence of desirable clues), so in general subjective limitations cannot render knowledge untrue to its object. At most they only mean greater ignorance and consequently greater likelihood of false judgment. The exigencies of life to be met remain just as numerous; the basis of judgment is more meager; hence error will probably be more frequent. Yet it remains true that no experience, however limited, is or can be intrinsically misrepresentative.

How much of reality we can grasp, doubtless depends upon our human limitations. The relativity of knowledge to the mind means such limitations, but it does not mean that the real object is a *ding an sich*. Unless we grossly suppose that what humans can know is all there is to know, such limitation can lead to no untruth of our knowledge to reality. In this matter, as in many others, theory seems to suffer from a tendency to extremes—to hold either that the reality we know is all there is, or else that we cannot truly know any. The golden mean seems both modest and sensible. Knowledge has two opposites, ignorance and error. The relativity of perception may mean ignorance or it may not. If I can observe things from every angle, the restriction to one perspective at a time will not mean necessary ignorance, especially since other perspectives can be predicted from the present one. But if perception were restricted to a single angle, that relativity would mean ignorance. This will be true for limitations of the mind in general.

Ignorance of whatever sort increases the likelihood of error, because it means that in practice we must go forward on grounds of judgment less sufficient. But the given itself is never misrepresentative; always it is true revelation of the real, however partial. The notion that it can be untrue to the real reflects both a misapprehension of the significance of the truth of judgment and the old and meaningless fallacy that the function of sensory awareness in knowledge is to provide a qualitative replica of the independent object. Ignorance, however great, cannot make of reality a *ding an sich;* it does not vitiate such knowledge as we have, and that knowledge is of the independent reality.

Idealists are wont to draw an opposite sort of conclusion from the same general considerations; that is, to urge that the conception of reality beyond all human power to know is meaningless, precisely because of the relativity of knowledge in general to the mind. It is true and important, that we can conceive no kind of reality whatever except in terms of some possible experience; but the idealist fails to do justice to our human power to transcend, by indirect methods, limitations of direct experience. He should be careful not to deny, by implication, that the blind man can believe in color. In a sense, the blind man does not know what he believes in; nevertheless he meaningfully believes in something that he can neither perceive nor imagine. It is very likely true that if we conjecture that reality has aspects forever beyond the reach of human beings, we must do so by the metaphor of some mind differently organized than our own. But when we know that other humans have greater auditory range than ourselves, and can reasonably suppose that insects possess senses which directly register stimuli which we do not, what prevents us from conceiving that there **are** ranges of the real beyond the direct apprehension of any human, or even of any animal that happens to exist? It is further true that we must have *some* sort of conception in terms of which to ascribe reality of any type; otherwise the ascription of reality itself means nothing. But if the idealist puts his challenge in the form, "How can we *know* there is a kind of reality we cannot *know?*" the different significance of the word "know" in its two occurrences needs to be considered. Mr. Russell has pointed out that we know there are numbers which nobody will ever count. To "know" a number is to know whether it is odd or even, prime or factorable, etc., or at least to be in position to determine this. To know that there *are* numbers not thus known, is to know a *principle* of the relation of every number to others, by which further counting is always possible, and hence to know that some numbers will always be uncounted. Similarly we may know (or have good reason to conjecture) that there are certain systematic relations in reality by which what is directly perceptible to us is connected with what is not. If it is a question how we are to conceive what should be beyond experience, then we may warn the idealist that he ought to be careful of this point lest he spoil his own argument. He has a final metaphysical interest in the power of human beings to transcend their own finitude. This is a case in point; in fact, it is the general case. We transcend our own limitations in terms of what we should or might experience if—. That is the nature of possibility in general. We transcend actual experience in terms of possible experience. But we transcend the actually given only as we abstract from something which is a fact; the nature and extent of such abstraction determines the degree and kind of possibility which is in question. There is no limit to the number and kind of restrictions of human experience which we can thus speculatively transcend.

Can I see both sides of this coin in my hand? At this moment when I am looking at the obverse, I cannot see the reverse side. But if I should turn it over, I should see the reverse. Seeing both sides of the coin is both possible and impossible—possible on condition, impossible without that condition. Taking my limitations severely enough, any possibility can be ruled out except the actuality. The meaning of a possibility which transcends the actual lies in the truth of some "If—then" proposition, the hypothesis of which is contrary to fact. As we progressively transcend the limits of the actual by our "if" the possibility in question becomes a more and more attenuated sort, but at no point, while our "If—then" proposition still has any meaning, can we say this possibility is not genuine.

Now, as has been pointed out, the ascription

of any reality beyond immediate experience requires and represents such affirmation of the possible. To repudiate all such transcendence is to confine reality to the given, to land in solipsism, and in a solipsism which annihilates both past and future, and removes the distinction between real and unreal, by removing all distinction of veridical and illusory. The ascription of reality is, then, the affirmation of possibility, and the kind of reality ascribed conforms to the nature of the possibility affirmed. As we progressively transcend our actual limitations, the reality conceived becomes more and more abstract and undetermined in its nature. But at no point, while our hypothetical statement still retains a vestige of meaning, is the conception of the corresponding real completely empty. The conception of other minds, different from our own, is a perfectly meaningful "if" by which we go one step beyond the actual situation of the blind man with respect to color. The reality thus speculatively affirmed is one degree more blank and dubious, but the existence of such reality still has meaning.

It is not, however, with the idealist's argument upon this point that we are principally concerned. The more important consideration for us is that meaning of "independence" of the object which is compatible with the relativity of knowledge. The idealist argues from this relativity of knowledge to the mind to the conclusion that the object is completely mind-dependent. In this, he misinterprets the nature of relativity and forgets the possibility that the object as known may be coincidently determined by two conditions and thus relative to both.

Since the idealistic argument is different from the phenomenalist's, let us vary our illustration of relativity in general.

An alpha-particle is shot out from a radium-atom, describes a certain path, and is arrested by a screen. The mass of the particle, its velocity, and its time of flight, are all such as to be inexpressible except with reference to some observer or frame of motion. The determination of each of these properties will vary for different relative motions of the observer and the system containing the alpha-particle. But does this variation mean that velocity and mass are not properties of an independent reality which can be observed in these various ways? If that were true, then there would be no objective physical difference between an alpha-particle and a beta-particle or a rifle bullet. The physical identification of the object would depend altogether upon the relative motion of it and the observer. But if the properties were not in some sense determinate independently of any frame of motion, then they would not be determinate in relation to the observer. Specify the relative motion of two systems, and these properties must have fixed values, representing the physical nature of the object. For any observer, in relative motion to it such and such, an alpha-particle shot out by an atom of radium will have a determined velocity x and mass y.

That is, there are certain properties of the object, as an independent reality, which can only be described in terms of some observer or frame of motion. But specify this relationship and the true description is thereby fixed. What is it that determines this? It cannot be the relative motion already specified. It is fixed by the objective real character of the thing. If human observers, directly or indirectly, see the motion of the particle and measure its mass and velocity, then what they *observe* will depend on them (their relative motion). But this condition in terms of them being specified, what they *observe* will depend on *what* they observe. This "what" is a determinate thing in some sense independent of the relative motion, though describable only in terms of *some* such relation. Under all conditions, this independent "what," along with the relative motion, enters into the determination of what is *observed*.

In other words, the observed mass, velocity, etc., of the objectively real thing is a function of two variables, the relative motion of observer and observed and the independent character of the thing observed. Specify both of these and the value of the function, observed mass or observed velocity, is completely determined. Specify either, and the value of this function then depends upon the other. Specify neither, and the function is then completely indeterminate.

Say to the physicist: "An alpha-particle is shot out from a radium-atom. What is its velocity and mass?" He will reply: "Your question is not strictly answerable until you specify the relative motion of the system and the observer. But since it is an alpha-particle, I can tell you the mass and velocity for any observer you please. The fact that it is an alpha-particle determines a series of velocities and masses relative to observers in all possible motions relative to the path of it." But say to him: "The relative motion of two systems, *A* and *B*, is one hundred thousand miles a second, directly toward each other. Something moves in system *A*. What is its mass and velocity as measured by an observer on *B*?" Obviously he will reply by asking what you are talking about. Or he might answer: "Until you specify what the thing and its state are for *some other* relative motion of observer and observed (say, rest), I cannot tell you its mass and velocity relative to the motion of the two systems which you mention."

Now the objective reality, alpha-particle, is identified by certain observable properties, mass and velocity amongst them. Suppose it were not identifiable by molecular combinations into which it enters or by any other properties which are not affected by motion, so that it could be known *only* through characteristics which are thus relative. We may then imagine ourselves to make rejoinder to the physicist: "What I mean is indescribable except in terms which are relative to the motion of the observer. How, then, can I tell you the nature and state of the thing I mean in any terms that are not dependent on the motion of the observer?" He might reply: "There is a systematic connection between masses, velocities, etc., in terms of *one* relative motion and in terms of any other. So it is unnecessary for you to try to answer in other than relative terms. The description in terms of *any* relative motion, if that motion be specified, will be a sufficient description of the nature and state of the thing. But surely you do not expect me to deduce the nature of the thing from the single condition of its motion relative to the observer."

The parallel in the case of the relativity of the object known to mind is obvious. "Thing as known" is a function of two variables; it depends on the mind, but also it depends on the thing. This thing can only be described in terms of its relation to some (actual or hypothetical) mind. But this does not alter the fact that if "thing as known" were not determined by a condition which is independent of the mind, it would not be determined at all. The parallel holds also in that the thing as known in one relation to a mind (say, from one perspective) enables us to predict its character as known in other such relations. So far as this is the case, its (relative) nature as known is a sufficient determination of its nature in general, or independent of any particular relation of this sort.

The fallacy of idealism lies in arguing: "The nature of the thing as known always depends on the nature of the mind. Therefore the object cannot exist or have character independent of the mind." This is as if one should argue "The mass and velocity of an alpha-particle always depends on its motion relative to the observer. Therefore it can have no mass and velocity, and cannot exist, independent of this relative motion." In one sense of the word "independent" it *is* true that the mass and velocity of an alpha-particle has no meaning independent of its relative motion. And in a strictly parallel sense, it is true that the nature of the object, independent of the knowing mind, is undetermined; and independent of any and every mind, is meaningless. But there is no need for us to trip over the ambiguities of the word. The mass and velocity of an alpha-particle at least has two independent conditions; its motion relative to the observer is only one of them. We cannot argue from "dependent on its relative motion" to "completely determined by its relative motion." Similarly we cannot argue from the fact that it is meaningless to try to describe a thing out of relation to mind to the quite different thesis that the real object known is completely determined by the mind which knows it. If it should be said that while the object is not determined by its particular relation to a particular mind, it is determined by relation to mind in general, we may revert to the analogy once more. Mass and velocity apart from relation to some frame of motion is always undetermined; but it is *not* determined by such relation in general (if that means anything).

To revert to a previous illustration, the idealistic argument may be parodied: "The size of Cæsar's toga is relative to the yardsick or to some other standard of measure. No size without a yardstick. The size of things is through and through yardstickian. To be sure, the fallible yardstick in my hand may not determine size in general, but the yardstick in the Bureau of Standards determines both my yardstick and all sizes that there are. It creates size."

If the mind were the *only* condition of the thing as known, then the nature of the mind being specified, objects in general would be completely determined. One could say, "Given human mind possessed of such and such organs and interpreting data in such and such categories, what will be the reality it knows?" And there would be an answer in general and in particular.

Idealism has often boggled over the fact that it could not deduce the particular content of experience and knowledge. The questions, "Why do I have just this experience? Why do I find just this reality and no other?" must have an answer. Either that or it must be recognized that the particularity of experience is itself an ultimate—if inexplicable—datum; that the given is a condition of reality independent of the mind. Berkeley, of course, has his reply to this question: There is a reality, God, independent of my mind, which is responsible. The post-Kantian idealists, not sharing Berkeley's empiricism, have either neglected this problem or, like Fichte, have said that it is no part of the business of philosophy to deduce the particular. But he fails to face the question: Granted the idealistic thesis, *can* the particular be deduced?* Philosophy, he might rightly claim, is not interested in the fact that I now see a blue blotter or that there are elephants in Africa. But his claim is that *all* the conditions of experience and reality are contained in mind. Outside of minds is nothing which could determine, or help determine, what minds know. If that be true, then mind being specified, not only the form or general character of knowledge but also the content in all its particularity, must be determined. It would still not be the business of philosophy to

---

*Schelling, however, acknowledges the justice of the challenge and seeks to meet it—with amazing results. Starting from the Fichtean premise, $A = A$, he deduces eventually the electrical and magnetic properties of matter! *System d. transcendentalen Idealismus, sämmt. Werke* (1858), Bd. I, 3, pp. 444–450.

make the deduction for each particular item, because the particular items would not be of general interest. But it *is* a matter of general interest that all such items are thus deducible—if that be a fact. We might except some inductive proof of this deducibility—the deduction of the elephants in Africa—as an illustration. If the mathematician should tell us, "All the facts of physics can be deduced from the system of quaternions," but should reply to our request for a deduction of the law of gravitation by saying, "Particular physical facts are of no interest to the mathematician and no part of his business," we should draw our own conclusions.

That idealism may argue that reality is exclusively mental or spiritual by maintaining that the condition of this particularity is *another* spiritual being, we are not here concerned. Such argument (or dogmatic assertion) is metaphysical and is, or should be, quite distinct from the argument from the relativity of knowledge.

It is a much more important consideration, I believe, that unless the content of knowledge is recognized to have a condition independent of the mind, the peculiar significance of knowledge is likely to be lost. For the purpose of knowledge is to be true to something which is beyond it. Its intent is to be governed and dictated to in certain respects. It is a real act with a real purpose because it seeks something which it knows it may miss. If knowledge had no condition independent of the knowing act, would this be so?

It is most important to discover precisely what, in terms of knowledge, can be meant by "the independence of the object." Whether the subject-object relation is universal in reality or not, clearly the answer must be compatible with its universality in *knowledge*. It must, further, be independent of any supposed qualitative identity of the content or perception with the object, since such identity is probably meaningless and in any case is unverifiable.

It may be asked, "What would it mean for a mind to know an object, when the supposition of the qualitative identity of given content of perception with the object is ruled out?" The answer, in terms of the theory here presented, will be clear: It means that we are able to interpret validly certain given items of experience as sign of other possible experience, the total content of such further possible experience, related to the given in certain categorial ways, being attributed to the object, as constituting what we know of it and *what we mean by attributing reality to it*. If this conception seems to leave us in the air about the "nature of the object," let us first inquire what further question it is to which we seek the answer. We might find that there is no such further question which is meaningful.

In terms of experience and knowledge, the in-

THE RELATIVITY OF KNOWLEDGE 193

dependence of reality—its independence of the
knowing mind—means, first, the *givenness* of
what is given; our realization that we do not create this content of experience and cannot, by the
activity of thinking, alter it. Second, it means the
truth of those "If—then" propositions in which
the process of possible experience, starting from
the given, could be expressed. The "if" here depends upon our own active nature for its meaning, as has been pointed out, but the content of
the "then" clause, and the truth of the proposition as a whole, are things with respect to which
the knowing mind is not dictator but dictated to.
I may confront the given with different attitudes
and purposes; I may be differently active toward
it and, starting from it, I may proceed into the
future in different ways. But *what I should then
find;* what eventuations of experience are genuinely possible; that is something independent of
any purpose or attitude of mine. These, I seek
correctly to anticipate in my present interpretation of the given. If they do not obtain in reality,
my present "knowledge" is false. Whether they
obtain or not, is determined independently of my
mind. If not, then it is not determined at all, and
knowledge and error are, both of them, purely
subjective and meaningless.

Third, the independence of reality means the
transcendence by reality of our present knowledge of it; it means that I can ask significant

Russell's law of the excluded middle

questions about my object which *have* an answer when that answer is something which I cannot give. In terms of experience this means that, starting from the given in certain ways, I can safely predict the accrual of *something* the particular nature of which I cannot now determine. For example, if I examine the contents of this drawer, either I shall find a piece of chalk or I shall find none. So much I know; but I do not know now—and cannot discover merely by taking thought—*which* of these alternatives I should find true. There is that in the object which I do not now know; I know something to be determined in reality which is neither implicitly nor explicitly determined in my knowledge of it. This, and all similar questions I could ask and could not now answer, witness the independence of my object.

If the idealist should find that there is nothing in such "independence" which is incompatible with his thesis, then it may be that between a sufficiently critical idealism and a sufficiently critical realism, there are no issues save false issues which arise from the insidious fallacies of the copy-theory of knowledge.

CHAPTER VII

THE A PRIORI—TRADITIONAL CON-
CEPTIONS

The position so far arrived at emphasizes the
fact that there is no knowledge of external reality
without the anticipation of future experience.
Even that knowledge implied by naming or the
apprehension of anything presented, is implicitly
predictive, because what the concept denotes has
always some temporal spread and must be identified by some orderly sequence in experience.
Hence we are inevitably confronted—as any theory of knowledge must be—with the problem of
Hume's skepticism: Are there any *necessary* connections in experience? Can conceptual order,
which is of the mind, be imposed upon a content
of experience which is independent and not yet
given? This is the problem of the a priori.

There is no knowledge without interpretation.
If interpretation, which represents an activity of
the mind, is always subject to the check of further experience, how is knowledge possible at all?
That the interpretation reflects the character of
past experience, will not save its validity. For
what experience establishes, it may destroy; its
evidence is never complete. An argument from

past to future at best is probable only, and even this probability must rest upon principles which are themselves more than probable. For the validity of knowledge, it is requisite that experience in general shall be in some sense orderly—that the order implicit in conception may be imposed upon it. And for the validity of particular predications, it is necessary that a *particular* order may be ascribed to experience in advance.

Thus if there is to be any knowledge at all, *some* knowledge must be a priori; there must be some propositions the truth of which is necessary and is independent of the particular character of future experience. But traditional conceptions of the a priori have broken down, largely because the significance of its necessity and its independence have been misconstrued.

"Necessary" is an ambiguous word; its contradictory is, in one meaning, "contingent," in another "voluntary." The necessary character of a priori truth, which is genuinely opposed to its contingency, has been confused with some psychological or other necessity, which the mind is under, of accepting it. What contradicts necessary truth must be genuinely impossible to happen. But it is not therefore impossible to believe. What is a priori does not compel the mind's acceptance. It is given experience, the brute-fact element in knowledge, which the mind must accept willy-nilly. The a priori represents the activity of mind itself; it represents an attitude in some sense freely taken. That we elicit some formula as a principle means that we take it as forbidding something or denying something which in some sense has significance. That which is utterly incapable of any alternative is utterly devoid of meaning. The necessity of the a priori is its character as legislative act. It represents a constraint imposed by the mind, not a constraint imposed upon mind by something else.

And the a priori is independent of experience, not because it prescribes a form which experience must fit or anticipates some preëstablished harmony of the given with the categories of the mind, but precisely because it prescribes *nothing* to the content of experience. That only can be a priori which is true *no matter what*. What is anticipated is not the given but our attitude toward it; it formulates an uncompelled initiative of mind, our categorial ways of acting. Truth which is a priori anticipates the character of the *real;* otherwise, it would possess no significance whatever. The real, however, is not the given as such, but the given categorially interpreted. In determining its own interpretations—and only so—the mind legislates for reality, no matter what future experience may bring.

If we are to understand this nature of the a priori, traditional misconceptions must first be cleared away. In general these are three: (1) that the a priori is distinguished by some psychological criterion such as the "natural light" or some peculiar mental origin such as innateness; (2) that it is distinguished by some peculiar mode of proof, or logical relation to experience in general, usually called "presupposition"; (3) that the a priori legislation of mind can not apply to experience unless what is given in experience is already limited or determined in some consonant fashion; that the validity a priori of our categorial interpretation requires also a priori modes of our receptivity or intuition.

The first of these need not detain us long: innate ideas are a dead issue. Psychological undeniability, even if it exist, would not be proof of truth. It is entirely conceivable that the animal man should be so organized that certain fallacies should be peculiarly impelling to his mind. And historically it is observable that what has appeared undeniable and been accepted as axiomatic over long periods of time may still be false. Nor is it implausible that there should be truths which are a priori, having a warrant not drawn from the particular character of particular experiences, which nevertheless should be grasped only with difficulty and not specially impressive to most men. Moreover, if the criterion of the a priori were a certain impulsion of the mind, then there would be no difference amongst truths on this point. As Bosanquet has pointed out, all discovered truth lays upon the mind the same impulsion to belief; this character belongs to all propositions once they are established.

The source of this rationalist conviction that the a priori must have some peculiar psychological warrant, is fairly easy to make out. Universal propositions drawn from experience are contingent and problematic unless they have some prior warrant. Knowledge which is certain can not be grounded in the particulars of experience if it is to apply to particular experiences in advance; it can only come from the possession of some universal by which the particular is implied. Nor can these universals be reached by generalization. Hence there must be universal truths which are known otherwise than through experience. Such universal propositions cannot be logically derived unless from other such universals as premises. Hence there must be *some* universal truths which are *first* premises logically underived and representing an original knowledge from which we start. Such propositions must be axiomatic, self-evident.

However, this notion of innate truth or self-illuminating propositions is not particularly consonant with rationalistic theory. The essence of human reason is a *mode* of thought, not a particular content; it has to do with the validity of conclusions, not with original premises natively possessed. Post-Kantian rationalism realizes this and, influenced no doubt by Kant's deduction of the categories, turns from psychological compulsion as the ground of the a priori to a conception of *logical* necessity. First, or highest, principles are no longer regarded as immediately evident, but are now supposed to be distinguished by a peculiar criterion of proof. They are "necessary presuppositions" of some class of more particular facts, of science, or of experience in general.

The meaning of "presupposition" here is far from clear; probably it has no single meaning, and no discussion could be altogether just to the variety of its uses. But in general, what seems to be intended is the designation of certain principles as logically prior to that which "presupposes" them, with the added thought that what is thus prior is thereby proved to have the character of necessary truth—necessary, that is, if facts of science or experience in general are taken for granted.

So far as this is what is meant, the fallacy committed by the notion that principles can be proved true a priori by being presupposed by science or experience, is so simple that it is extraordinary that it could ever have gained currency. Correctly speaking, what is logically prior to a fact or proposition will imply that fact or proposition, but it will not, in general, be implied by it. In the language of mathematics, if A is logically prior to B, then A must be a sufficient condition of B or at least one of a sufficient set of conditions; but "sufficient condition" must not be confused with "necessary condition." Physics presupposes mathematics in the sense that it exhibits particular instances of general mathematical principles, while mathematics contains no necessary reference to physics. In the same sense, all the special sciences presuppose logic. But if what is presupposed in this sense be regarded as thereby established or proved necessary, the fallacy involved is easily detected. If I assert that two feet and two feet are four feet, I do not thereby commit myself to the proposition $2 + 2 = 4$. It is required only that this be true of linear measure. Gases under pressure or living organisms might—for all that is here in question—be governed by very different laws. The particular fact does not even require that there should be *any* general laws of mathematics.

There can be little doubt that this fallacy has played its part in traditional conceptions of the a priori. Presuppositions, so called, are always general in their import. That which presupposes them is more particular. Now A is not a necessary condition of B unless "A is false" implies "B is false," which is the same as to say that B implies A. Hence no general principle is a necessary condition of any particular fact or proposition unless that particular implies the general principle. And even if this should be the case, it would be the

particular and not the general which was, so far,
logically prior and the original premise.

If we avoid this fallacy and take "*A* presupposes *B*" to mean "*A* is necessary condition of
B," *i. e.*, "*B* implies *A*," then we should be so
cluttered up with presuppositions that the fine
glamor of the word would be lost. Presuppositions would be truly necessary conditions—that is,
relatively necessary; necessary *if*—but the necessary conditions of any proposition are as numerous as the things that it implies. The necessary
conditions of any particular fact of experience
are merely its logical consequences. Obviously, it
is not intended to reduce a priori principle to the
status of one among the numerous consequences
of the particular fact. Furthermore, the only necessity which could thus be established would be
relative to the fact in question. If that fact be
contingent, as the particular content of experience is, then its presuppositions will, unless otherwise supported, share precisely that contingency.

The metaphysical respect in which presuppositions have been held reflects the vast influence
exercised by the geometry of Euclid upon historic
rationalism. This respect is, of course, entirely
justified; but along with it went a conception of
geometrical method and of deduction in general
which, although perhaps inevitable to an earlier
day, is quite unwarranted. According to this view
the logically first principles, or presuppositions,

are self-evident axioms which, through the process of deduction, shed the glory of their certainty on all the propositions deduced from them. But here it is to be observed that the ground of certainty of the first principles has nothing to do with their logical priority. The criterion of their truth is their self-evidence or undeniability; they loan their indisputable character to their consequences instead of deriving it from the fact of being logical foundation of these consequences. If they were not self-evident they could derive no certainty or necessity from the fact of being thus presupposed. The connotation of the phrase "a priori" was fixed in terms of this ancient conception according to which all systematic knowledge was supposed to find its warrant through deductive derivation from such self-evident beginnings. Literally connoting "by deduction" it came to mean "necessarily true" because only such first principles of deduction as were taken to be necessary or self-evident were then acceptable.

To-day, however, when this conception of deduction has been given up in mathematics and elsewhere, when "postulate" or the colorless "primitive proposition" has replaced the self-evident axiom, when non-Euclidean geometries have been recognized to have precisely the same logical structure as Euclid, and when it has been shown that various sets of postulates may give rise to the same deductive system, we have less than no excuse for retaining the notion that a presupposition is more certain than its consequences. Where the body of facts which a deductive first principle implies is considerable and well-established, and there are no implications of it which are known to be false, the presupposition gains that kind of verification which particulars can give to general principles—that is, the partial and inductive verification of it as an original hypothesis. But to regard a presupposition as established by what presupposes it, except in this inductive sense and with the same contingency as the consequences of it, has not even the warrant of historical confusion.

The traditional rationalist conception that metaphysical first principles can be shown to be logically indispensable, or that what is logically prior is thereby proved to be certain or self-evident, is one to which the actual structure of logical and mathematical systems lends no support. In genuinely rigorous deductive systems, as these are understood today, "logically prior" means only "deductively more powerful" or "simpler." The supposed necessity, or logical indispensability, of presuppositions most frequently turns out to be nothing more significant than lack of imagination and ingenuity. The plurality of possible beginnings for the same system, and the plurality of equally cogent systems which may contain the *same* body of already verified propositions but differ in *what else* they include, dispel the notion of indispensability in what is logically prior.

A less important but equally persistent fallacy is the notion that at least some necessary truths can be established by the fact that to deny them is to reaffirm them—that they are implied by their own contradictories. It is wise to walk cautiously here, because the logical facts are quite complex. The most frequently offered illustrations of re-affirmation through denial are not even good cases of a proposition implied by its own denial. For example, the fallacy of arguing from the undeni-able existence of thinking to the self which does the thinking vitiates Descartes's use of the "I think." But quite apart from that, the man who should assert "I am not thinking," so far from contradicting himself, would give the best possible evidence of the truth of his statement. The propo-sition, "I am not thinking," does not imply, "I am thinking." It may be that the attitude of will which we suppose to underlie the making of *any* assertion is such as to be incompatible with the admission, "I am not thinking," so that we may be sure that whoever could make such a statement would find himself at cross purposes. But the rea-son for this is contained neither in the proposition nor in any implication of it. There is here no logi-cal inconsistency whatever.

Other examples of the supposedly self-contra-dictory—the statement of Epimenides the Cretan that "All Cretans are liars," etc.—have been so frequently discussed in current literature that consideration of them may be omitted here. Most of these commit what Mr. Russell calls a "vicious circle" fallacy by ignoring the systematic ambiguity of type which characterizes such propositions. As a corrolary, the supposed "necessity" which attaches to their contradictories is equally fallacious.

However, there are propositions which are genuinely implied by their own denial, and hence propositions whose denial leads to their reaffirmation. And all such belong to the class what may quite reasonably be called "necessary." (I should omit further consideration of such logical technicalities, which must be getting boresome to the reader, except that this particular point will be of some importance later on.) The curious fact is, about such genuine examples of propositions implied by their own denial, that they are not thus proved true. To see that this is so, we must first examine the nature of reaffirmation through denial. Whoever asserts a self-contradictory proposition does not in one and the same breath affirm and deny the content of his assertion. He affirms it in fact; he denies it by implication only. Or to put it otherwise; he affirms it, and the question whether he also denies it is the question of what his assertion implies.

Now the most obvious illustrations of such

propositions whose denial genuinely implies them come from the field of logic; in fact, they all belong to logic when that subject is interpreted in the rational way as including all purely formal truth. And the content of logic includes all principles of inference.

Whoever, then, denies a principle of logic, may either draw his own inferences according to the principle he denies, or he may consistently avoid that principle in deriving his conclusions. If one deny a principle of inference, but inadvertently reintroduce it in drawing conclusions from his statement, he will indeed find that he has contradicted himself and admitted what originally be denied. But if he denies a principle of inference and consistently reasons in accordance with his own statement, he need incur no self-contradiction whatever.

It is a fact that for one who stands within a given system of logic, the denial of one of its principles will imply the principle itself. But this signifies nothing more profound than the fact that deductions in logic are inevitably circular.* In deducing our theorems of logic, we must make use of the very principles which the deduction is supposed to demonstrate. If then, I use "bad" logical premises but "good" logical reasoning, I shall

---

*Omitting from consideration the development of logic, as a purely abstract system, by the "operational" instead of the "postulatory" method. These omitted considerations serve to strengthen, not to weaken, what is here set forth.

contradict myself, quite as surely as if I use two premises which are mutually inconsistent. Perhaps an example here will be of assistance. Take the law of contradiction in the form, "That X is A and X is not A, is false." Its contradictory will be, "X is A and X is not A." Let us take this last statement as a premise and draw the inference from it.

(1) "X is A and X is not A" implies its latter half, "X is not A."

(2) "X is not A" implies "It is false that X is A."

(3) "It is false that X is A" implies "That X is A and X is not A, is false." (Just as " 'Today is Monday' is false" implies "That today is Monday and it is raining, is false.") Thus from the denial of the law of contradiction we have deduced the law of contradiction itself. But we have done so only because, though denying it in the premise, we have reintroduced it in step (2) of the reasoning. If we had, consistently with the premise, refused to take step (2), we should never have got any such conclusion.

Every good or correct logic, then, will be such that its principles are undeniable without contradiction; the denial of any one of them leads to formal inconsistency. But this is true only because so long as we remain within our system of logic, we shall use the very principle in question in drawing inferences from the denial of it, and thus beg the question of its truth.

A good logic must be circular. But what should lead any one to suppose that this character belongs exclusively to systems of good logic? Apparently those who set store by the "reaffirmation through denial" have committed the fallacy of illicit conversion; they have reasoned: "A logic whose principles are true will give their reaffirmation through denial. Therefore, whatever principles meet this test must be true."

All logic and pseudo-logic is similarly circular. A little ingenuity suffices to construct a bad logic in which, reasoning badly according to our bad principles, we always get consistently bad results. And if we deny one of these principles, still by sticking to our bad method of reasoning, we can reaffirm the bad principle in conclusion.* Since

---

*One family of such systems—consistent in their own terms, and such that the denial of any principle lends to its reaffirmation as a consequence—is determined by the presence in the system of the proposition

$$q < [p < (p < q)]$$

where p, q, etc. are propositions, and $p < q$ represents "p implies q," or "if p is asserted, q may be asserted." This proposition allows of two distinct meanings of $p < q$, neither of which coincides with the usual one; and the properties of this relation may be further specified in a variety of ways. Some of the systems in this family might be regarded as "good" logic, but most of them are "bad." Such a "bad" logic may be developed logistically from the following formal postulates:

A. $- (- p) = p$ (Def. of $-p$, the denial of p)
B. $- (p < - p)$
C. $(p < q) < (- q < - p)$
D. $[p < (q < r)] < [q < (p < r)]$
E. $(q < r) < [(p < q) < (p < r)]$
F. $(p < q) < (- p < - q)$

Postulate F is obviously false as a general law of implication. It is interesting that postulate B seems to exclude the possibility that any proposition should lead to its own denial as a consequence, yet if P be any principle of the system, we can prove that $- P < (- P < P)$ Hence the assertion of $(- P)$ leads to the assertion $(- P < P)$.

a bad logic, whose principles are false, may still be such that the denial of any one of these principles will lead to its reaffirmation, it follows that the test of "reaffirmation through denial" does not in logic prove the truth of the principle thus reaffirmed.

It should be added, to avoid misunderstanding, that in spite of what has just been said, the test of self-criticism or circularity is a valuable test of any deductive development of logic. That the principles proved are precisely the principles used in the demonstration of them, is here a matter for congratulation. That the method of our proof coincides with the result of it, is a test of both method and result. It is not a test of truth, however; it is a test of formal or methodological consistency. The error of taking self-criticism to be a test of logical truth lies in overlooking the fact that a thoroughly false logic may still possess this merely methodological consistency.

One further bit of explanation seems required also. I do not mean to say that there are no necessary propositions. Whoever takes a given logic to be true will find its principles undeniable without contradiction (*i. e.*, in his logic) and therefore necessary. Some logic is true, and hence some logical principles are necessary. The point is simply that the truths of logic are not proved by any such procedure—since, as proof, it always begs the question.

Precisely the point which I wish here to make is that logical "necessity" has here no connotation of the inescapable. What is a priori is not true because the mind is so constituted that it finds such truth unavoidable; however fantastic or practically negligible any alternative supposition may be, there still *are* such alternatives, which may be self-consistent. Doubtless what is fundamental, as logic is fundamental, has its roots in the nature of the human mind, but not in such wise as to be either self-evident or the only self-consistent possibility. If it should be such that it must be assumed or it cannot be proved, that, so far from proving truth, would be a character which it shares with delusions and absurdities. There will still be alternatives of assumption in the presence of which the mind is uncompelled. Whatever was genuinely *imposed* upon the human mind would not be a priori; it would have just that brute-fact character which distinguishes the given.

It is here that rationalist conceptions, by their confusion of logical and psychological, fall into further difficulty. The a priori is recognized as not being given as the content of experience is given. But if the a priori have psychological self-evidence or inescapability of any sort, then it must be absolute datum in some sense or other. Either the mind would find these truths belonging to it as soon as it became conscious, with sufficient clear-

ness, of its own possessions, or it would acquire
them at some particular date in some particular
moment of illumination, and would recognize that
the ground of this new realization was not previously there in the mind. In the former case, the
a priori would belong to the mind only in the
sense that the individual body does; the infant
would find it as he finds his ears or finds that he
can move his arms. It would be a commonplace of
reality, but it would have no higher character than
that of uniformly evidenced fact. There would be
no guarantee of it beyond the guarantee of uniform experience up to date. On the other alternative, it would have the character which belongs to
such illumination as may be received from an external and authoritative source, and the truth of
it would depend upon some sanction superior to,
or at least independent of, his own mind. Yet it
is of the essence of rationalism to recognize the
a priori as a peculiar possession of the mind itself,
in a sense not compatible with either of these conceptions.

This point of the relation of the a priori to the
mind, is really of prime importance, for upon it
depends that assurance, superior to the assurance
we can have of generalizations from experience,
that nothing future experience can reveal will
falsify it. Whatever experience may bring, the
mind will be there; whatever belongs to the mind
itself is assured in advance. This is the one point

upon which all conceptions which recognize an a priori have agreed. The conception which retains this significance and avoids the fallacies and contradictions pointed out above, is one which outrages traditional ideas, but at bottom it is simple and, I think, can be made obvious. The a priori has its origin in an act of mind; it has in some sense the character of fiat and is in some respects like deliberate choice. The a priori is a peculiar possession of mind because it bears the stamp of mind's creation. And the criterion of creativity is not inevitability but exactly its opposite, the absence of impulsion and the presence of at least conceivable alternatives. But I dare not press a point of view so novel until there has been further consideration of points which historical conceptions and problems will serve to exemplify.

In particular, if the a priori is to be thus conceived as made by mind, shall we not fall into another difficulty: How, then, shall we know that it can be imposed upon a reality which is independent? It is here, of course, that we find the grounds of skepticism in general and of Hume's in particular. The human mind, by its nature and by the manner of its activity, imposes certain interpretations upon experience. Every such interpretation would, if valid, limit the character of reality and the possibilities of future experience. We can have no assurance that such limitations characterize the independent real or bound what future experience may bring.

It is for this same reason that Kant recognizes, in addition to the categories, another a priori element in knowledge and makes the distinction of phenomenal and real. The content of experience is limited by the forms of intuition, which are imposed not by the active interpretation of the mind but by the passive modes of its receptivity.* The categories are subjective modes of the mind's interpretation or synthesis of the content of intuition. How, then, can we be assured that they will be valid of experience in general? An indispensable part of Kant's answer is that the object in experience must itself be subjective or phenomenal. It must be limited by the very fact of being experienced in such wise as to make universally possible the mind's modes of categorial synthesis. That which can not validly be thought under the categories can not be given in intuition. Thus the objects of knowledge are the objects of experience. The limitations of thinking are also the limitations of sensing; the possibility of knowledge is assured by the fact that experience is not of the independent real but of phenomena already informed by our receptivity.

*It is difficult, of course, to interpret Kant, with any assurance of accuracy, upon this point. In the *Transcendental Aesthetic* the distinction of forms of intuition as modes of our receptivity from any mode of mind's activity, seems sufficiently clear. In later sections, reference to the "synthesis of apprehension" and such passages as the one headed, "Of the a priori grounds of the possibility of experience" raise doubts about the principle of this separation. But certainly the division between those conditions which the mind actively imposes on the object and those which it passively imposes in intuition must be there, else the whole procedure of the *Critique* falls to the ground.

This manner of meeting the skeptical difficulty is both unnecessary and impossible. It is impossible because if there were conditions imposed upon experience by our receptivity, mind could not recognize them as its own. At most it could only conjecture that they belonged to it and not to the nature of the independent real, or to that *portion* of reality to which experience so far had been confined. Lacking any certain criterion by which the limitation of the content of experience could be ascribed to mind, such conditions would appear simply as limitations of what was given, whose continuance in all future experience would be as problematic as any empirical generalization. And this answer to skepticism is unnecessary, because mind may limit reality (in the only sense which the validity of the categories requires) without thereby limiting experience. The active interpretation by mind imposes upon given experience no limitation whatever.

Every beginning student of Kant asks sooner or later, "But how does Kant know that phenomena are *not* things in themselves?" And the only answer that can be given is that if what could be experienced were limited only by what existed to be experienced, then the limits of experience could be discovered only through experience itself. Any conclusion rgarding them would then be probable only, since it would be argument from past to future. If the limits belong to reality and not to the mind, then knowledge of them a priori is not possible.

Perhaps this answers the question why Kant, consistently with the rest of his procedure, must distinguish phenomena from things in themselves. But it omits the real question how we can *know* that the limitations of experience are due to the mind and are not simply those of an independent reality which experience reveals. If there are limitations of experience which are imposed not by the activity of thinking addressed to the given, but before that given is given, or in its being given, how shall we distinguish what mind is responsible for from what independent reality is responsible for? This can only be done either by knowing the unknowable reality or by some criterion of what mind is responsible for in given experience. This must take the form, "Even if it existed to be experienced, we could never experience X (let us say, non-Euclidean space)." And this reminds us of another objection that the beginning student makes: "How do we know that we shall keep on having the kind of mind we have and not wake up tomorrow in a non-Euclidean or timeless world?" Probably the answer is that we do not know this; that Kant in fact supposes it possible (since he believes in immortality); but that it is useless to mix our problems in this way; for discussion of the validity of mundane knowledge and of science, the general character of human experience is a datum in the sense of setting the problem of explanation. But this does not answer the question how, if we *should* wake up in so novel a world, we should know that the change was in *us*, in the forms of our receptivity, and not merely in external reality.

We cannot conceive any limits of possible experience in general. Or to speak more exactly; the limits of the possibility of experience are the limits of meaningful conception. "Possibility of experience" is ambiguous, and "conception" as that word is ordinarily used, is ambiguous in a parallel fashion. The sense in which I can conceive a non-Euclidean reality is the sense in which I can give meaning to an "If—then" proposition in which the "if" states some intelligible condition and the "then" ascribes some content which supposedly would be *experienced* under the conditions of that "if." How abstract and fantastic such an "if" may become, without losing meaning altogether, and how tenuous the speculatively conceived reality which is thus ascribed, we have seen in the previous chapter. But in precisely the same sense that "reality" is ascribed, in that sense some possibility of experience is predicated. We can conceive limits of *human* experience only by conceiving the possibility of an experience which we do not have. When the possibility of experience is speculative, the reality in question *and the limitations which it transcends* are equally speculative. Where that possibility has some basis in *actual* experience, a limitation may be *known*, but it is known *by generalization from experience* and the prediction of its continuation in all future experience has precisely and only such assurance as may attach to empirical generalizations. We cannot know a priori and with absolute certainty that any limitation of experience will be permanent. I can and do conceive my individual experience as limited by certain personal peculiarities such as near-sightedness and range of auditory sensibility. But I discover this limitation by comparison with other persons and by conceiving something, which I do not have, as possible experience intelligibly related to the kind I do have. Whether such limitation is permanent or temporary, is merely a question for empirical science to answer; the oculist or aurist may tell me. I conceive all human experience to be similarly limited by human sensibility, as compared with that of some other animal, or perhaps only some dreamed-of being whose sensibility should be affected by stimuli which affect none of ours. We cannot literally imagine such experience any more than the blind man can imagine red; nevertheless it is not beyond our powers of conception. It is an identical proposition that no conceivable experience or reality is beyond our powers of conception.

Let us not forget the issue which is in question.

The skeptic asks how we can know that modes of conception or understanding or interpretation which are of the mind can be validly imposed upon an independent reality and all future experience. The Kantian answer is that the object of knowledge is not independent reality but phenomena, which are limited by human modes of receptivity, and that these, in the nature of the case, will hold for all future experience. This answer is unnecessary because we have a much simpler one before us; it is an identical proposition that no conceivable experience or reality is beyond our powers of conception. What is beyond our powers of conception has no meaning; the word which is supposed to denote it is a nonsense syllable. Experience does not need to be limited in order that we should be able to understand it; we can understand *anything* in one way or another.

Furthermore, whatever is understood is in some sense or other conceived as possible of experience. The very manner in which we attach a meaning, for example, to "non-Euclidean space" is assurance that if we should experience it we could understand it. The conception of non-Euclidean space is a fairly definite one, and the sense in which it could be understood, if experienced, is definite in the same measure. Other conceptions of what transcends actual experience are more tenuous; the "possibility" of experience which is in question is more abstract and the meaning of the hypothesis is vague in like degree. But what is absolutely and in every sense beyond the possibility of experience is likewise beyond all meaning. An absolute and a priori limitation of experience could not be known. The kind of limitations which I attribute to myself or to human beings in general is the kind which I associate with sense-organs or some biological characteristic; and whatever evidence of them there may be is empirical. We know that we shall never experience directly certain ranges of vibration because we have no sense-organs which are affected by them. But we know this a posteriori only, and with whatever probability attaches to the continued correlation between certain sensory apparatus and certain modes of stimulation, or between our subjective experience and these particular organs. That our experience will persist in having this limitation, is probable only, however fantastic the alternative. If it be asked, "How do we know a priori that there are certain limits which will characterize all future experience," the answer is that we can have no such knowledge. We shall experience what we shall experience. We might experience anything you please, imaginable or unimaginable, which can be phrased at all. And if we experienced it, we should proceed to understand it, either by finding a consistent categorial interpretation or by condemning it as hallucination (which, after all, would be a categorial un-

derstanding of it.) The only limitation which need
be imposed upon possible experience in order that
it may be brought under the categories is the limitation to what can be understood. The alternative
to what can be understood cannot even be phrased.
And what is limited only by nonsense syllables is
not limited at all.

It may be objected: Exactly the contingency
which is supposed to be ruled out by the Kantian
conception is the possibility of a fantastic experience in which all that order upon which science relies, all my knowledge and modes of interpretation, would be worthless. Unless experience
is limited a priori, what rational ground of assurance have we that knowledge may not be thus
invalidated? The answer is in part that which the
queen gave in the episode of the wishing carpet:
"If this were real, then it would be a miracle. But
miracles do not happen. Therefore I shall wake
presently." We have no absolute assurance in advance that our experience at some particular time
in the future will meet the criteria of *physical*
reality. But we *are* sure in advance that if it does
not, it will not be experience of the physically real.
Kant creates an artificially difficult problem for
himself by his use of the term "experience" as if
experience and the phenomenally real coincide.
Did the sage of Konigsberg have no dreams! In
fact, this procedure is quite usual. We first forget all that part of experience which is under-

stood by being classed as dream or illusion, and think of "experience" as something to the content of which reality must be assigned. We then proceed—when confronted with the skeptic's challenge—to terrify ourselves with the possibility of an "unintelligible" experience such as any prosaically-minded person would immediately dispose of, if it were reported to him, with the verdict "dream" or "insane imagination." The categories are required to cover the totality of experience only if the categories "dream," "illusion," "hallucination," are included. An a priori principle of interpretation is not required to bring all experience within that category whose principle it is. Precisely what it expresses is the criteria of reality, of a certain type such as the physical. Its universal applicability to experience is satisfied if whatever experience does not conform to the criteria in question can be repudiated as not real (*e. g.*, not physical reality). Obviously any experience is intelligible if the absence of certain types of order mark it as unreal and, therefore, not in question. And could any one's experience be understood without repudiating much of it as non-veridical? *A priori principles of categorial* *interpretation are required to limit reality; they are not required to limit experience.* The contingency of illusion, dream, or even of insanity may be real possibilities of future experience; that has nothing to do with the validity of the categories.

In this connection, it is also of importance to raise another and related question: Has it ever been claimed, or could it reasonably be claimed, that knowledge of the particular can be a priori? In the sense that this particular can, and must be, subsumed under some universal of which knowledge is possible a priori; Yes. But in the sense that mind, confronted with a given content of experience, can with absolute certainty refer it to its proper category, and thus interpret what is now given in such wise that no further experience could invalidate that interpretation; No. The particular phenomenon may always be non-veridical or the subject of mistaken apprehension; and whether it be such, we look to further experience to reveal. The usual phrasing of our dictum with respect to the particular might be such as: "This material object must have mass," or "The sum of two sides of this triangular plot must be greater than the third." But the empirical object is always such that we are capable of being deceived about its "true nature." This presentation may not be a real material thing; the plot may not be truly triangular. Strictly such knowledge of the particular is always complex: "This is a material object and material objects must have mass." "This plot is triangular, and the sum of two sides of a triangle must be greater than the third." The first half of these represents the subsumption of the given under a category; the last half, a principle of that category. Clearly it is the principle only which is a priori. The interpretation by which the given is referred to a category is always such that it may possibly be erroneous; its validity can never be known with certainty, independent of all further experience. That the categories condition experience in the sense of imposing on its content an irrevocable order and connection, or an interpretation not subject to doubt in the particular case, it is not possible to believe. The only sense in which categorial interpretation can be a priori is the sense that the *principle* of this interpretation is not subject to recall even if, in the particular case, what is given should fail to conform. That is a priori which we can maintain in the face of all experience *no matter what*. In the case of an empirical law, a mere generalization from experience, if the particular experience does not fit it, so much the worse for the "law." But in the case of the categorial principle, if experience does not fit it, then so much the worse for the experience.

The question of the possibility of knowledge a priori, is not the problem: How can we know in advance that experience which should not conform to our categorial principle is impossible? It is the problem: How do we know in advance that if it does not conform to our principle it will not be veridical, or will not be real in the category which is in question? The former question can

have no answer unless by some impossible dogmatism about the limitation of experience by a
mind which is itself above or behind experience,
and hence unknowable. And even this hypothesis
of transcendent mind does not assure the permanence of its conditions unless by some further dogmatism which assumes its continuity unchanged.
The latter question has an obvious answer: We
know that any experience which does not conform
to our categorial principle will not be veridical
because the principle states the *criteria* of reality
of that categorial type.

If it be asked further: "How do we know, in
these terms, that we may not be presented in experience with what will not fit into *any* category
and thus be wholly unintelligible," the answer is
in part by reference to that systematic ambiguity
of the term "reality" which was pointed out in
Chapter I. What is not reality of one sort is
reality of another; what we do not understand in
one way, we shall understand in another. The
subsumption of the given under the heading
"dream" or "illusion" is itself a categorial interpretation by which we understand certain experiences. Even "the unintelligible" is a sort of category, a temporary pigeon-hole in which items are
filed subject to later classification when we have
some further light on them or it becomes more
imperative to understand them. It would be a
hardy soul who would insist that no content of

experience is unintelligible at the moment when it is given, or that there is any time-limit on the unintelligibility of particular items of experience. The notion that all content must be immediately and absolutely intelligible and categorized, in being admitted to experience, is just one of those respects in which rationalistic theory is too pretty to be true.

It might even be suggested, without going beyond the bounds of plausibility, that the assumption that nothing can be finally and absolutely unintelligible, is a sort of ideal of reason, or represents a willingness to bet on our capacity to triumph over *any* apparently chaotic character of experience and reduce it to some kind of intelligible order. Our dictum that no experience can be intrinsically unintelligible, is saved from being falsified by experience in general by the fact that it sets no time-limit on our efforts to understand, and hence no failure can be final. As a report of our actual dealings with the given, the generalization "All experience is understood" would be a bit absurd.

It is, however, more important and more just to observe that intelligibility is always a matter of degree. Nothing is *completely* understood. And some partial interpretation is always possible. That very repudiation by which the non-veridical is ruled out from a certain category, is itself such partial interpretation and represents a beginning of our understanding of the experience in question. Thus the ascription of intelligibility and unintelligibility is always relative—relative to our present powers and relative to those interests which make interpretation in some particular way momentarily important or desirable. With reference to our present understanding, all experience is both. The notion that, in categorizing the given, the mind understands it completely and has done with it for all time, is an unwarranted assumption which the Kantian point of view seems to inculcate without explicitly making. And it is implausible as soon as it is mentioned.

Hence if we take the problem of the a priori to be concerned with our foreknowledge of absolute limits of the possibilities of all future experience as such, the question how we can have such knowledge has no valid answer. But if we take it to relate to our knowledge in advance of the principles to which all *veridical* experience must conform, it has an obvious one. The principles of categorial interpretation are a priori valid of all possible experience because such principles express the criteria of the veridical and the real. No experience could possibly invalidate them, because any experience not in conformity, which might be evidence against them, is automatically thrown out of court as not veridical in that category, and hence not pertinent to them. Knowledge of such a priori principles requires only reflective self-consciousness because it is simply knowledge of those criteria which we apply in classifying experience in one or another fashion, interpreting it in one or another way. A categorial principle is a sort of purposive attitude taken in the interests of understanding and intelligibility with which we confront the given. It does not preclude any imaginable or unimaginable content of experience in the future, but only precludes our interpreting it in a fashion contrary to our predetermined attitude or bent.

If any be inclined to press the matter further, and raise the question how we can be positively assured that our minds will not alter in these fundamental attitudes, I shall reply that we can not have any such final assurance. And it is not important that we should. For a theory which refers the a priori to a transcendent, absolute, and universal mind, this question has its difficulties. But the theory here presented does not depend on the hypothesis of such a mind. It is compatible with the supposition that categorial modes of interpretation may be subject to gradual transition and even to fairly abrupt alteration. As will be pointed out in the next chapter, such alteration in categorial interpretations is a fact of social history but one which does not have the subversive results which might be imagined. There is no reason why it may not be a fact of the developing mind of the individual as well. To be sure, the continuity of fundamental attitudes and purposes is the core of personality; the supposition that, without any rationale, these may become altered, is simply the supposition that a new and abnormal personality may replace our present one. This is admittedly possible, but it is not a contingency against which the theory of knowledge is supposed to provide.

Chapter VIII

THE NATURE OF THE A PRIORI, AND THE PRAGMATIC ELEMENT IN KNOWLEDGE

In experience, mind is confronted with the chaos of the given. In the interest of adaptation and control, it seeks to discover within or impose upon this chaos some kind of stable order, through which distinguishable items may become the signs of future possibilities. Those patterns of distinction and relationship which we thus seek to establish are our concepts. These must be determined in advance of the particular experience to which they apply in order that what is given may have meaning. Until the criteria of our interpretation have been fixed, no experience could be the sign of anything or even answer any question. Concepts thus represent what mind brings to experience. That truth which is a priori rises from the concept itself. This happens in two ways. In the first place, there is that kind of truth, exemplified most clearly by pure mathematics, which represents the elaboration of concepts in the abstract, without reference to any particular application to experience. Second, the concept in its application to the given exhibits the predetermined principles of interpretation, the criteria of our distinguishing and relating, of classification, and hence the criteria of reality of any sort. This is most clearly evident in the case of those basic concepts, determining major classes of the real, which may be called the categories, though in less important ways it holds true of concepts in general.

For both these ways in which the truth is fixed, independently of experience or in advance of it, it represents the explication or elaboration of the concept itself. *The a priori is not a material truth, delimiting or delineating the content of experience as such, but is definitive or analytic in its nature.*

The a priori as thus definitive or explicative, representing principles of order and criteria of the real, meets all the requirements which emerge from the discussion of the preceding chapter. Since it is a truth about our own interpretative attitude, it imposes no limitation upon the future possibilities of experience; that is a priori which we can maintain in the face of all experience, come what will. And although it represents the contribution of the mind itself to knowledge, it does not require that this mind be universal, absolute, or a reality of a higher order than the object of its knowledge. The a priori does not need to be conceived as the inscrutable legislation of a transcendent mind, the objects of which, being limited by its forms of intuition, are phenomenal only. Hence the distinction of the legislative mind as ultimate

reality from its object which is not thus ultimate,
falls away, and with it the difficulty of knowing the
mind and of recognizing what is a priori as that
which is determined by our own active attitude.
The a priori is knowable simply through the reflective and critical formulation of our own principles of classification and interpretation. Such
legislation can be recognized as our own act because the a priori principle which is definitive, and
not a material truth of the content of experience,
has alternatives. It can be recognized as due to
the mind itself by the ordinary criteria of responsibility in general—that a different mode of acting is possible and makes a discoverable difference.
Where there is no possibility of refraining from
our act or acting otherwise, there can be no discoverable activity—indeed, there is no act. As
has been pointed out, if what is a priori sprang
from a transcendent mind, acting in unalterable
ways, it never could be known to be our own creation or distinguished from those facts of life
which are due to the nature of the independent
real. What can be known to be a priori must meet
the apparently contradictory requirements that it
may be known in advance to hold good for all experience and that it have alternatives. The principle of classification or interpretation meets these
requirements, because the alternative to a definition or a rule is not its falsity but merely its abandonment in favor of some other. Thus the deter-

mination of the a priori is in some sense like free choice and deliberate action.

This meets also another difficulty which will already have presented itself to the reader. If the a priori is something made by mind, mind may also alter it. There will be no assurance that what is a priori will remain fixed and absolute throughout the history of the race or for the developing individual. From the point of view here presented, this is no difficulty at all but the explanation of an interesting historical fact. The rationalist prejudice of an absolute human reason, universal to all men and to all time, has created an artificially exalted and impossible conception of the categories as fixed and unalterable modes of mind. One result has been to limit the usefulness of the conception, so that what we could call, in ordinary parlance, "the categories of physics" or "the categories of biology" would not serve as examples of "the categories" because it is obvious that the fundamental principles and concepts of any natural science change progressively with its development. This, in turn, has served to obscure the large and important part played in science by that element of categorial order which cannot be determined by merely empirical fact but must be provided by the scientist himself in his setting of the problem and fixing the criteria by which the meaning of experimental findings is to be interpreted. Thus the most impressive examples of human knowledge have been too little drawn upon in discussions of epistemology.

The assumption that our categories are fixed for all time by an original human endowment, is a superstition comparable to the belief of primitive peoples that the general features of their life and culture are immemorial and of supernatural origin. The grand divisions of our thought-world differ from those of our early ancestors as our modern machines differ from their primitive artifacts and our geographical and astronomical outlook from their world bounded by a distant mountain range or the pillars of Hercules and shut up under the bowl of the sky. Certain fundamental categories are doubtless very ancient and permanent: thing and property, cause and effect, mind and body, and the relations of valid inference, doubtless have their counterparts wherever and whenever the human mind has existed. But even here, the supposition of complete identity and continuity is at variance with facts which should be obvious.

For all primitive peoples, for example, and for some who distinctly are not primitive, the properties of a thing are not localized in time and space, as for us. Almost anything may be a talisman or fetish, whose action takes place (without intermediaries) at a distance and in a time posterior to its destruction by fire or by being eaten. Things also have doubles, inscrutably operating in that other-world whose influence mysteriously interpenetrates the realm which we call "nature." Furthermore, the long-persistent problem in physics of action at a distance increasingly comes back to haunt us and to unite with new problems of physical interpretation which threaten to drive us once more to dissipate the "material thing" throughout all time and space; to find its manifestation and even its very being in a spatio-temporal spread of events indefinitely extended.

That the present distinction of mind and body corresponds only roughly with that division in ancient thought; that body of inert matter and mind which does not occupy space are no older than the advent of that esoteric doctrine which dawned in Europe with the Greek mysteries and Christianity—this can hardly escape us. This mode of distinction contrasts with the tripartite division into body, mind, and spirit, and with the five-fold and n-fold divisions of more easterly cultures. It is also obvious that the pressure of modern science in the field of biology and our present uneasiness about this twofold nature of the individual, augur some departure from the clarity of Cartesian dualism.

The *names* of our categories may be very old and stable, but the *concepts*, the modes of classifying and interpreting which they represent, undergo progressive alteration with the advance of thought.

Probably those modes of thought embodied in logic and in the forms of language are more fundamental than others. And very likely what we recognize as explicit categories are always superficial as compared with more deep-lying forms which only the persistent and imaginative student can catch, in some vague and fleeting insight, because they are so nearly the marrow of our being and so all-pervasive that they can hardly be phrased in significant expression. These go back to the point where mind is continuous with the objective and indistinguishable from it. For we can know our own nature only in so far as we comprehend or vaguely imagine what it would mean to be other than we are. We can recognize the presence of mind only where mind makes a discoverable difference. If we should think of mind as what the rationalists suppose—superimposing on reality a rigid mask of form outside which mind itself could never catch a glimpse—then this altogether universal and un-get-overable form could never become self-conscious. It would remain—in Fichte's phrase—the "Great Thought which no man has ever thought." It would be not of mind but of the objective reality; it would be the Absolute which forever conditions but never can be known. But the idealistic rationalist can not eat his cake and have it too; the mind which can be recognized as such is *ipso facto* finite and limited by discoverable bounds. That mind is thus

continuous with the finally mysterious—the is-ness
of what is—we must of course grant; in the contemplation of mind we contemplate one aspect of
the Great Fact in the presence of which all explicit thought is silenced. But the categories are
not the form of that which, having no alternative
and no bounds, is formless. They are the explicit
bounds of that which, if it transcend them, must
—fall into some other category. They are divisions within the comprehensible in general, but
not the shape of comprehensibility itself.

It will be well to make clear that the conception here presented does not imply that because
the a priori is something made by mind and capable of alteration, it is therefore arbitrary in the
sense of being capriciously determined. That it is
not, and cannot be, determined by the given,
does not imply that it answers to no criteria whatever. That type of a priori truth which pure
mathematics illustrates—that is, the elaboration
of concepts in abstraction from all questions of
particular applications—answers only to the criteria of self-consistency. Just to the extent that
the development of such a purely analytic system is withdrawn from every consideration of useful application, its truth is simply truth to the
original meanings embodied in its basic concepts.
But when concepts are intended to be applied in
experience, and a priori principles are to determine modes of classification and interpretation,

the case is different. Here mind is still uncompelled by any possible content of experience. But knowledge has a practical business to perform, the interests of action which it seeks to serve. The mode of the mind's activity answers to our need to understand, in the face of an experience always more or less baffling, and of our need to control. There is also another factor which helps to determine what modes of attempted comprehension will be most easily and most widely useful. While that absolute human reason which the rationalist supposes to be completely and universally possessed by every human is a myth, nevertheless man, being a species of animal, has characteristics which mark him as such, and some of these at least are reflected in the bent of human thought. Some modes of thought are simpler and come more naturally to us than others which still are possible and which might, indeed, be called upon if an enlarged experience should sufficiently alter our problems—just as some modes of bodily translation are more easy and natural, though these may be somewhat altered when the environment includes a sufficient number of automobiles and airplanes. Moreover, the fundamental likeness in our modes of thought, which represents whatever community of nature marks our original mental endowment, is continually enhanced by the fact that the needs of individual humans are mostly served by coöperation with others. "The human mind" is distinctly a social product, and our categories will reflect that fact.

In brief, while the a priori is dictated neither by what is presented in experience nor by any transcendent and eternal factor of human nature, it still answers to criteria of the general type which may be termed pragmatic. The human animal with his needs and interests confronts an experience in which these must be satisfied, if at all. Both the general character of the experience and the nature of the animal will be reflected in the mode of behavior which marks this attempt to realize his ends. This will be true of the categories of his thinking as in other things. And here, as elsewhere, the result will be reached by a process in which attitudes tentatively assumed, disappointment in the ends to be realized, and consequent alteration of behavior will play their part.

Confirmation of this conception of the a priori could only come from comprehensive and detailed examination of at least the major categories of thought and the underlying principles of common-sense and scientific explanation. Such a task cannot be undertaken here; at most only a few illustrations can be offered with the hope that they are typical.

The paradigm of the a priori in general is the definition. It has always been clear that the simplest and most obvious case of truth which can be known in advance of experience is the explicative proposition and those consequences of definition which can be derived by purely logical analysis. These are necessarily true, true under all possible circumstances, because definition is legislative. Not only is the meaning assigned to words more or less a matter of choice—that consideration is relatively trivial—but the manner in which the precise classifications which definition embodies shall be affected, is something not dictated by experience. If experience were other than it is, the definition and its corresponding classification might be inconvenient, useless, or fantastic, but it could not be false. Mind makes classifications and determines meanings; in so doing, it creates that truth without which there could be no other truth.

Traditionally propositions which have been recognized as analytic have often not been classed with the a priori; they have been regarded as too unimportant; sometimes they have even been repudiated as not truth at all but merely verbal statements. The main reasons for this cavalier attitude have been two; in the first place, it has been overlooked that the real itself is a matter of definition and that the dichotomy of real and unreal is that first and basic classification which the mind confronted with experience must make. And second, the powerful sweep and consequence of purely logical analysis has not been understood.

The clearest example of this power of analysis is to be found, of course, in mathematics. The historical importance of mathematics as a paradigm of a priori truth needs no emphasis. Almost one may say that traditional conceptions of the a priori are the historical shadow of Euclidean geometry. But in mathematics much water has gone under the bridge since the time of Kant, and in the light of the changes which have come about, these traditional conceptions are proved totally impossible. The course of this development will be familiar to the reader; only the outstanding features of it need be mentioned.

Though there are anticipations of current mathematical conceptions as far back as Plato, the movement which led to their present acceptance dates principally from the discovery of the non-Euclidean geometries. In developing these systems, it was obviously impossible to depend on intuitions of space, either pure or empirical. If Euclid is true of our space, then no one of these geometries can be; and if Euclid is not true and certain, then the main ground of the supposition that we can rely on intuitions of the spatial is discredited.* Hence in developing the non-Euclidean systems, all constructions such as helping-lines, and any step in proof which should de-

*Euclid and a non-Euclidean system cannot both be true of space while corresponding denotations of terms are maintained. The discovery that they may both become true of space with systematic difference in the denotation of terms played its part in the logic of modern geometry.

pend not upon pure logic but upon the character of space must be dispensed with. If a step in proof cannot be taken by rigorous logic alone, it cannot be taken at all. When it was found thus possible to develop the non-Euclidean systems without appeal to any extra-logical aids, a similar revision of Euclid was carried out, eliminating all explicit or implicit reliance upon constructions, superpositions or other appeal to spatial intuition. This new method, together with certain indicated generalizations, constituted the so-called "modern geometry."

Next it was demonstrated that not only geometry but other branches as well can be developed by the deductive method, from a relatively few assumptions, and likewise without reliance upon empirical data. As a result all pure mathematics is found to be abstract, in the sense of being independent of any particular application. Because if all the theorems follow logically from the definitions and postulates, then we can alter at will what we let the terms, such as "point" and "line," denote without in the least disturbing any step in the proofs. *Whatever* "point" and "line" may mean, given these assumptions about them, these consequences—the rest of the system—must also hold of them, since the theorems follow from the assumptions by rigorous and purely logical deduction.

The question of the truth of the mathematical

system *in application* was thus completely separated from its mathematical or logical integrity. Still further changes went along with this. The "truth" of initial assumptions lost all meaning in any other sense than their exhibition of certain patterns of logical relationship to be adhered to throughout. The distinguishing assumptions of a non-Euclidean geometry, for example, so far from being self-evident, were supposedly mere arbitrary falsehoods with respect to their most obvious empirical denotation. The term "axiom" was replaced by "postulate" or "primitive proposition." In the interest of logical simplicity alternative sets of assumptions which would give the same system of propositions were investigated. What should be initially assumed and what proved became a question merely of such logical simplicity. It became customary to speak of the truth of mathematics as hypothetical or to say that what mathematics asserts is only the relation of implication between postulates and theorems. It is truth about certain patterns of logical relationship established by initial definition or postulate.

Further, it became clear that the distinction between those assumptions of the form called "definitions" and those termed "postulates" was relatively arbitrary and unimportant. Logically it makes little difference except for simplicity of procedure, how far the order of a system is set up by propositions in which "is" means logical equiva-

lence and how far by those in which it means only
the one-way implication of concepts or subsumption of classes. Since the content of the concepts
of pure mathematics is simply that order to which
they give rise, that manner of development in
which essential relationships are exhibited as the
definitive meaning of the concepts is truest to the
nature of the subject.

The completion of this last refinement of mathematical method was made by Whitehead and
Russell in "Principia Mathematica."* It was here
proved that the initial assumptions of mathe-

---

*This development is still too recent for the exact bearing of its
consequences to be clear in all respects. Points concerning which there
may be some doubt are as follows:

(1) Can this method, without alteration, be completely carried out
in geometrical branches? Some concepts needed in geometry are
dealt with in volume III, but volume IV, which was to complete this
subject, has not appeared.

(2) There are certain assumptions, such as the "axion of infinity"
which appear as *hypotheses* to some theorems which, apparently, require them. It is not known whether this procedure is entirely avoidable without abandoning certain classes of theorems which have their
place in usual mathematical developments.

(3) Consistency and independence are of the essence of mathematics, since they concern its logical integrity, apart from all questions of application. It is possible to think, in view of usual mathematical procedures, that tests of consistency and independence involve implicit appeal to intuition or to applications. By the method
of "Principia" it is not clear how it is possible to deal with such
problems. Independence proofs have been applied to logistic systems
by N. Bernays and others, but only by a reversion to those familiar
devices the logic of which is precisely the point in question. Professor
H. M. Sheffer has offered a general method for testing consistency
and independence without reference to any possible application (See
his "General Theory of Notational Relativity," privately circulated).
The method of dealing with usual branches in this way must wait
upon his further publication.

(4) It is questionable whether logistic methods employed in "Principia" are in all respects acceptable as "proof" and whether they do
not, in certain ways, import illicit assumptions of "existence." But
if there are defects of this sort, it is highly probable that they are
avoidable.

matics can all be dispensed with, except the definitions. The truths of mathematics follow merely from definitions which exhibit the meaning of its concepts, by purely logical deduction. Judgment of such mathematical truth is, thus, completely and exclusively analytic; no synthetic judgment, a priori or otherwise, is requisite to knowledge of pure mathematics. The content of the subject consists entirely of the rigorous logical analysis of abstract concepts, in entire independence of all data of sense or modes of intuition. The definitions which embody these concepts are not required to be true in any other sense than that they should be precise and clear; the formulation of them represents an act of mind which is legislative or creative and in some sense arbitrary; it answers to no criteria save self-consistency and adequacy to whatever purposes the elaboration of the system itself may be supposed to satisfy. It may still be true that "concepts without precepts are empty," but it must be granted that there is a kind of knowledge of "empty" concepts. Or at least such admission can be avoided only by a restriction of the term "knowledge" to exclude pure mathematics and logic. The importance of such a priori analytic knowledge is witnessed by the basic character of these subjects for all other sciences.

Pure mathematics stands between logic on the one side and the empirical application of mathematics on the other. Logic is in some respects the illustration *par excellence* of the a priori, since its laws are the most completely general of any. The laws of logic cannot be proved unless they should first be taken for granted as the principles of their own demonstration. They make explicit the basic principles of all interpretation and of our general modes of classification. And they impose no limitation upon the content of experience. Sometimes we are asked to tremble before the specter of the "alogical" in order that we may thereafter rejoice that we are saved from this by the dependence of reality upon mind. But the "alogical" is pure bogey, a word without a meaning. What kind of experience could defy the principle that everything must either be or not be, that nothing can both be and not be, or that if X is Y and Y is Z, then X is Z? If anything imaginable or unimaginable could violate such laws, then the ever-present fact of change would do it every day. The laws of logic are purely formal; they forbid nothing but what concerns the use of terms and the corresponding modes of classification and analysis. The law of contradiction tells us that nothing can be both white and not white, but it does not and can not tell us whether black is not white or soft or square is not white. To discover what contradicts what we must turn to more particular considerations. Similarly the law of the excluded middle formulates our decision that whatever is not designated by a certain term shall be designated by its negative. It declares our purpose to make, for every name, a complete dichotomy of experience, instead—as we might choose —of classifying on the basis of a tripartite division into opposites and a middle ground between the two. Our rejection of such tripartite division represents only our penchant for simplicity and similar considerations.

Further laws of logic are of like significance. They are principles of procedure, the parliamentary rules of intelligent thought and action. Such laws are independent of the given because they impose no limitations whatever upon it. They are legislative because they are addressed to ourselves —because definition, classification, and inference represent no operation in the world of things, but only our categorial attitudes of mind.

Furthermore, the ultimate criteria of the laws of logic are pragmatic. Indeed, how could they be anything else? The truth of logic is not material truth but a truth about the modes of self-consistency. Since this is so, logic must be the test of its *own* consistency, and hence of its own truth, as well as the test of the consistency of everything else. But if logic tests its own truth, then what can be the test of truth in a genuine issue of logic, which is not a question of mere inadvertance on one side or the other? Those who suppose that there is *a* logic which everyone would agree to if

he understood it and understood himself, are more
optimistic than those versed in the history of logical discussion have a right to be. The fact is that,
as was pointed out in the preceding chapter, there
are several logics, markedly different, each self-
consistent *in its own terms* and such that whoever, using it, avoids false premises, will never
reach a false conclusion. Mr. Russell, for example, bases *his* logic on an implication relation such
that if twenty sentences be cut from a newspaper
and put in a hat, and then two of these be drawn
at random, one of them will certainly imply the
other, and it is an even chance that the implication will be mutual. Yet upon a foundation so remote from ordinary modes of inference the whole
structure of "Principia Mathematica" is built.
This logic is utterly self-consistent and valid in
its own terms. There are others even more strange
of which the same may be said.* Genuine issues
of logic are those which stand above such questions of the merely self-critical integrity of the
logical system. There are such issues, and these
cannot be determined—nay, cannot even be argued—except on pragmatic grounds of human
bent and intellectual convenience. That we have
been blind to this fact, and that much good paper
and ink has been wasted by logicians who have
tried to argue on some other grounds what are
only questions of convenience or of value, itself

*See p. 209, footnote.

reflects traditional errors in the conception of the a priori.

Pure mathematics and logic exemplify that type of the a priori which have the highest degree of abstraction from experience—whose concepts are so general that we may call them "empty." Concerning these, there may be a question whether there will not be issues of an entirely different sort when we attempt to apply them in experience. One may say, for example, that when geometry becomes abstract and freed from all necessary reference to our intuitions of the spatial, the question of the *truth about space* becomes an entirely separate one, and one with respect to which there must be reference to forms of intuition or something of the sort, or there will be nothing which is determinable a priori at all. Similarly one may say that if arithmetic as a purely abstract deductive system has no necessary reference to the character of countable objects, then its a priori truth is of no value for the anticipation of the behavior of concrete things. This will be true, of course, and of importance. If there should be a priori truth *only* with respect to concepts in utter abstraction from experience, and if this a priori character were to vanish when these concepts are given a concrete denotation, then the significance of the a priori for the natural sciences and for common practice would be largely, if not completely, lost.

But there *is* an a priori truth of concepts which have concrete denotation. Let us consider the example of arithmetic. Arithmetic depends *in toto* upon the operation of counting or correlating, a procedure which can be carried out in any world containing identifiable things, regardless of the further characters of experience. Mill challenged this a priori character of arithmetic. He asked us to suppose a demon sufficiently powerful and maleficent so that every time two things were brought together with two other things, this demon should always introduce a fifth. The conclusion which he supposed to follow is that under such circumstances $2 + 2 = 5$ would be a universal law of arithmetic. But Mill was quite mistaken. In such a world we should be obliged to become a little clearer than is usual about the distinction between arithmetic and physics, that is all. If two black marbles were put in the same box with two white ones, the demon could take his choice of colors, but it would be evident that there were more black marbles or more white ones than were put in. The same would be true of all objects in any wise identifiable. We should simply find ourselves in the presence of an extraordinary physical law, which we should recognize as universal in our world, that whenever two things were brought into proximity with two others, an additional and similar thing was always created by the process. Mill's world would be physically most extraordinary. The world's work would be enormously facilitated if hats or locomotives or tons of coal could be thus multiplied by anyone possessed originally of two pairs. But the laws of mathematics would not be affected. It is because this is true that arithmetic is a priori. Its laws prevent *nothing;* they are compatible with anything which happens or could conceivably happen in nature. They are true in any possible world. Mathematical addition is not a physical transformation. The only bringing together it implies is in the mind; if translation in general affected numerical alteration, we should always count things *in situ,* but we should count and add as usual. Physical changes which result in an increase or decrease of the countable things involved are matters of everyday occurrence. Such physical processes present us with phenomena in which the purely mathematical has to be separated out by analysis. It is because we shall always separate out that part of the phenomenon not in conformity with arithmetic and designate it by some other category—physical change, chemical reaction, optical illusion—that arithmetic is a priori. *Its laws constitute criteria of our categorial classification and interpretation.* As this example serves to illustrate, such categorial interpretation of the concrete and empirical throws out of court whatever would otherwise violate the a priori principles which embody the category, but it does not thereby legislate anything phenomenal out of existence.

Perhaps, however, we have gone too far. Mill's illustration is of an alteration of experience in general which is too simple and too poorly carried out to make it plausible that our categorial interpretation would be different in such a world. But if translation in general affected numerical alteration then an entirely different mode of categorial interpretation might better serve the purposes. Our present categories would not—*could not*—be prohibited but other modes might more simply reduce the phenomenal to order and facilitate control. Or in such a world, arithmetic might be confined to mental phenomena—since these would be exempt from the effects of change of place—and numerical principles would be laws of psychology. If we were jelly-fish in a liquid world, we should probably not add at all, because the useful purposes served by such conceptions would be so slight. Still if some super-jelly-fish should invent arithmetic by a *jeu d'esprit* (as Hamilton invented quaternions) he would find nothing in any possible experience to controvert it, and he might with some profit apply it to his own distinct ideas.

The ideal illustration of the a priori in applied geometry would be a consideration of physical relativity, showing how geometrical truth may turn upon the place where the dividing line is drawn between the properties of *space* and those of *matter*. Applied geometrical principles are a priori true of all space-filling things. But this a priori truth has its pragmatic aspect since there are these alternatives about the manner in which the category of "the spatial" shall be bounded. But to carry out this illustration in detail would be beyond my competence.*

Incidentally it may be pointed out that the ideas which have gained currency through relativity-theory make clear the nature of Kant's mistakes in the supposition of a limited form of spatial intuition. For Kant, the spatial or geometrical has to do with relations of the simultaneous; the shape of a triangle, for example, is something instantaneously imaginable. But for celestial triangles, such instantaneous intuition has no meaning; what exists or happens at a distance is not directly verifiable here and now; a passage of something through time, as well as space, is inextricably bound up with the determintion of the distant fact. Hence the imagination of a "curved-space" need not mean something like flattening out a hemisphere without disturbing the relations of great circles on its surface. It means only imagining *certain uniform sequences* to characterize our experience of the spatial under certain conditions. The "unimaginable" character of curved-

*The reader may also be referred to Poincaré's "Science and Hypothesis," the section on "Space and Geometry."

space in the sense that we cannot visualize a non-Euclidean triangle on the blackboard, has nothing to do with the matter. Triangles on different scales have different "shapes" in non-Euclidean space, and triangles big enough to "verify" the nature of space are too big to "imagine." Our ancestors who believed the earth was flat could certainly "imagine" a non-Eucidean space, in the only sense which is required, since the geometry of the earth's surface is (in an obvious sense) Riemannian.

The a priori element in natural sciences goes much deeper than might be supposed. All order of sufficient importance to be worthy of the name of law depends eventually upon some ordering by mind. Without initial principles by which we guide our attack upon the welter of experience, it would remain forever chaotic and refractory. In every science there are fundamental laws which are a priori because they formulate just such definitive concepts or categorial tests by which alone investigation becomes possible.

A good example of this is to be found in Einstein's little book "Relativity."* The question under discussion is the criteria of simultaneity for events at a distance. Suppose the lightning strikes a railroad track at two places, A and B. How shall we tell whether these events happen at the same time? "We . . . require a definition of simultaneity such that this definition supplies us with

*Pp. 26–28: italics are the author's.

a method by which . . . we can decide whether or not the lightning strokes occurred simultaneously. As long as this requirement is not satisfied, I allow myself to be deceived as a physicist (and of course the same applies if I am not a physicist) when I imagine that I am able to attach a meaning to the statement of simultaneity. . . .

"After thinking the matter over for some time you then offer the following suggestion with which to test simultaneity. By measuring along the rails, the connecting line *A B* should be measured up and an observer placed at the mid-point *M* of the distance *A B*. This observer should be supplied with an arrangement (*e. g.*, two mirrors inclined at 90°) which allows him visually to observe both places *A* and *B* at the same time. If the observer perceives the two flashes at the same time, they are simultaneous.

"I am very pleased with this suggestion, but for all that I cannot regard the matter as quite settled, because I feel constrained to raise the following objection: 'Your definition would certainly be right, if I only knew that the light by means of which the observer at *M* perceives the lighting flashes travels along the length *A–M* with the same velocity as along the length *B–M*. But an examination of this supposition would only be possible if we already had at our disposal the means of measuring time. It would thus appear as though we were moving here in a logical circle.'

"After further consideration you cast a some-

what disdainful glance at me—and rightly so—
and you declare: 'I maintain my previous definition nevertheless because in reality it assumes
nothing whatever about light. There is only *one*
demand to be made of the definition of simultaneity, namely, that in every real case it must supply
us with an empirical decision as to whether or not
the conception which has to be defined is fulfilled.
That light requires the same time to traverse the
path *A–M* as for the path *B–M* is in reality
neither a supposition nor a hypothesis about the
physical nature of light, but a *stipulation* which
I can make of my own free-will in order to arrive
at a definition of simultaneity.' . . . We are thus
led to a definition of 'time' in physics."

As this example well illustrates, we cannot even
ask the questions which discovered law would answer until we have first by a priori stipulation
formulated definitive criteria. Such concepts are
not verbal definitions nor classifications merely;
they are themselves laws which prescribe a certain
behavior to whatever is thus named. Such definitive laws are a priori; only so can we enter upon
the investigation by which further laws are
sought. Yet it should also be pointed out that such
a priori laws are subject to abandonment if the
structure which is built upon them does not succeed in simplifying our interpretation of phenomena. If, in the illustration given, the relation
"simultaneous with," as defined, should not prove

transitive—if event A should prove simultaneous with B and B with C, but not A with C—this definition would certainly be rejected.

Indeed *all* definitions and *all* concepts exercise this function of prescribing fundamental law to whatever they denote, because everything which has a name is to be identified with certainty only over some stretch of time. The definition provides criteria of the thing defined which, in application, become necessary or essential laws of its behavior. This is especially evident in the case of scientific definitions because the "things" of science are of a deep-lying sort, representing uniformities of behavior of a high order.* If definition is unsuccessful, as early scientific definitions mostly have been, it is because the classification thus set up corresponds with no natural cleavage and does not correlate with sufficiently important uniformities of behavior. Early attempts to reduce phenomena to law are based upon the "things" of common-sense which represent classification according to properties which are relatively easy of direct observation and impressive to the senses. When such attempts fail, it is largely because of this superficiality of initial classification. The alchemist's definitions of the elements, for example, are the clue to his indifferent success; the definitive properties pick out amorphous groups which have little significance of further uniformity. Not until such crucial

*See Appendix A.

properties as combining weights become the basis
of classification is it possible to arrive at satisfactory laws of chemistry. The earlier definitions can
not be said to have been false; they were merely
useless, or insufficient to the purposes in hand. A
large part of the scientific search is, thus, for
✳ *things worth naming.*

We have reached a point today where we understand that the typical procedure of science is
neither deduction from what is self-evident or
relatively certain nor direct generalization from
experience. If any one method is more characteristic of science than another it is that of hypothesis and verification. But we seem still to overlook the fact that the *terms* in which hypothesis
and law are framed themselves represent a scientific achievement. We still suffer from the delusion
that fixed and eternal categories of human thought
on the one side are confronted with equally fixed
and given "things" on the other. Is it not obvious,
to dispassionate observation, that scientific categories and classifications are subject to progressive modification or even abrupt alteration, and
that these have a directive and controlling influence upon the other phases of scientific research?
And here too, as in hypothesis and verification, the
development takes place, not by logical derivation
from antecedent principles nor by direct formulation of empirical content, but by the hazarding of
something by the mind and its retention or re-

pudiation according to the success or non-success of what is based upon it. The test of success here is not, however, simple conformity with experience, as in the testing of hypothesis, but is the achievement of intelligible order amongst the phenomena in question, and responds also to such criteria as intellectual simplicity, economy, and comprehensiveness of principle.

The reader will perhaps feel that, in so far as this is true, what is here represented as a priori is nothing of the sort but is merely something that we learn from experience. But if so, I hope that he will reread the illustration from Einstein, with due regard for the logic of it. However much the give and take between the purposes of science and discovered fact may contribute to alter the procedure by which those aims are sought, and may induce new basic principles and categories, still the naming, classifying, defining activity is at each step prior to the investigation. We cannot even interrogate experience without a network of categories and definitive concepts. Until our meanings are definite and our classifications are fixed, experience cannot conceivably determine anything. We must first be in possession of criteria which tell us what experience would answer what questions, and how, before observation or experiment could tell us anything.

The uniformities which science seeks are of a high order and represent a further reach of those same purposes exhibited on a humbler scale by the uniformities of common sense comprehension. The categorizing and classifying activity of thought is, thus, more deliberate and self-conscious in the case of science and, by comparison, easier to observe than in the case of common sense. Because scientific categories are in some part built upon more basic distinction, the functioning of them as criteria of the real is less frequent and perhaps less important. It is, nevertheless, sometimes to be observed in the interplay between new principles of scientific interpretation and residual phenomena which are unexplained or reports of observation which are regarded as possibly involving error. If Röntgen had been unable to repeat the experience in which he first saw the bones of his hand, that perception would have been discredited. Because no one but their discoverer could see the "N-rays" with any assurance, and it was found that he saw them when the refracting prism was removed as well as with it, they were discarded as illusory. The phenomena of hypnotism remained for a long time in the limbo of the dubious, and even today offer a difficult problem of separation of veridical phenomenon from illusion, self-deception and the like. The phenomena of "dual personality" would challenge a very fundamental category if only there were not so much doubt about what it is that is "dual" and whether it is genuinely dual. To choose a different sort of ex-

ample, when the eclipse-photographs which figured in the discussion of relativity were examined,
the question was raised whether the star-displace-
ments as measured on them represented simply
the bending of light-rays or were due in part to
halation of the sensitive film. Thus, for a moment
at least, so fundamental a problem as that of
abandoning the categories of independent space
and time was intertwined with the question whether
the position of dots on a photographic plate represented authentic star-photographs or was due to
something which took place inside the camera.

What needs to be observed here is at once the
continuity of scientific problems of a high order
with the apparently simple and fundamental criteria of the real, and the fact that such decisions
of reality or unreality are themselves interpretations involving principles of the same order as
scientific law. They are such as forbid, for example, the non-biological transformations and
non-physical successions which occur in dreams.
A mouse which disappears where there is no hole,
is no real mouse; a landscape which recedes as we
approach, is but illusion. The reality of an object
of a particular sort is determined by a certain
uniformity of its behavior in experience. The formulation of this uniformity is of the type of natural law. So far, such laws are a priori—for this
particular sort of thing; the experience which fails
to conform to the law is repudiated as non-veridical.

This situation is most paradoxical; principles of the order of natural law are reached by some generalization from experience—that is, from *veridical* experience; there are no generalizations whatever to be had from the unsorted experience of real and unreal both. But what experience is *veridical*, is determined by the criterion of law. Which is first, then; does the content of experience validate the law or does the law validate the experience in attesting its veridical character? The answer is that the law is first precisely so long as and so far as we are prepared to maintain it as criterion of the real. But the "reality" which is in question is likely to be of a highly specific sort. The authentic photograph of stars and the picture affected by halation, for example, are both real, both physically real, both photographs even, in a certain sense. What is an "authentic photograph" has to be very precisely defined in the case in point and is so defined as to exclude the effect of light reflection from the back of the glass of the photographic plate. The manner of this definition or classification obviously will require a correlation of photograph and thing photographed of the type set forth in certain physical laws. In the particular case, failure to exhibit such lawful relationship condemns the phenomenon as not authentic or not real—that is, not really this very specific sort of thing.

Thus all concepts, and not simply those we

should call "categories," function as criteria of reality. Every criterion of classification is criterion of reality of some particular sort. There is no such thing as reality in general; to be real, a thing must be a particular sort of real. Furthermore, what is a priori criterion of reality in one connection may be merely empirical law in some other—for example, the law correlating photograph and thing photographed, or the law of the behavior of solid bodies in translation which condemns the mouse that disappears without a hole, or the laws of perspective which exclude a landscape which recedes as we approach it. *The determination of reality, the classification of phenomena, and the discovery of law, all grow up together.* I will not repeat what has already been said so often about the logical priority of criteria; but it should be observed that this is entirely compatible with the shift of categories and classifications with the widening of human experience. If the criteria of the real are a priori, that is not to say that no conceivable character of experience would lead to alteration of them.

For example, spirits cannot be photographed. But if photographs of spiritistic phenomena, taken under properly guarded conditions, should become sufficiently frequent, this a priori dictum would be called in question. What we should do would be to redefine our terms. Whether "spook" was spirit or matter, whether the definition of "spirit" or of "matter" should be changed; all this would constitute one interrelated problem.

What would prove to you that the relative motion of a body effected a foreshortening of it and altered its mass? If the answer is "no conceivable experience" and you are able to formulate a definition of "mass," a conception of motion, and of ideally exact measurement in terms that do not conflict with one another and with your other physical conceptions, there is no possible ground on which you could be proven wrong. To a mind sufficiently resolute for an independent space and time, no possible experience could prove the principles of relativity. The question, "How long shall we persist in holding to our previous categories, when confronted with star-photographs and the displacement of spectrum-lines (or with spiritistic phenomena or evidence of telepathy)?" is one which has no general answer. A stubborn conservatism can be proved unreasonable only on the pragmatic ground that another method of categorial analysis more successfully reduces all experience of the type in question to order and law. Confronting such a problem, we should reopen together the question of definition or classification, of criteria for this sort of real, and of natural law. And the solution of one of these would probably mean the solution of all. Nothing could *force* a redefinition of "spirit" or of "matter." A sufficiently fundamental relation to human bent or to human interests would guarantee continuance unaltered even in the face of unintelligible and baffling experience. And no equipment of categories and concepts which the mind is likely to achieve will enable us to understand experience completely and in every respect. In such problems, the mind finds itself uncompelled save by its own purposes and needs. What is fixed datum and must be conformed to, is only that welter of the given in which not even the distinction of real and unreal is yet made. The rest is completely and exclusively our problem of interpretation. I *may* categorize experience as I will; but what categorial distinctions will best serve my interests and objectify my own intelligence? What the mixed and troubled experience will be—that is beyond me. But what I shall do with it—that is my own question, when the character of experience is before me. I am coerced only by my own need to understand.

It would indeed be inappropriate to characterize as a priori a law which we are prepared to alter in the light of further experience even though in an isolated case we should discard as non-veridical any experience which failed to conform. But the crux of the matter lies in this; beyond such principles as those of logic and pure mathematics whose permanent stability seems attested, there must be further and more particular criteria of the real prior to any investigation of nature. Such definitions, fundamental principles and criteria the mind itself must supply before experience can even begin to be intelligible. These represent more or less deep-lying attitudes, which the human mind has taken in the light of its total experience up to date. But a newer and wider experience may bring about some alteration of these attitudes even though by themselves they dictate nothing as to the content of experience, and no experience can conceivably prove them invalid.

It is the a priori element in knowledge which is thus pragmatic, not the empirical. The pragmatists generally have neglected to make the separation of concept and immediacy, with the result that they seem to put all truth at once at the mercy of experience and within the power of human decision or in a relation of dependence upon the human mind. But this would be an attempt to have it both ways. The sense in which facts are brute and given cannot be the sense in which the truth about them is made by mind or alterable to human needs. To be sure, this a priori element in knowledge runs very deep; it is present whenever there is classification, interpretation, or the distinction of real from unreal—which means that it is present in all knowledge. So I suppose it must be admitted, in the last analysis, that there can be no more fundamental ground than the pragmatic for a truth of any sort. Nothing—not even

direct perception—can force the abandonment of
an interpretive attitude, nor indeed *should* move
us to such abandonment (since illusion or mistake
is always possible) except some demand or purpose of the mind itself. But certain important
ends, such as intellectual consistency and economy, completeness of comprehension, and simplicity of interpretation, occupy a place so much
higher, for the long-run satisfaction of our needs
in general, that they rightfully take precedence
over any purpose which is merely personal or
transitory. In the popular mind especially, pragmatism too often seems to connote the validity of
rather superficial and capricious attitudes—for
instance, the justification of belief from no deeper
ground than personal desire. It is this insufficient
regard for intellectual integrity, this tendency
to trench upon high-plane purposes from low-
plane motives which marks the kind of "pragmatism" which is to be eschewed. We must all be
pragmatists, but pragmatists in the end, not in
the beginning.

In another respect also, there is a connotation
of "pragmatism" which more or less prevails,
which is inapplicable to the theory here presented.
Concepts and principles of interpretation are subject to historical alteration and in terms of them
there may be "new truth." But the situation in
which this happens needs analysis. It does not
mean the possibility of new truth in any sense in

which new truth can genuinely contradict old truth. This may not at first be clear. New ranges of experience such as those due to the invention of the telescope and microscope have actually led to alteration of our categories in historic time. The same thing may happen through more penetrating or adequate analysis of old types of experience—witness Virchow's redefinition of disease. What was previously regarded as real—*e. g.*, disease entities—may come to be looked upon as unreal, and what was previously taken to be unreal—*e. g.*, curved space—may be admitted to reality. But when this happens *the truth remains unaltered and new truth and old truth do not contradict.* Categories and concepts do not literally change; they are simply given up and replaced by new ones. When disease entities give place to mere adjectival states of the organism induced by changed conditions such as bacteria, the old description of the phenomena of disease does not become false in any sense in which it was not always false. All objects are abstractions of one sort or another; a disease entity is found to be a relatively poor kind of abstraction for the understanding and control of the phenomena in question. But in terms of this abstraction any interpretation of experience which ever was correctly made will still remain true. Any contradiction between the old truth and the new is *verbal only*, because the old word "disease" has a new meaning. The old word is retained but the old concept is discarded as a poor intellectual instrument and replaced by a better one. Categories and precise concepts are logical structures, Platonic ideas; the implications of them are eternal and the empirical truth about anything given, expressed in terms of them, is likewise through all time unalterable.

In the typical case in which old methods of interpretation are discarded in favor of new ones, it requires new empirical data, which offer some difficulty of interpretation in the old terms, to bring about the change. Any set of basic concepts has vested interests in the whole body of truth expressed in terms of them, and the social practices based upon them. The advantage of the change must be considerable and fairly clear in order to overcome human inertia and the prestige of old habits of thought. Such new and recalcitrant data, which bring about the change, complicate the problem of comparing the "new truth" with the old. The factors which need to be considered are: (1) the two sets of concepts, old and new, (2) the expanding bounds of experience in which what is novel has come to light, (3) the conditions of the application of the concepts to this new body of total relevant experience.

In the case of the Copernican revolution, for example, it was the invention of the telescope and the increasing accuracy of observation which mainly provided the impetus to reinterpretation. But these new data were decisive only in the pragmatic sense. Those who argued the issue supposed that they were discussing a question of empirical fact. But since there is no absolute motion, the question what moves and what is motionless in the heavens is one which cannot be settled by experience alone. The fixed stars prove to be a highly convenient frame of reference, resulting in relatively simple generalizations for the celestial motions, and enabling celestial and sublunary phenomena to be reduced to the same equations, while almost insurmountable complexity and difficulty attend the choice of axes through the earth. Theoretically, however, if any system of motions is describable with respect to one set of axes, it is also describable in terms of any other set which moves with reference to the first according to any general rule. Let us imagine for a moment that this theoretically possible description of astronomical and physical phenomena in terms of a motionless earth had been worked out for all the data now at hand. In terms of which set of concepts, old or new, should we have the truth? Obviously in both. The one would be comprehension and simple truth; the other so complex as to be almost or quite unworkable. But they would no more contradict each other than a measurement in pounds and feet contradicts one in grams and meters.

This situation is not altered by any thought that newly discovered fact may play another than the pragmatic rôle and be decisive of truth in a deeper sense. Nobody has ever supposed that what were only hypotheses or empirical generalization of a high degree of probability were incapable of being disproven by new facts. To the extent that newly discovered empirical evidence may render old principles theoretically impossible, the old truth never was anything but hypothesis and is now proved flatly false. It is not, I hope, the point of the pragmatic theory of knowledge to reduce all truth thus to hypothesis. That would be nothing but a cheerful form of skepticism.

Rather the point of the pragmatic theory is, I take it, the responsiveness of truth to human bent or need, and the fact that in some sense it is made by mind. From the point of view here presented, this is valid, because the interpretation of experience must always be in terms of categories and concepts which the mind itself determines. There may be alternative conceptual systems, giving rise to alternative descriptions of experience, which are equally objective and equally valid, if there be not some purely logical defect in these categorial conceptions. When this is so, choice will be determined, consciously or unconsciously, on pragmatic grounds. New facts may cause a shifting of such grounds. When historically such change of interpretation takes place we shall gen-

uinely have new truth, whose newness represents
the creative power of human thought and the
ruling consideration of human purpose.

The separation of the factors, however, reveals
the fact that the pragmatic element in knowledge
concerns the choice in application of conceptual
modes of interpretation. On the one side, we have
the abstract concepts themselves, with their purely
logical implications. The truth about these is absolute, in the fashion in which pure mathematics
offers the typical illustration. Such purely abstract a priori truth answers only to the criteria
of consistency and adequacy. It is absolute and
eternal. On the other side, there is the absolute
brute-fact of given experience. Though in one
sense ineffable, yet the given is its own fashion
determinate; once the categorial system, in terms
of which it is to be interpreted, is fixed, and concepts have been assigned a denotation in terms
of sensation and imagery, it is this given experience which determines the truths of nature. It
is between these two, in the choice of conceptual
system for application and in the assigning of
sensuous denotation to the abstract concept, that
there is a pragmatic element in truth and knowledge. In this middle ground of trial and error, of
expanding experience and the continual shift and
modification of conception in our effort to cope
with it, the drama of human interpretation and
the control of nature is forever being played. That

the issues here are pragmatic; that they do not touch that truth which still is absolute and eternal—this is the only thing that would save those who appreciate the continually changing character of this spectacle from skepticism.

Chapter IX

THE A PRIORI AND THE EMPIRICAL

So far, various aspects of, and elements in, knowledge have been considered, for the most part separately. The results may now be brought together, and the relation of the various factors considered with more care. Quite commonly, the different types or phases of knowledge—of presented objects, of a priori principles, of empirical generalizations—are all lumped together, and either what is true of one type only is applied to all, or in some other fashion an omnibus explanation is attempted which will include them all under one formula. No theory devised by such procedure can ever be more than partially successful.

The following need to be distinguished: (1) the immediate awareness of the given, such as might be supposed to be reported in statements like "This looks round," "This feels hard," "This tastes sweet"; (2) knowledge of presented objects, such as is expressed by, "This *is* hard," "This is a sweet apple," "This penny is round"; (3) the a priori elaboration of wholly abstract concepts, like the formulations of pure mathematics, apart from any question of possible applications; (4) the categorial knowledge of interpretative principles and criteria of reality, which is that form of a priori knowledge which arises when concepts have a fixed denotation and are applied to the given; (5) empirical generalizations, which are universal but not a priori.

The difference of the first two is especially easy to overlook; the first—"This looks round"—is a direct report of the momentarily given; the second—"This penny is round"—represents the conceptual interpretation of this given, and implies much which is not given.

As has been made clear in preceding chapters, the term "knowledge" is here restricted in a manner which may seem arbitrary but at least answers to definite criteria; that only is called "knowledge" which is verifiable and has a significant opposite "error." There is, in the knowledge of presented objects and of objective properties, a distinguishable element of awareness which is indispensable to this knowledge but which, by itself, cannot be knowledge in the meaning here assigned. It is this awareness of immediate and recognizable qualia which may be supposed to be expressed by "This looks round," etc. So far as such a statement is merely a report of the immediately given, it is neither verifiable nor stands in any need of verification. Nor is it subject to any possible error. If the subject of the report is the immediate feeling itself, there is no possibility of being mistaken about it, though all sorts of misapprehension about the experience reported might arise in the mind of another person to whom the report might be addressed, due to poor choice of language or to the ineffable character of individual immediate experience.

It has also been pointed out that such immediate awareness is an element *in* knowledge rather than a state of mind occurring by itself or preceding conceptual interpretation. Without the relational element which conception introduces, immediacy is inarticulate. It is questionable whether a state of pure esthesis is a genuine mental possibility. In any case, it is not necessary to assume its existence. The sense in which such immediacy is prior to its interpretation is the sense in which interpretation is subject to change. Cognition of the external world is *active* just so far as conceptual interpretation is subject to correction and alteration, on occasion. In the case of such a *new* interpretation, the immediate awareness is literally and temporally antecedent; but that there is a first moment of such apprehension, in which there is such awareness and *no* interpretation, it is not necessary to believe. In all cases, however, it is the content of the given which determines (in part) the interpretation, not the interpretation which determines the immediate to fit it. In that sense also the awareness of the given is prior to its interpretation.

Predications of the second sort—"This is hard,"

"This penny is round"—express something much more complex than the immediate feeling of pressure or the givenness of a "round" or "elliptical" presentation. As predications of objective properties, these represent an interpretation put upon the content of immediate awareness which implicitly predicts further experience. Being thus predictive, they are judgments which are subject to verification and liable to error.

Strictly, the nature of the judgment as interpretation of the given is more complex than the statement of it. This is obvious in the case of the example, "This penny is round"; calling what is presented "a penny" is interpretive to at least the same degree as judging it to be round. What the subject expresses is an interpretation as much as the predicate. A similar thing is true of all predications in which the subject is something *named;* the distinction between subject and predicate is merely one of emphasis or nuance—it reflects a difference between what is already granted or obvious and what needs explicit assertion. The two statements, "This penny is round" and "This is a round penny," do not represent materially different interpretations of what is given.

Similar considerations hold for all predications of objective character to anything given, except those in which the subject is mere demonstrative like "this" which supposedly serves merely to point to the given. Even such demonstratives, moreover, attribute to the "this" which is indicated that kind of continuance and lawful relation to other things which is the mark of the objective. The point of using the demonstrative lies in its indication of a reality which is not subjective but whose existence and asserted character is verifiable, by ourselves and other persons, over a stretch of time. Hence the difference between assertions about a "this" and predications about something named lies only in the more extended and more definite character of the interpretation which the use of a name as the subject term implicitly takes for granted. And in all such predication the application of the subject term, as of the predicate, is an interpretation of given experience.

The fact that the denotation of a demonstrative is, in all ordinary parlance, "this (thing or objective property) which is presented," and not "this *presentation*," draws our attention to the fact that the attempt to exemplify the mere report of immediate awareness—as by the illustrations, "This tastes sweet," etc.—can be only approximately successful. Here also the demonstrative denotes an object, not the presentation itself. Otherwise there would be no predication, because subject and predicate would coincide and what we are trying to express would take the form "Sweet taste tastes sweet" or simply the ejaculation "Sweet taste!" The use of predication is completely pre-empted to the conveying of the objective, and there is no language whatever, unless of primitive cries, which expresses awareness of the given as such. The expressive ejaculation or cry is, so to speak, the salutation of the real or the acknowledgment of an existent. Such salutation or acknowledgment, however, represents an essential element in knowledge—that which distinguishes the truth from lies; that fact of presentation which is our confrontation with reality.

Concerning our knowledge of presented objects, it may be noted further that there is no difference which is important in the present connection between the predication of an objective property and the predication of substantive character or thinghood. So much is evident from the practical equivalence of "This penny is round" and "This is a round penny." The kind of interpretation involved and the general manner of its verification is the same whether it is a property like roundness or a substantive character such as being a penny which is in question.

By how much does the interpretation which characterizes our knowledge of objects transcend what is given? What is involved in its complete verification? Obviously in the statement "This penny is round" I assert implicitly *everything the failure of which would falsify the statement*. The implicit prediction of *all* experience which is essential to its *truth* must be contained in the original judgment. Otherwise such experience would be irrelevant to it. All that further experience the failure of which would lead to the repudiation of the apprehension as illusory or mistaken is predicted in the judgment made. Now suppose we ask: How long will it be possible to verify in some manner the fact that this penny is round? What totality of experience would verify it completely, beyond the possibility of necessary reconsideration? I have here no theoretical axe to grind, but it seems to be the fact that *no* verification would be absolutely complete; that all verification is partial and a matter of degree. Even after the penny itself has ceased to exist, a sufficiently important connection with other matters might still lead to a revival of the question whether it is really true that a round penny lay before me on my desk on the twenty-ninth of January, 1926, at four o'clock. And however difficult it might be at such later time to gain new and decisive evidence, theoretical tests of what would increase or decrease the probability would be capable of formulation. Is it not the case that the simplest statement of objective particular fact implicitly asserts something about possible experience throughout all future time; that theoretically every objective fact is capable of some (partial) verification at any later date, and that no totality of such experience is absolutely and completely sufficient to put our knowledge of such particulars beyond all possibility of turning out to be in error? So far as this is true, *all interpretation of particulars and all knowledge of objects is probable only,* however high the degree of its probability. Every such judgment about the real external world remains forever at the mercy of future possible experience. Between the immediate awareness, "This looks round," and the objective interpretation, "This is round," there lies all the difference between this present moment and all time; between an experience which is now complete and *had,* and a totality of possible experience which is unlimited and inexhaustible.

Perhaps this conclusion that the verification of empirical particulars is always partial, will be more evident if we investigate the alternative. Let us suppose that, for some interpretation of a particular given experience, there is some finite and limited totality of later experience which, together with the presentation itself, will absolutely and finally verify our interpretation as an empirical fact so that nothing further could possibly require the retraction of it. Let us suppose the presentation to be given and interpreted at time t_0. And let us imagine the verification to be complete at time t_1. Now let us ask: Will the total significance of this empirical fact be exhausted at time t_1, so that consideration of it will enable no *further* prediction of anything which would be discoverable at some still later time, t_2? We shall hardly be inclined to answer in the affirmative, since such an answer would mean that, after the date t_1, the fact would have no further consequences and its existence or historical verity would be no longer determinable. Because if at time t_2 there should be no consequences of this fact, which would be lacking if the event had not taken place, then there will be absolutely no means, at time t_2, whereby it may be discovered whether there *was* any such fact or not. Hence there can be no such time, t_1, after which no consequences predictable from the interpretation of the presentation at t_0 will accrue. The verifiable consequences of any fact last as long as time itself. Now suppose further that at some date, t_2, we put ourselves in position to meet the consequences of this fact, which was accepted as completely established at t_1. And suppose that these consequences fail to appear, or are not what the nature of the accepted fact requires? In that case, will there still be no doubt about the accepted fact? Or will what was *supposedly* established at t_1 be subject to doubt at t_2? And in the latter case can we suppose it was absolutely verified at time t_1? Since no single experience can be absolutely guaranteed to be veridical, no limited collection or succession of experiences can absolutely guarantee an empirical fact as certain beyond the possibility of reconsideration.

This is not an argument; as argument, it would

be *petitio principii*. But I believe that, having followed out these consequences, the reader will be inclined to repudiate the supposed alternative and to grant the thesis that the interpretation put upon the empirically given is always something temporally inexhaustible, hence never completely verified, and is always probable only.

Incidentally this conclusion serves to answer a question which may have occurred to the reader in an earlier chapter: If knowledge is knowledge only as it is predictive and verifiable, does it cease to be knowledge when it is completely verified? We now see the answer to be that knowledge—the knowledge of empirical particulars at least—never *is* completely verified. This also throws light upon the nature of the concepts of things and of objective properties, which are applied to the given in interpreting it. It has been noted that what any concept denotes has always a temporal spread. In appealing to the reader to grant the considerations of the preceding paragraphs, I likewise ask him to grant, by implication, that this temporal spread is unlimited and that the existence of things and properties has a sort of unlimited duration, as was suggested in Chapter IV in the reference to the "fallacy of simple location" in time.

The empirical knowledge of particular objects is probable only. Yet underlying it there is and must be an element of the a priori, else there would be no criteria of its empirical truth and not even a valid probability. When we make the judgment, "This penny is round," the subject "penny" and the predicate "round" both express implicitly certain a priori criteria which are definitive of the meaning of these terms in application. Being a penny, or being round, means a hundred and one various sequences in further possible experience. That these sequences would actually accrue under suitable conditions is implicitly predicted in applying these concepts to the given presentation. To be really round, this presented object must alter in appearance in certain characteristic ways with change of perspective; it must feel in certain ways if handled; and if it be measured with precision instruments, the results must be thus and so. Furthermore, it must *not* alter in certain other ways which would oblige us to explain that the angle of vision or some trick of eyesight, etc., had led us into error. Such explication of what is implicit in the concept sets the criteria by which further experience will verify (or falsify) the present judgment. If this setting of criteria were not a priori and incapable of being overturned by the eventualities of experience, then such experience would not be a test of the truth of the predication, or even establish a probability of it. That is to say, when we make the judgment, "This is round," what we suppose ourselves to know requires two propositions to express it fully:

(1) "If this is round, then further experience of it will be thus and so (the empirical criteria of objective roundness)" and (2) "This present given is such that further experience (probably) *will be* thus and so." The first of these is a priori; the second is our statement of the probable empirical truth about the given object.

Unfortunately, I must ask the reader to go with me a little further in this analysis of the knowledge of empirical particulars. There is no escape for us, because the truth about it happens to be quite complex. Certain further considerations have, in all probability, already suggested themselves to the reader. First, in the light of preceding paragraphs it is evident that the empirical criteria of, let us say, roundness which we can have explicitly in mind at any one moment, will not be the completely sufficient criteria because the empirical eventualities which would *completely* verify the roundness of the given thing are too utterly complex and extended to be thus explicit. When we actually *define* "roundness" in words, we refer the meaning of one term to others, and (supposing the definition to be well-made and adequate) *both the subject term defined and the predicate which defines it* have a meaning which, in application, are of this complex sort which it is not possible to express completely, or have explicitly in mind, at any one moment. So to speak, the terms of a definition are all in one plane, in which the definitive relations are finitely specifiable. But each term is a point of reference in another dimension (that of denotation) and its meaning in this dimension is not thus exhaustively expressible in a few words. That a meaning in denotation must have this complex character is due in part to the fact that no object can be apprehended in isolation. Any appearance of an object is conditioned also by other objects, particularly by my own body. It is such conditions which are expressed in the "if" clause of those "If—then" propositions in which the predictions implicit in an interpretation may be made explicit.

That such complexity of consequences is always implicit in every concept, may be more evident if we reflect upon the example of some mathematical concept. For instance, the analytic consequences of the definition of "triangle" are as numerous as the geometrical theorems concerning triangles—that is, unlimited in number.

We may further note that we may—indeed *must*—have this unlimited meaning in denotation in mind in a figurative sense, when we do not have it in mind explicitly. The possession of the concept or meaning is utterly irrelevant to any experience whatever, unless we could—with sufficient time and attention at least—say whether certain eventualities of experience would or would not be compatible with its application. For example, the detective who should be assigned the problem

whether I did or did not have a round penny before me at a certain time, could not possibly exhaust in any statement all the evidence which
would, if discovered, be pertinent to it. But if he
did not have it in mind in the figurative sense, all
the Sherlock Holmesing in the world would not
help him a bit because he would not be able to
recognize evidence when he found it. We are, even
the best of us, more or less stupid and might not
be capable of specifying whether a given eventuality is or is not pertinent to our problem. That
is to say, it may be true in some degree that we do
not have the meaning of our concepts in mind
even in the figurative sense. But so far as we are
thus stupid, we simply do not know *what* we mean
when we use the terms; that part of the (ideal)
meaning of the language we apply to our presented experience is simply erased in our case;
and we are condemned by our lack of intelligence
not to understand what we are trying to think and
talk about.

However, this stupidity which in some degree is
inevitable to all of us, and this fact that much of
our meaning, when we interpret given experience,
is in mind only in the figurative sense, is not particularly embarrassing, either theoretically or
practically. Because while the empirical eventualities which would exhaust the denotative meaning
of our interpretative concept are too numerous to
state or have in mind explicitly, those which we

shall be called upon to meet in any brief period are not. And we can—with wit and luck—keep ahead of experience and be explicitly prepared to interpret it by the time the evidence is presented. Furthermore, such explicit eventualities as we *do* have in mind represent knowledge which is a priori, however far they fall short of *exhausting* our interpretive meaning.

A second point which needs at least passing mention is the fact that the a priori element in our knowledge of particulars is complex in another fashion also. This element has been expressed above by the proposition "If this is round, then . . ." So far we have observed that the "then" clause is compounded of empirical eventualities apparently unlimited in number. We must now observe, further, that each one of these is conditional. "If this is round, then if I take two steps to the right, it will look more elliptical." "If this is round, then if it be measured with precision instruments, the result will be thus and so." "If this is round, then it will *not* look elliptical if it is viewed from directly in front. This conditional character of the propositions expressing the predictions implicit in the interpretation of the given, has already been discussed in Chapter IV; and hence need not detain us longer here.

These first two points may be schematically summed up by saying that the a priori element which must underlie the empirical knowledge of particulars is expressible by some set of propositions of the form: If this is round, then condition A being provided, empirical eventuality M will accrue. If this is round, then condition B being provided, empirical eventuality N will accrue. And so on. The totality of the complex "then" classes expresses the complete and a priori meaning of the concept "round" in denotation. Some of these we have explicitly in mind—granted intelligence, we shall be prepared with those with respect to which experience will shortly present us pertinent evidence. Others we have in mind in the figurative sense that we should be explicitly prepared if called upon to include them in, or exclude them from, what we mean by "being round." Still others, perhaps, which belong to an *ideal* denotation of "roundness" we may not have in mind at all. So far as this last is true, we are stupid and are unprepared to understand experience.

There is still one most important point about our knowledge of empirical particulars which remains to be observed. It has been said that what we must know, for example, in order to interpret a given presentation as that of a round object is (1) the a priori proposition, "If this is round, then further experience of it will be thus and so," and (2) "This present given is such that further experience (probably) *will be* thus and so." It will have occurred to the reader that we could not possibly know anything like the second proposition

except by a generalization from previous experience—"Things which look as this does, under conditions like the present, usually turn out to satisfy
the criteria of roundness in further experience."
In general, we must rely upon past experience for
our knowledge of what empirical eventualities are
likely to be connected with any given type of appearance—that is, for our knowledge as to what
presentations are appearances of what objects. In
every case, interpretation of the given requires
empirical generalization.

But it is particularly necessary to recognize
that the subject of *this* type of generalization
from experience is not the *object* presented (or
the class of such objects) but the *presentation itself* (or the class of such). Our recognition of the
object—"This is a round penny"—is the interpretation itself. But the recognition of the *presentation* is simply the classification of it with other
qualitatively similar appearances. The basis of
our interpretive judgment is the fact that, in past
experience, what appeared as this does, under circumstances like the present, has turned out to be,
for example, a round penny—in a sufficiently
large proportion of cases to warrant probable
judgment.

This kind of generalization is seldom explicit.
Our collation of the given with similar appearances in the past is too swift and instinctive for
that. This is presumably the element in human

knowledge which is evolutionally basic and is shared by us with the other animals. But occasionally at least it needs to be explicit; and there is one familiar example which may serve as illustration. The physician is often called upon to diagnose a case, not by some decisive test, but by "the picture" which the case presents. (A clinical picture is, of course, much more complex than any single presentation, but it is, so to speak, preëminently presentational in character, requiring to be identified by direct inspection and difficult or impossible to put in words.) If the physician decides, "This is measles," he does so by means of a generalization from past experience. The subject of this generalization is the class of clinical pictures like the present one. The basis of the judgment is the frequency with which such appearances in the past have been followed by a later case-development which answers to the elaborated medical concept "measles." The ascription of this concept is an interpretation, whose main significance is that of prognosis.

Our knowledge of objects in general is such a diagnosis of appearances. Without our recognition of the presentation by its classification with qualitatively similar ones in the past, and our recollection of the further eventualities in these cases, no interpretation would be possible. That such recognition is ordinarily spontaneous and unconsidered, does not alter the logical character of it as a generalization.

In empirical knowledge there are, thus, two elements concerning which we have certainty; the recognized qualitative character of the given presentation is one and the a priori elaboration of some concept (or the partial elaboration which is explicit with us) is the other. But the applicability of the concept to the presentation is probable only, because such application is an interpretation which is predictive. The probability, or degree of assurance of such interpretation, reflects a generalization from experience. It is an argument from past to future or from the uniformity of experience. In short, in spite of the elements of certainty underlying it, which have been pointed out, the validity of our knowledge of presented objects depends upon the same general considerations that govern empirical generalizations of the types more frequently recognized. Oftentimes it has been supposed that we have a kind of certainty in our recognition of objects, and this has been designated as "knowledge by acquaintance." But such is not the case. What we are directly "acquainted with" are not objects but presentations. Seeing is believing, but quite often the belief based on seeing turns out to be a false one.

Thus there are, on the theory here presented, very much the same problems to be met concerning empirical knowledge, as on various other theories. But the incidence of those problems is different; and this, as we shall discover in later chapters, makes a difference in the manner in which they can be met. A brief comparison, even though inadequate, may be of assistance here. Ordinarily the problem of empirical knowledge in general, when phrased by reference to usual forms of predication, is viewed as the problem how we can know with certainty that what is denoted by the subject of the proposition whose truth is in question will also have the properties denoted by the predicate. How may we be assured that all X's are Y's; that all masses obey Newton's law; that all events have causes, that the sum of the angles of a triangle will be 180 degrees? The problem is that of the *necessary connection of what is denoted by two concepts.*

Now I believe it should be obvious, no matter what theory of knowledge is held, that there is only one ground on which the necessary connection of X and Y, such that all X's will certainly be Y's can be known; that is, that if we find that the concept Y is inapplicable to any particular, then the concept X will be retracted as likewise inapplicable. If we know with certainty in advance that all men are mortal, we know it because if we discover any being not to be subject to the accident of death, then, however like a man he may appear, we shall refuse to recognize him as human. We can know that the sum of the angles of a triangle must be 180 degrees only if in case we find this not so in a particular instance, we shall retract the concept "Euclidean triangle" as inapplicable to the thing in question. Whenever this is so, the subject concept implies or includes the predicate concept and the proposition is a priori because the judgment is analytic.

If the problem of empirical knowledge is supposed to be "How can we be assured that objects met with in experience and identified as X's will never turn out not to be Y's?" then, again, I believe it should be clear on any theory of knowledge that we can never have such assurance, especially if it is remembered that there is no a priori certainty that perception in any particular case is not illusory or subject to the accident of mistaken identification. That is to say, it should always have been clear, if we remember that "experience" as we are confronted with it includes the non-veridical, that the application of concepts in naming and recognizing objects, itself implies characters of the object which are not now presented but wait upon further experience to be revealed.

Remembering this, it will be evident that the only kind of a priori knowledge of the empirical for which there is room in a consistent theory is that kind which consists in knowing the empirical eventualities, implicit in the application of our subject-concept, which are indispensable to the *correctness* of such application. We do not need any limitation of possible experience to be assured of this. If a thing is not an X unless further experience will corroborate a certain Y-character of it, then, let experience be what it will, all X's must be Y's. It is true that this leaves *all* empirical knowledge—except the hypothetical—subject to the tests of later experience, in the sense that such future experience may invalidate our identification and naming of objects. But my point is that no theory ever presented can do more, unless we can be absolutely certain of our recognitions of objects in momentary experience. Such certainty of momentary identification is something which no theory has ever claimed explicitly, though *most* theories have, as a matter of fact, proceeded *as if* it were possible.

Take, for example, geometrical knowledge. Kant claimed a *synthetic* ground of our knowledge of the necessary connection between "the triangular" and "figures having interior angles which sum up to 180 degrees." This synthetic ground was supplied by the limitation of possible human experience to the Euclidean space-form. But did Kant suppose that this limitation of possible experience enabled us to glance at a plot of ground and say with a priori certainty that the sum of its angles was exactly 180 degrees? If not, could one claim—accepting Kant's theory—that this a priori limitation of experience in any fashion assured to our knowledge of this particular plot of ground (or of any other particular) a certainty which future experience might not

trench upon? There can be no doubt that the answer must be negative. What, then, as regards our
knowledge of the empirical, is the supposed advantage of this synthetic element supplied by the
limitation of possible experience? Absolutely all
that it assures us, about any empirically given
object, is that, *if* it be truly triangular, then the
sum of its angles will be 180 degrees; and whether
this condition is satisfied in any particular case,
it leaves subject to the test of future and more
exact determination.

One may further inquire: If we can never, in
a momentary apprehension of anything, be absolutely certain that it is a real Euclidean triangle,
how are we to know that the class of objects actually identifiable as triangles have this further
property of the sum of their angles, unless by the
fact that if they do not have it, then we shall retract the ascription of real triangularity as inapplicable to them? We now see this plot of
ground: it looks triangular. In this momentary
experience, there is absolutely no way in which we
can tell that it is not. Suppose we proceed to measure its angles with a theodolite, and find that the
sum is 181 degrees. Does the Kantian, or any
other, theory deny this possibility? If not, then
the only ground on which we can know that what
is actually identifiable as triangle will have the
further property in question is, in the last analysis, some ground which will lead to the repudia-

tion as "not-triangular" of that which fails, in further experience, to give the required measure of its interior angles, even though, as presented at a certain moment, it was indistinguishable from a real triangle.

Let us take one step further. If a good Kantian must still grant, in the interests of veracity, that the generalization "All figures which are momentarily indistinguishable from the triangular have angles which sum up to 180 degrees" would be false, then how can it be claimed with plausibility that experience of a world in which the laws of Euclid do not hold would be impossible to human beings? If in *one* case we can see as triangular a figure the measure of whose angles exceeds 180 degrees, in what sense would it be impossible that this should be *universally* true? How would a form of intuition prevent us from seeing just as we now do a space whose properties would be Riemannian?

Is it not fairly obvious that the real question about the applicability of Euclid to our space is not the question of what we can imagine or could conceivably experience; but is the question whether the character of experience in general is such that the procedure by which the failure of any spatial object to verify the Euclidean properties is put down to mistaken apprehension is one which gets on better (*i. e.*, better serves our interests of reducing experience to order and securing control) than would any general revision of our whole system of geometrical conceptions?

The situation in which we find ourselves as a result of modern developments in geometry is in accord with this conception of a priori knowledge and its relation to the empirical. As modern mathematics discovers, the concept "triangle" (and the other basic concepts of geometry) include a logically sufficient ground for *all* the properties of triangles, without any synthetic element which is supposed to limit experience. To be sure, this means entire separation of the question of abstract geometrical truth from the truth of experience. This last becomes a question of empirical generalization—or more accurately, it is the complex question: Which of the alternative systems of geometrical concepts will best succeed in its application to experience; it being remembered that what such application requires is that any geometrical concept will be retracted as inapplicable when experience fails to verify the essential geometrical properties—*i. e.*, that all *divergence* of experience from our chosen geometry is to be explained on other grounds, or relegated to the status of mistaken apprehension?

From this point of view, the development of the conceptual system in the abstract is a priori; the question of the applicability of one of its constituent concepts to any single particular is a matter of probability; and the question of appli-

cation *in general* is the question of the *choice* of
an abstract conceptual system, determined by
pragmatic considerations.

We find that there is much more in the abstract concepts than Kant thought—that as a
fact the whole geometrical system can be drawn
from them by purely logical analysis; and we find
that in any case the application to *particulars* is
no better than probable. Under these circumstances, it is extremely dubious what advantage
would accrue if we *could* find a ground for a priori
truth which was synthetic and consisted in some
limitation of the possibilities of intuition. And we
find the supposition that there *is* limitation and
that we can know it, vitiated by the fact that we
most certainly *could* have an experience in which
Euclidean-appearing things should, upon further examination, turn out to have non-Euclidean
properties. The *only* question about a priori truth
in application which is left to be determined is
the question what shall be accepted as the empirical *criteria* of triangularity, straightness, and
so on. This is at once the question *what* kinds of
sequences in experience are to be regarded as
ground for attributing mistake to *previous identifications* of spatial characters in things, and the
question *what* abstract system shall be our choice
for application to experience in general. The
chosen system becomes criterion of the veridical
in experience, that is, its concepts become *criteria*

of reality of a certain sort. It is this question of the choice of conceptual systems for the interpretation of experience which, on the view here presented, is a matter of pragmatic choice, whether that choice be made deliberately, or unconsciously and without recognition of its real grounds.

If, now, the reader will generalize from this illustration in terms of the geometrical, he will have before him the distinguishing characteristics of the present theory of the relation between a priori truth and the content of experience. While other concepts than the mathematical do not usually have their consequences so systematically worked out, nevertheless all concepts give rise to an a priori truth which is purely analytic and independent of any application to experience. Such analytic consequences of a single concept, in isolation, will be relatively meager and relatively trivial. But how complex, far-reaching, and important the analytic consequences may be when three or four such abstract concepts are conjoined, modern systems of mathematics serve to illustrate. That which *any* such concept denotes is always something which, in terms of experience, must have a temporal spread. What is required to determine its applicability, is some orderly sequence in experience, or some set of such. At any given moment, such applicability is verifiable only approximately or in degree. It is thus that the application of the concept to experience may be secured without loss of its a priori character: its logical consequences, which time alone can verify, become *criteria of its applicability*. Later experience which does not accord will lead to the retraction of the concept as inapplicable to the particular to which it was assigned by previous interpretation. Thus the logical requisites a priori of the concept become, in its application to experience, the criteria of reality of a certain sort. The application a priori of Euclidean geometry to nature means, for example, that whatever apprehended particular turns out, in the course of experience, not to have the properties logically implied by the concept "Euclidean triangle" will be condemned as *not a real triangle*, however much it may have looked like one.*

Up to this point, there has been no consideration of the last of the five distinct kinds of apprehension or knowledge mentioned at the beginning of the chapter, *i. e.*, empirical generalizations, ordinarily so-called. We have found that a certain kind of empirical generalization enters into the judgment of truth about empirical particulars. But these are not of the type ordinarily called "generalizations" since the subject of them is the presentation itself; they are usually not expressed at all and are indeed, as we found, dif-

*For a note concerning a further problem about the application of abstract conceptual systems to experience, see Appendix E.

ficult to express in language without including reference beyond themselves to objective and enduring things. Customarily what is meant by "empirical generalization" is a universal proposition the subject of which denotes a class of *objects*. It is distinguished from the a priori in application by the fact that the connection between subject and predicate is not necessary but contingent.*
A simple illustration may be here of service. The proposition "All swans are birds" is a priori because if any creature originally designated as a "swan" should be discovered to lack some distinguishing character of birds, the name "swan" would be withdrawn. The applicability of the predicate term is logically requisite to the applicability of the subject. But the proposition "All swans are white" is an empirical generalization because white color is not included as essential in the denotation assigned to "swan." The former proposition can not be falsified by any possible experience because its truth has a purely logical warrant; it represents the implication of a concept. But the latter proposition has no such logical warrant and *may* be falsified by experience; black creatures having all the essential properties of swans may be discovered. It is to be noted that any universal proposition asserts the nonexistence of some class of things: that all swans are birds requires that there be no non-bird swans;

*See Appendix F.

that all swans are white, asserts that the class of
swans of different color is a class which has no
members. But the proposition which is a priori
does *not* assert any limitation of experience; it
asserts only that whatever lacks some essential
property, X, is not to be classified under some
concept, A. That all swans must be birds, does
not legislate out of existence any possible creature. The empirical generalization, however, *does*
require for its truth a limitation of nature and of
experience: that all swans are white, excludes certain conceivable creatures from existence. It is
thus that the a priori proposition is assured with
certainty in advance, while the empirical generalization requires for its theoretical certitude a
verification which extends to all reality.

The empirical generalization is forever at the
mercy of future experience, and hence probable
only, while the a priori proposition is forever certain. But as the above example points out, this
does not represent any greater assurance about
the content of future experience, or of nature, in
the one case than in the other; it represents only
an intention of interpretation or classification
which maintains a connection between two concepts regardless of experience in the one case but
not in the other. Since the a priori in general is
definitive and analytic, not synthetic, the case is
the same for all a priori propositions.

This particular example is trivial because the

classification "swan" is not a very comprehensive
one; its systematic interconnection with other
classes and categories is relatively slight and unimportant. But more impressive examples can be
given to illustrate the same point—that the a
priori does not dictate to nature but concerns our
interpretation of empirical facts. For example,
the law of gravitation is a posteriori because, if
it fails of verification, we shall still not abandon
the concept "mass," or any of the other terms,
but only the relation between them stated by the
law. By contrast, geometry is a priori because if
the sum of the angles of what is identified as a
Euclidean triangle turn out to be other than 180°,
we shall condemn the experience as "mistake";
and if a sufficient number of such attempted verifications have, without exception, the same result,
we shall abandon the Euclidean character of our
space but not the meaning of "Euclidean triangle." I should suppose that the probability of
Newton's laws and of those theorems of celestial
mechanics which are purely geometrical is of the
same order of magnitude. Certainly there is nothing in the a priori character of geometry to give
us any superior assurance that experience will
conform to it. In so far as certain principles operate as criteria of reality and apparent exception to them condemns the experience as illusory,
the a priori may seem to have another significance.
But this is only because "*nature*" *is itself a cate-*

gory—the very fundamental and important category of the physical: what is extruded from it is
still an absolutely given and un-get-overable fact
of experience, requiring to be dealt with in some
other way if we are to understand it at all. It is,
in fact, easy to exaggerate the cleavage between
the physical and the merely mental or psychological, such as the illusory, as one may observe by
a serious consideration of the question whether
mirages and mirror-images belong to nature or
are merely mental.

The facts which I should like here to emphasize
are mainly two. In the first place, that no substantive conception, determined a priori, is able
to confine particular experiences within its conceptual embrace with absolute assurance; that all
identifications of objects and all *material* truth
about future experience remains probable only.
The supposition that any theory may secure for
the a priori a different significance than this, is
a delusion. The impossibility of it will become apparent if we remember two things: that experience includes dream, illusion, and mistake as much
as "the physical"; and that no theory, even on its
own showing, can attribute an a priori certainty
which is not hypothetical to predications about the
particular presented thing. In the second place,
I would emphasize the fact that the whole body of
our conceptual interpretations form a sort of
hierarchy or pyramid with the most comprehen-

sive, such as those of logic, at the top, and the least general, such as "swans," etc., at the bottom; that with this complex system of interrelated concepts, we approach particular experiences and attempt to fit them, somewhere and somehow, into its preformed patterns. Persistent failure leads to readjustment; the applicability of certain concepts to experiences of some particular sort is abandoned, and some other conceptual pattern is brought forward for application. The higher up a concept stands in our pyramid, the more reluctant we are to disturb it, because the more radical and far-reaching the results will be if we abandon the application of it in some particular fashion. The decision that there are no such creatures as have been defined as "swans," would be unimportant. The conclusion that there are no such things as Euclidean triangles, would be immensely disturbing. And if we should be forced to realize that nothing in experience possesses any stability— that our principle, "Nothing can both be and not be," was merely a verbalism, applying to nothing more than momentarily—that dénouement would rock our world to its foundations.

On the one hand, every concept, however unimportant, gives rise to a formal truth exhibiting its structure, which it is beyond experience to invalidate and which in its own little way is a criterion of reality. The concept "swan" determines what is, and what is not, a real *swan;* though what is not a swan is, perhaps, some other kind of bird. And on the other hand, *no* concept or principle, however basic, can be *guaranteed* to bring lucidity and comprehension by being applied to particular experiences in a predetermined way. Even the laws of logic prescribe only what is real *thing*, or properly determined *event*, and do not prevent those evanescent appearances and puzzling transitions of experience which it baffles us to understand. On the one side, there is the Platonic heaven of our concepts, with the beautiful clarity of their patterned interrelations, and their absolute truth. On the other side there is the chaos of given experience. The bringing of these two together is a matter of trial and error; is that empirical and material truth which is never more than probable, and is subject to continual revision in the process of our learning. That kind of revision which means the abandonment of certain concepts as not truly applicable to certain areas of experience is more fundamental and important than the mere giving up of empirical generalizations previously held. But it is only a deeper-lying phase of that process which the progress of our understanding may necessitate.

The truth of the a priori is formal only; but we cannot capture the truth of experience if we have no net to catch it in—that is its immense importance. But so far as the validity of all material truth depends upon the predictability of particular experience, the problem of our knowledge of it is that of the validity of our probability-judgments. That there may be no such valid knowledge because "there are no necessary connections of matters of fact," represents a problem which is still to be met.

Chapter X

THE EMPIRICAL AND PROBABLE

The only knowledge a priori is purely analytic; all empirical knowledge is probable only. In affirming such a view, one assumes a heavy burden of proof; the whole history of the theory of knowledge (unless we go back to Plato) seems to enforce the conclusion that such a conception must inevitably lead to skepticism. The presumption would seem to be that if the only general propositions which are absolutely certain are of the conceptual, and if all empirical truth, including that about particular objects, is only probable, then there can be no genuine knowledge of nature at all; even genuine probability will be lacking, for probability itself must rest upon some antecedent certainty. More particularly, it may be felt that the knowledge of nature requires some ground of *order* in reality, or in the content of experience, which assures its consonance with our modes of conception; that is, that there must be knowledge a priori of some "metaphysical" and synthetic truth, as contrasted with the merely logical truth of the analysis of concepts, in order to bridge the gap between abstract ideas in the mind and the reality presented in experience. Lacking this, knowledge of nature, since it is predictive, will find no basis for its validity.

At once, it should be remarked that there is an absolute certainty of the empirical which has been recognized—the immediate apprehension of the given. Such direct awareness is not indubitable knowledge of an *object*, but the content of it is an absolutely given fact. This immediate presentation is our confrontation with reality and is requisite to the distinction of particular empirical truths from falsehood. Immediate qualia constitute the ultimate denotation in experience of our concepts, and the specific character of the given plays its indispensable part in any verification. It is difficult, if not impossible, to express the content of the given without importing what is not given; and our awareness of it has not been called "knowledge," because with respect to it there can be no error. Nevertheless, it functions as an absolute ποῦ στῶ for the knowledge of nature.

For the rest, as I shall hope to show, the conception that our knowledge of nature is a knowledge of probabilities, is the only one, compatible with demonstrable facts, which can save it from reduction in the end to mere "animal faith." And furthermore, for the validity of empirical generalizations as *probable* knowledge—or more accurately, as knowledge of probabilities—no a priori truth other than the merely analytic is required.

It is true that, in order that the difficulties posed by skepticism may be met, it is essential that there be *some* knowledge which is more than probable, and that such knowledge should be pertinent to nature and experience. But as has been pointed out in the last two chapters, this is secure: there is in all science, and in common-sense knowledge, an element which is absolute and certain because it is a priori. The determination of the criteria of reality, in its various categories, and of principles of interpretation, antecedent to particular experiences, is purely analytic. Our concepts in general, without which no knowledge would be expressible and nothing in experience would be thinkable, give rise to such analytic and certain truth. As the matter is usually conceived, this knowledge which we find to be a priori would be included in what is meant by "knowledge of nature," since it delimits, for example, the physical and prescribes basic laws which must be true of all physical reality. So far the point to be noted is, that there is a knowledge of nature which is more than probable *because it is not merely empirical*, or dependent on the content of the given. This is important because, as has been noted, one form which the skeptical difficulty takes is that empirical knowledge cannot be even probable unless *some* knowledge is more than probable. The validity of probability-judgments rests upon antecedent general truths which must be certain. If *all* knowledge should be empirical and such principles therefore mere generalizations from ex-

periences, then *these principles* would be only
probable; with the result that the knowledge which
depends on them and is ordinarily called "probable" would be only probably probable. Hence in
ways which are obvious, any statement which we
could make would require the qualification "probable," and knowledge would disappear in an infinite regress of such qualification. It is the
thorough-paced empiricism of a position such as
Hume's which leads to this difficulty. Or to put it
in another way, Hume's skepticism results, not
from the absence of necessary connections of empirical particulars, but from failure to observe the
ways in which the necessary connections of *ideas*
are pertinent to the interpretation of the empirically given and hence are antecedent determinations of *reality*.

Nevertheless, it is true that when our a priori
conceptions are applied to given particulars, the
truth to which they give rise is only hypothetical, or if stated categorically, is probable only.
Amongst universal propositions which refer to
nature, we must distinguish between empirical
generalizations which are synthetic—such as the
law of gravitation, for example—and analytic
principles which exhibit the consequences of our
concepts, such as those of geometry. The former
are probable only. The latter are a priori and certain; but their a priori certainty is either that of
abstract conceptual systems, or when they are

given denotation and application, it is hypothetical, and when mention of the hypothesis is omitted, they are not certain but are merely probable. Thus a geometrical principle, when applied to a concrete presented object, is a priori and certain in the form, "If this plot of ground is triangular and our space is Euclidean, then the sum of these angles is 180 degrees." But when the hypothesis is dropped and we assert, "The sum of these angles is 180 degrees," the judgment is probable only, because there is no a priori and complete assurance that the concept "Euclidean triangle" is genuinely applicable to this plot. Likewise if the judgment is empirical but general such as "The sum of the angles of any plane triangle is 180 degrees," it is probable only, because there is no complete assurance of the Euclidean character of space. Or if Euclidean conceptions are made definitive of space and hence criteria of "the spatial" —as they might be—then such an a priori determination must be accompanied by our preparedness to relegate any divergence of presented phenomena from Euclid to some other category— to interpret them, for example, as physical refraction of light or as optical illusion. But the presence or absence of such divergent characters in some set of phenomena would not be determinable a priori or with absolute certainty. For example, there still could be no complete assurance that what are designated as "celestial triangles" bounded by light rays, were purely *spatial* phenomena, unaffected by some *physical* law of the bending of the rays. Hence any general empirical proposition about the set of actual phenomena, meant to be denoted by "celestial triangles," will still be probable only, because there will be no complete assurance that they have a right to the name and conform in all respects to what the a priori laws of space require of real triangles.

As has been pointed out, every concept is criterion of some restricted kind of reality and, on the other hand, even basic or categorial concepts are not criteria of reality in general but only of reality within that category. Every presentation is an absolute fact; is the presentation of reality of some sort or other. But it does not follow that what is presented is classifiable in some particular category, such as the spatial or the physical, without mistake. Identification of what is presented as an object of a certain type, or a particular kind of reality, is an interpretation put upon the presentation, which is implicitly predictive and hence transcends the given and is subject to verification or falsification by further possible experience. If we know the properties of triangles or of space a priori, still the empirical judgment, "This is a Euclidean triangle," is no more than probable. Therefore the necessary connection between "Euclidean triangle" and certain geometrical properties does not assure the geometrical truth about any particular presented object or any collection of such.

Our subsumption of the given under concepts is, thus, always contingent upon future experience, and the a priori knowledge of universal principles does not secure any a priori knowledge of empirical particulars. I think it will be clear that the connection between universal principles and empirical particulars has frequently, if not generally, been left a little vague, and open to the unwarranted inference that the certainty of the universal means an equal certainty about the particulars, because the particular follows from the universal. It is true that "All triangles are thus and so" implies "This triangle is thus and so" (provided "this triangle" exists). But the point is, of course, that any presented *this* may not be a triangle but only an approximation to, or slight deformation of, a triangle, or something whose difference from the triangular is momentarily— or for a thousand years—incapable of detection.*

It has likewise been, most frequently, left a little vague just what is meant by "knowledge of nature" or "empirical knowledge." And this vagueness also is probably traceable to a failure of logical precision. Propositions of the general

---

*We may remind ourselves that the Platonic distinction between knowledge which is a priori and of the idea, and opinion, which is probable and of the empirical, is based precisely upon the point that no sense-particular is exactly subsumable under any concept.

form "All A is B" may have either of two meanings—but not both at once.* They may mean (1) "The concept A includes or implies the concept B" or (2) "The class, or collection, of A's is included in the class of B's." In the first (the intensional) meaning, such a proposition is a priori true or a priori false; there need be no appeal to experience to determine the implications of concepts. The second meaning is still not quite precise until it is clear how membership in the class of A's is to be determined. If it is determined by ideal conformity to the concept A, then obviously it will follow from the fact that this concept implies B, that the class of A's so determined is contained amongst the B's. But in that case, membership of any given particular in the class is always subject to possible doubt. If, however, the term "A's" is used denotatively to specify in extension a certain group of particulars, then it does not follow from the fact that the concept A implies the concept B, that a group of particulars called A's will indubitably have the character of B's. "Empirical knowledge" usually does—and certainly ought to—mean a knowledge of particular things pointed out or otherwise determined in extension. With this meaning, the empirical knowledge that a group of objects called "A's" will have the character of B's does not follow (as anything more than probable) from the

*See Appendix F.

a priori certainty that the concept A implies the concept B. The difference between the a priori, analytic, and intensional, on the one hand, and the empirical and extensional, on the other, is the difference between "*If* this is an A, then necessarily it is a B" and "This is an A; therefore it is a B." The former may be certain when the latter is not. Hence the difficulty that a priori knowledge of universal truths does not lead to any corresponding empirical knowledge which is indubitable—if this is supposed to be a difficulty—is not peculiar to the conception here presented that a priori truth is analytic. Any theory whatever will have to meet this point unless the relation of universal concepts and particular objects is somehow misconstrued.

There is, to be sure, an important difference between that knowledge of particulars which would be subsumable under a priori principles if only the applicability of the concepts in question were assured and a knowledge of particulars which is supported only by inductive generalization—for example, between the inference from observed triangularity to other geometrical properties (if applied geometry is a priori) and the inference from observed physical character to gravitational behavior (laws of gravitation being inductive generalizations). In the one case, we know with certainty that if our identification and naming is not erroneous then the object will have certain

further properties; in the other we know only that
if our identification is correct, it will *probably*
have certain further properties. But in both cases,
our knowledge of the presented thing is probable
only because there is no complete certainty of its
subsumption under the concept which is in question.

Thus the *compatibility* of an a priori truth
such as is here maintained with the thesis that empirical knowledge in general is no more than
probable, turns upon the previous point that the
knowledge of individual objects and of particular
occurrences of objective properties always involves the application of a concept to something
presented, and that this identification of the
given as genuinely a case which falls under the
concept is something which immediate experience
does not make absolutely certain. Such identification is an interpretation which is essentially
predictive and depends also upon a prior generalization from experience. The identification is
made on the basis of certain immediately presented qualia which, in past experience, have
proved more or less reliable clues to those further
characters which are necessary to verification of
the objective nature of the thing presented and
to its valid subsumption under the concept used
to name it. This interpretation reflects a judgment of the form, "That which presents the immediate qualia here given usually (and hence in

a particular case, probably) has the objective character in question."

This fact about the application of concepts to presented things emphasizes the general likeness of all empirical knowledge. Knowledge of individual objects, as much as of generalizations or laws, runs beyond what is given and asserts a certain regularity or predictable interconnection between experiences. *Every* objective judgment is such that it can be verified only by some progression in experience. Since there is no indubitable knowledge of objects in direct awareness, the knowledge of things as much as the knowledge of laws is at the mercy of the future. Empirical knowledge depends on prediction, on an argument from past to future, on the presence of some particular uniformity in experience; and the general problem of its validity is the same which is posed by Hume's skepticism. How this validity can be assured without appeal to the dependence of the content of experience upon the mind, or to the limitation of experience in conformity to requirements of intelligibility, or to some other such metaphysical presumption—this is, I should suppose, the outstanding problem which remains to be considered.

At once, however, it is to be noted that this problem here assumes a form different from that in which it has usually been considered, in three respects.

In the first place, that part of Hume's skepticism which is concerned with necessary connections questions the possibility of the knowledge of laws only and does not (explicitly at least) put in question the possibility of the identification or recognition of things. When it is seen that the validity of both these kinds of knowledge turns, for the most part, on the same considerations, the problem is considerably altered. At first glance it seems to be rendered even more difficult, because the scope of the skeptical doubt is enlarged. But, as will appear later, this is not the case. It means that a world without law must likewise be a world without recognizable things. The recognition of objects requires that same kind of order or reliable relatedness which law also requires.

In a way, this means that the proof which Kant attempted in his deduction of the categories may be secured without the Kantian assumption that experience is limited by modes of intuition and fixed forms of thought. Because the deduction of the categories consist at bottom in this: that without the validity of categorial principles no experience is possible. And a careful examination of Kant's argument reveals the fact that he uses the term "experience" to mean "objective experience," "valid experience," "experience of actual and identifiable objects," even though he does not make this quite explicit. He certainly does not mean that the categories are requisite to the experience of a buzzing blooming confusion. Indeed, in some passages of the "subjective deduction" the argument turns precisely upon the consideration that the only alternative to a categorized and orderly experience is a meaningless flux of mere *schwarmerei*. Very likely the reader will incline to be harder upon the present attempt than upon Kant's famous argument, and to hold that it may not here be proved that knowledge is valid by showing that the only alternative is chaos. However, in advance of the argument, I think we may see that the question of the validity of empirical knowledge stands on a different footing when we recognize that this *is* its only alternative than when we suppose, as Hume apparently does, that we may take our world as a world of recognizable identifiable things while still doubting the validity of all generalizations such as natural law.

The second remark which is in point is that nothing in the foregoing touches the very important fact that the principles of interpretation and classification and the criteria of the real are a priori and certain in advance of experience. This has an important bearing upon the problem of the validity of empirical knowledge in general, because it means that *experience must, a priori, conform to certain principles in order to be pertinent to any particular investigation or to the validity of any particular law of nature.* Nothing is real in all categories; everything is real in some category. A set of categories adequate to the understanding of experience in general must meet this last requirement. It is *not* a priori certain that any given experience is validly interpretable in a particular category—for example, the physical. But we *do* know with certainty and a priori that *if X* is a physical thing, then it will conform to certain general principles which can be laid down in advance because they constitute criteria of the physical. When we study the sciences of physical reality, we have this a priori knowledge of principles to which the given must conform if it fall within the class of those phenomena which are significant in this connection. Thus we are provided, a priori, with a basal minimum of law within the field, as a sort of Archimedean point for all investigation. This does not enable us to apply our basal principles which are a priori to some particular given without the possibility of mistake. We may still be in error by confusing a subjective and psychological phenomenon—an afterimage, for example—with a physical thing. But it does enable us to be certain that nothing which concerns us in the study of physical nature can violate our fundamental principles. To fail to conform is to be repudiated as not pertinent to our present study.

Furthermore, if we should be possessed of an adequate set of categories, then we may be certain a priori that whatever does not conform to the principles of a particular category will conform to the principles of some other which is coördinate. We play a sort of game of "animal, vegetable, or mineral" with experience, by which it will be impossible for it to get out of the net of our understanding, no matter what may be the content of it.

The third important difference between what it is necessary here to establish and the problem as posed by Humian skepticism, is that it is the validity of empirical knowledge as *probable* judgment only which requires to be assured. If more than this is needed to save us from skepticism, then, once for all, there is no answer to the skeptic. The particular point of doubt, I should suppose, is whether probable knowledge and empirical generalizations can be valid if, as is here maintained, all necessary connections are logical only and do not limit the content of experience. The validity of probability and of induction is commonly supposed to rest upon some ground of order and connection beyond the merely logical—some "uniformity of nature" which could conceivably be absent from our experience. No such metaphysical presupposition would be compatible with the account of knowledge here given. For us, then, the validity of empirical knowledge turns upon the nature of the alternative when all assumption of more than merely logical necessity in nature, or of conformity a priori to any order which could conceivably be absent, is dispensed with.

For this, the first essential is an examination of what is essential to the validity of probable judgment from the purely logical point of view. It is, fortunately, unnecessary to enter upon a complete theory of inductive generalization and probability. Indeed, examination of this question could be dismissed altogether were it not that certain errors about the logical character of probable judgment have become entangled with the more fundamental question of the epistemological and metaphysical foundations of our knowledge of the probable. We must discuss these merely logical facts not to get them into the picture but to keep them out.

"Probability" has many different meanings and the first requisite is to avoid certain verbal confusions which are possible. Ordinarily, we phrase the empirical generalization, or other statement which we know—or should know—to be probable only, as if it were absolutely certain. As economy of language, this is excusable and even unavoidable. But if we thus state, for example, Newton's law of gravitation as absolute truth, we must not confuse what is stated with the judgment of any informed and intelligent person who makes the statement. The intent of the judgment is not the statement judged probable, but *that* it is probable. If in such a case we assert briefly that A is

B, our judgment is, "It is probable that A is B" or "that A is B is highly probable," or "A is B has a probability represented approximately by the fraction m/n." Now a common supposition seems to be that our knowledge of the law of gravitation is invalid if there are facts of nature which do not conform to the law. But if this is probable knowledge, it is a very simple and obvious fact that its validity does not require such conformity. The judgment "A is B is probable" does not require for its truth that A is B; it requires only that this should be genuinely probable. What the genuineness of a probability requires concerning the independent facts to which it relates, we need not, for the moment, inquire. But at least it is undeniable that the judgment, "A is B is probable," may be absolutely true when the judgment "A is B" would be absolutely false. Unless this is the case, there is no real difference between probable and certain knowledge. Nobody will contest this; yet I think we may discern behind a good deal of the questioning about the validity of probable knowledge, the confused thought that if what we know is "A is B is probable" but in fact A is not B, then such knowledge is invalid. Certainly it is a question in what its validity consists, but equally certainly this does not consist simply in accord between what is probably true and the objective fact.

Another pertinent consideration has to do with

the relation between the probable judgment and those facts which constitute the ground of it and hence stand to it in the relation of premises to conclusion. It has always been clear, of course, that it is impossible to tell whether a given judgment of probability is valid without examining the data on which the judgment is based. Every text on the elements of probability-theory contains some such illustration as the following: Let four hands of whist be dealt and each player inspect his hand. Let the quæsitum be the probability of four aces in one hand. This probability will be different (1) for A who is not a player and does not examine any hand (2) for a player B, who observes that he holds no aces, and (3) for another player, C, who finds one or more aces in his hand but not four. If we represent the value of the probability for each by the letter designating the person, then $B > A > C$, though for each it is the same objective state of affairs whose probability is in question. In other words, a correctly estimated probability is relative to the data upon which it is based, or the premises from which it is drawn. This is frequently phrased by the somewhat dubious formula, "Probability is relative to our ignorance."

Thus probable knowledge is always relative to him who has it, in the sense that it depends upon whatever other relevant knowledge he may possess. When some proposition or law is adjudged probable, there is always a tacit qualification which must be made explicit before the validity of the judgment can be assessed. For example, when the law of gravitation is declared to be probable, the real intention might be formulated as: "On the basis of what duly qualified persons —who may fairly be presumed to know all the relevant facts which are available—unite in reporting, this law is probable." The probability of the law is, very likely, different for me than for the scientist who knows the pertinent facts more directly. For him, the data are, in part at least, certain laboratory-tested facts. The rest of us—having no such laboratory experience—accept it on authority; which means that our judgment bears a less direct relation to the premised facts, and concerns the reliability of a proposition about which expert investigators agree. For the scientist something is simply true which for me is probable because he reports it. Hence for me, the conclusion about the law represents a compounding of probabilities. (Strictly, of course, the same thing is true for the scientist also, though in lesser degree.)

In this last respect, the illustration is typical of most probability-judgments. Nearly all the accepted probabilities rest upon more complex evidence than the usual formulations suggest; what are accepted as premises are themselves not certain but only highly probable. Thus our judgment, if made explicit, would take the form. The probability that A is B is a/b, because if P is Q, then the probability that A is B is m/n, and the probability of "P is Q" is p/q (where $m/n \times p/q = a/b$). But this compound character of probable judgment offers no theoretical difficulty for their validity in general, provided only that the probability of the premises, when pushed back to what is more and more ultimate, somewhere comes to rest in something certain, and provided also that there are *some* valid principles of probability in general—whether those commonly accepted or some others.* These two provisos, just stated, represent the prime requisites of the validity of probable judgment, concerning which there may be doubt.

The validity of the judgment that A is probably B does not, as we have just seen, concern any direct relation between the judgment and the fact or non-fact, A is B; it concerns the relation between the judgment and whatever are the relevant data upon which it is based. These may be verbally quite remote; the immediate premises are, very likely, themselves only probable, and perhaps in turn based upon premises only probable. Unless this backward-leading chain comes to rest

---

*Strictly, of course, there are theoretical difficulties about the compounding of probabilities, and in fact about almost every point in probability-theory. Except so far as they bear directly upon epistemological problems, I have neglected these: short of interpolating here a complete theoretical analysis of probability, no other course is possible.

finally in certainty, no probability-judgment can
be valid at all. But if it does thus finally come to
rest, the complexity of it is of no theoretical consequence. Such ultimate premises, however, must
be actual given data for the individual who makes
the judgment, hence the probability of a given
formulation may vary. from individual to individual, according to our individual knowledge of
a relevant sort.

All these facts are simple and fairly well recognized; I hope I shall be pardoned for repeat-
ing commonplaces in order to emphasize the following obvious consequences of them: (1) In the
only sense in which we can possibly suppose probable knowledge to exist at all, its validity is unaffected by the fact that it is subjective (that is,
relative to the data of knowledge possessed by the
individual, and very likely different for each);
and (2) Probable knowledge may be valid in spite
of the fact that what is judged probable may, in
any given case or any number of cases, be false.

There is a further important consequence of
the relativity of probable judgment. Unlike deductive inference, in which the conclusion is as
certain as the premises, the conclusion of a probability-inference must retain its reference to the
premises. The conclusion "A is probably B" is
elliptical; what is validly meant is "On the premises such and such, A is probably B." This might
easily be overlooked. One might say, "But since

my premises are true, it is true without qualification that *A* is probably *B*." So phrased, the conclusion "*A* is probably *B*" seems to refer directly
to some objective fact. But it is just this oversight which must be guarded against. As referring
directly to objective fact, some new bit of evidence or the next moment's experience may completely alter the probability—may turn what was
probable into something certainly true or certainly false or something more probable or less
probable than before. This is what happens when
we say that the probability of something is increased or descreased. If, in the earlier illustration, the man who has seen no hand of cards
should be shown a hand with no aces, the probability of four aces in one hand "is increased." But
the validity of his previous judgment is untouched, and the fact—if it be such—that there
are not four aces in one hand is unaffected. There
is no such thing as *the* probability of four aces
in one hand, or *the* probability of anything else.
Given all the relevant data which there are to be
known, everything is either certainly true or certainly false. Given anything short of this, what
the value of the probability is, depends upon what
data are thus given. There are always various
probabilities of the same quæsitum, on the basis
of various data or different relevant knowledge.
When the premises contain *all* the relevant knowledge which is available under certain well-defined

conditions, then reference to "the probability"—as in actuarial work, etc.—has a recognizable significance; it consists in tacit reference to this well-understood body of data. But clearly, this alters nothing in what has been said.

A "poor evaluation" of the probability of anything may reflect ignorance of relevant data which "ought" to be known, or it may reflect logical error in the relation of the probability conclusion to its premises. In the former case, there will be moral or practical delinquency, perhaps, but the validity of the conclusion is unaffected. It is in the latter case only that any probability-judgment can be genuinely invalid. That the validity of probability-judgment is thus unaffected by ignorance and is affected only by logical error, goes along with the fact that the conclusion necessarily retains reference to its premises.

The consequence of this which is most important is that *the probable judgment, if valid, is true*. There is no difference in the case of probability-inference between validity and truth. What the judgment "*A* is probably *B*" asserts is not that *A* is *B* or that any other objective state of affairs (except what the premises assert) holds good. It asserts that "*A* is *B*" has a certain probability on the basis of certain data. If the data are actual the probability is "actual"; if the data are merely hypothetical, the assigned probability shares this hypothetical character. But unless there has been logical error, the probable judgment is not only valid but absolutely true. There is no alternative to this account except that probability has no kind of truth, no validity, and no meaning of any sort.

Moreover, a probable judgment, once true, is always true. A probability cannot change, because probability has no meaning except by relation to its premises or ground. New data do not invalidate the previous judgment, because they constitute a new problem and mark a new probability. The probable judgment based upon specific data is not only eternally valid, if it is ever valid, but if it is valid, it is absolutely and eternally true.

As we have seen, there are two types of empirical generalizations with which we have to do: (1) those ordinarily so called, in which it is asserted that whatever may be validly named by some name has a certain further property, or properties, not implied by that name, and (2) those empirical generalizations of a subtler sort which underlie the naming of something presented. The first type include what are ordinarily called "natural laws"; what they ostensibly assert is that wherever a certain order is present in experience, a certain further order will accompany it. What those of the second type assert is that what presents a certain given appearance will exhibit in further experience the order requisite to the applicability of a certain concept.

For both types, the general character of the judgment is the prediction that something will hold of future experience because it has held in past experience. And in both cases, it is the validity of this as a probability which requires to be established. One difference between these two needs to be remarked: "natural laws" must have held in all past experience and are predicted to hold universally, while this is not necessary for our interpretation of presentations. If I assert "This is a sweet apple," the nature of my judgment might be expressed: "What looks like this, under these conditions, will probably have the sweet apple taste, digestibility, etc." This judgment reflects my past experience of appearances like that now given. But it is neither plausible nor necessary that what looks like this should have turned out in *all* past cases to be a sweet apple. It is sufficient for probable judgment that this should have been so in a certain proportion of cases.

The requirement of universality for natural law is, possibly, a bit artificial. What I mean is: there are any number of generalizations to be found in common sense and in practice which have the same general character as "laws" in other respects but which have not been universally substantiated in past experience and would not be regarded as invalidated by future exception:—Potatoes are good food; red-cedar shingles will last for twelve years; a banker's advice about investments will be safe;

the theatre-roof won't fall on your head. I think a little reflection will reveal that by far the greater part of life is guided by such generalizations which give rise to a probability in the particular case but are not without their exceptions. In fact, if laws of nature should have this character generally, nobody would be much upset outside of academic circles. A generalization with very few exceptions is almost as good as one with none, as a basis for action. I am not trying to argue that there are no unexceptionable empirical generalizations, nor to fudge the difference between certainty and probability. But I would point out that, granting all the universal truth and all the certainty that the most ambitious theory has ever claimed, if it were not for that more lowly knowledge of probabilities based on generalities which have their known exceptions, we should most of us be dead within the week. A theory which agonizes endlessly about certain knowledge of nature and neglects the probable, represents a somewhat artificial interest.

Thus we must recognize, alongside of those natural laws which are based upon past experience without exceptions and are predicted universally, empirical generalizations admitting of possible or actual exception but nevertheless having a certain probability in the individual case. Let us call these last "statistical generalizations" since they are exhibited at their best when supported by statistical procedures. There are various theoretical grounds—quite apart from the practical considerations urged above—on which it may be doubted whether such statistical generalizations and universally predicted empirical generalizations, or "laws," can be distinguished in the end. But examination of these may be omitted, since decision of this issue is not of ultimate importance for us here. In any event, our knowledge of a generalization is probable only, and the use of it depends simply upon its giving rise to a validly probable prediction in particular cases.

It is obvious that all empirical knowledge eventually goes back to knowledge of empirical particulars. Generalizations have their ground in the coincidence of such particulars. Knowledge of the particular functions also as the basis of the *applicability* of general principles which are not empirical but a priori. And knowledge of the particular is rooted in immediate experience. The first apprehension, so to speak, is of given appearances, having a specific and later recognizable character, and of their continuity with further and equally specific experience. Coincidence of such progressions in immediacy give rise to habits of action, which may become explicit in generalizations of the form "What appears like this will turn out thus and so." Granted that such coincidence in experience can establish probability for the future, we have in the immediate awareness of the given that certainty which becomes the basis of a probable knowledge of the particular object or the occurrence of an objective property.

The interpretation of the presentation is the application of a concept to it. The applicability of the concept requires, a priori, certain predictable sequences in experience, continuous with the given. The application itself is hypothetical; that the concept is genuinely applicable is not a priori but only probable. This probability is supported by a generalization from direct experience of the sort which has been pointed out; a statistical generalization to the effect that appearances like the given one, under circumstances like the present, are, in possible experience, continuous with such sequences as the applicability of the concept requires, in a certain proportion at least of cases.

This probable knowledge of particulars becomes in turn the basis for generalizations of the type more commonly recognized as such—propositions asserting a universal connection between what is denoted by some concept and a further character or property, not implied by that concept. Our knowledge of such generalizations represents a compounding of probabilities, since its assumed premises—the knowledge of particulars —are only probable, and the passage from these premises to the generalization itself is inductive and represents a connection which is not certain but probable only. But this *compound* probability has as its premises the immediate certainty of the given data in the experience of particular instances.

At this point, the alert reader will doubtless inquire if the validity of memory is not here assumed. The answer is, in brief, that this assumption is not necessary. Memory is a form of empirical knowledge, parallel in most respects to perception. As in perception, so in the case of memory, something is absolutely given—the present recollection. And like perception, memory as a form of knowledge is an interpretation put upon this presentation; an interpretation, moreover, which in the particular case is verifiable, in those ways in which all knowledge of the past is subject to verification. Also memories, like perceptions, may be roughly divided into different types, having different degrees of reliability, which we are able to assess. This, plainly, is the only view consonant with common sense and with obvious characters of experience. Hence we must conclude that memory in general is *probable* knowledge, and that so far as other forms of knowledge are based on memory, the probability of such knowledge is compound, to a degree not previously noted. But that does not introduce any new theoretical difficulty.

In fact, memory is in this respect like various other data which enter into the structure of our knowledge in general—particularly the reports of other people. Such reports are more or less reliable, as past verifications of such have attested. They enter into the body of data, upon which our further judgments are based, as more or less probable premises. So far as the experience supporting an empirical generalization is thus vicarious, the probability of that generalization is compound to an extent which it would not be if the experience were exclusively our own. Or to put it in another way, reports of others are a particular type of our own experience, having a probability which reflects our past experience of such reports and of their relation to our further experience pertinent to their truth. In various similar ways, our empirical knowledge is complex and remote from its bases in immediate experience. The probability attaching to it has a correspondingly compounded character.

Some may feel that such an account makes our empirical knowledge so complex and, when explicitly analyzed, so remote from its eventual grounds, that the kind of validity here assigned is little better than condemnation. But will not honest examination require the admission that our empirical judgments *are* thus logically complex; that ordinary statements of them usually proceed by taking much for granted which is not absolutely certain. Such artificial simplification is excusable, or even necessary, in the interest of the separation of problems, or for some other paradigmatic purpose. But it is in inexcusable in what purports to be an analysis of knowledge in general. If the truth should be complex and somewhat disillusioning, it would still not be a merit to substitute for it some more dramatic and comforting simplicity.

There are, moreover, certain mitigating considerations. In the first place, the complexity of empirical judgment and its remoteness from completely certain grounds, does not necessarily mean that its probability is diminished in like proportion. If the difference between the compounded probabilities and absolute certainty is slight, the eventual and resultant probability may likewise be very close to theoretical certainty. In the second place, the practical attitude which is expressed in ordinary judgment as if it were based upon some certainty is, in fact, one which is quite compatible with the failure of what we say to prove true. Such failure would not prove devastating to our attitude toward life as if an absolute truth had been destroyed. For example, if you ask me, I shall unhesitatingly assert, "This is a good fountain pen." But if next moment it refuses to write and thereafter can never be got to work properly, I shall not lie down and die because my knowledge is invalid and my universe has come apart. All my statement really means is that I have good enough grounds to think it highly probable—which is, in fact, the case. If it should be

pointed out that I am not even certain that this
is the same pen I have used heretofore, the experience of which was my basis of judgment, I shall
still not be disturbed in my practical attitude. I
shall say, "Oh, well, what of it? Life is too short
to bother about the difference between probabilities of that order and certainty." Which again is
quite true. My unhesitating practical attitude is
no mere "animal faith"; it is quite in accord with
the remote possibility that what I assert and act
upon may not be true—is logically remote from
ultimate certain grounds and most complex. My
attitude has a complete theoretical justification.
It is precisely the supposition that knowledge requires absolutely certainty about the empirical,
that closes the door to a theoretical justification
of it. Such a supposition has no theoretical support and no corroboration in our actual practical
attitudes. There is just about enough chance that
our trusted generalizations may be false to make
the pursuit of science pleasantly exciting. What
a dull business life would be if *everything* we ventured to act upon should turn out true! In a world
in which knowledge, as some have portrayed it,
would be valid, intelligence would be unnecessary,
since habit would be a universally safe guide.

If now the analysis of our empirical knowledge
can be supposed to be covered, let us turn to its
general character. It is that of a probability-
judgment which, when explicitly stated, affirms

that something has a certain degree of probability on the basis of premises which are, eventually, direct individual experience. The validity of such knowledge does not, of course, require that we should explicate all its complexity, or even that we should be able to. The man whose shrewd but untutored logical sense prevents his believing what logic would condemn, makes a *valid* judgment, whether he could provide the logical analysis of it or not. If our empirical judgments include only what a just logic would validate, they are sound. And in so far as we do not offend against logic, but hold to our empirical knowledge as probable in a degree which it truly is, the content of our knowledge is true. Experience next moment may destroy the generalization judged probable. But it will remain forever true that it *was* probable on the grounds from which we made our judgment. And that is all that any probability-judgment can validly mean.

Since valid empirical knowledge means only such probability, on grounds which genuinely establish it, and since any other than empirical knowledge is a priori, we have the important consequence that *just in so far as we are rational, what we believe is absolutely and eternally true.* What rational men entertain as highly probable may largely alter with the passage of time. Empirical generalizations, as usually phrased, may be overturned and others take their place. The growth of science may repudiate as "false" what, in its previous stages, was held "true." But a just appreciation of the nature of such knowledge as only probable has this consequence: let our ignorance be however large, our experience however circumscribed, we need believe nothing false, except as we fail to be rational and believe without valid grounds. Such avoidance of the unwarranted will not condemn us to sheer ignorance; we may at every stage possess a generous body of generalizations which, correctly assessed, are valid and are useful guides to practise. Indeed, will not a survey of the history of human thought compel the conclusion that only such a conception as this can save the reasonable-minded man from repudiating the attempt at scientific knowledge as chimerical?

However, it may be said that what the defense of knowledge requires is not a justification of it as a logically valid judgment, corroborated by reference to past experience but doomed perhaps to repudiation in the light of the future. Empirical knowledge is essentially predictive and its relation to the future is of the essence of its validity. There is no attempt to escape this point. I have so far spoken as if, in general, the argument from past to future is valid; as if *some* ground of induction is secure. The fundamental doubts which may be entertained of this will be the topic of the concluding chapter.

Two points may be noted here: first, a "law" having a high degree of probability may have to be abandoned in the light of future experience as not universal, and may yet remain a "rule of thumb" or statistical generalization which is true in the great proportion of cases and hence gives rise to a still valid probability in the particular case. The practical use made of laws which are superseded may, and often does, stand as still justified. The "laws" of the ancients are, oftentimes, such as would still be useful guides to action if we had no better. And second, we need to ask just what is necessary for the justification of probability-judgment as a basis for practical action. That what is probable must always be true, is an obviously impossible answer to this question. It is even impossible to demand that whatever is probable must in every instance be true in the majority of cases—in spite of some theories to the contrary. A probability may genuinely be valid in some instances even though beyond a certain point *no* case should be found in accordance with it. I think reflection will reveal that what is requisite to its justification as a practical attitude is that action in accordance with probabilities must *in general* be more successful than action which ignores them. In other words, it is essential that the world be such that probabilities *in general* are justified by the future—that the world is "orderly"; that there *are* certain stabilities extending through the past and future, and that the attitude which is based on past coincidence will in general be safer for the future than a different one. But this question is that same one concerning the existence of some basis for induction, which the next chapter will discuss.

CHAPTER XI

EXPERIENCE AND ORDER

Since empirical knowledge is exclusively a knowledge of probabilities, the validity of it in general depends upon the validity of induction and probability-judgment. The preceding chapter has been written as if some principles of such inference may be presumed as valid. That presumption, however, requires justification, particularly since the grounds upon which it is often supposed to rest have here been repudiated. Let us phrase the issue as sharply as possible: Concepts are of the mind. All knowledge is in terms of concepts, and the possibility of it depends upon their applicability to experience. The application of a concept requires always a certain orderly sequence in experience. But the content of experience is independent of the mind; that order is discoverable in possible experience, cannot be dictated by the knower. If generalization is to be possible—if concepts are to be applicable in distinguishable classes of cases, and if the connection of concepts in such generalizations is to find its application in reality—then the givenness of certain qualia, or complexes of such, must be a clue to expected sequences, and the occurrence of such sequences in the past must be a ground of their valid prediction for the future.

However, it is *not* requisite that such expectation and predication should be *certain*. Knowledge of particular objects is never beyond the possibility of mistaken apprehension; and empirical generalizations are, theoretically, never more than highly probable. What is requisite, then, in order that empirical knowledge should be valid, is that this connection of given qualia with expected sequences, and the connection between the sequences prescribed by one concept and that which is essential to some other, should be genuinely probable. In general there must be the possibility of arguing from past to future; not with certainty, but with probability.

Concerning probability-judgments, it has been pointed out, first, that their validity does not require that what is judged probable should be true—not even that the particular generalization should be true of any specifiable proportion of actual cases. Second, the probability-judgment is relative to the pertinent knowledge of him who makes it; and this relativity is no bar to its validity. Third, this relativity of the probability-judgment to its premises means that its validity, in the particular instance, consists in a certain relation between the conclusion and its ground; and means also that if it is valid it is true, absolutely and eternally. These three characters of probability-judgments rest upon obvious facts which cannot be denied without destroying the distinction between probability and certainty. It is an immediate consequence of them that a particular empirical judgment, if it represents a probability-inference justly drawn from its grounds, is absolutely true knowledge. The one remaining question is whether there are any valid principles of such inference according to which a particular empirical judgment may be justly drawn. If probability-judgment *in general* may be valid then there is no further ground of doubt that empirical judgments which are rational are true.

For the ideal completion of the argument, presentation and detailed examination of the principles of probability-inference and induction—as well as of our categorial concepts—would be in order. But the reader will not ask for that in the present book—another of at least equal length would be required. The particular ground of possible doubt is obvious enough: the applicability of concepts and the argument from past to future, require the presence of some order and uniformity. In an experience whose content is independent of the mind, it may be thought that such order could conceivably be lacking, and that the presumption of it is, therefore, dogmatic and without foundation. Pointing out that the validity of probability consists in a relation between the conclusion and its ground, and that the truth of what is judged probable is not directly relevant, does nothing to meet this present point. Precisely what is in question is whether a judgment which is in this sense subjective, confronting an experience which is independent, can be meaningfully relevant to the constitution of reality.

Since the applicability of concepts (or recognition of things by their appearances) as well as the validity of generalizations, is in question, the issue concerns the intelligibility of experience as well as the possibility of empirical knowledge. These two turn, for the most part, upon the same considerations.

The conclusion of which I shall hope to convince the reader is that no assumption of anything which could conceivably be false is necessary; that no sort of experience which the wildest imagination could conjure up could fail to afford a basis for intelligibility and probable judgment. The contrary assumption has frequently been due to the false conception that is *certainty* of apprehension and certainty of generalization which must be provided for. And some of those same confusions which we have found surrounding previous issues are involved here also.

I recognize that my burden of proof in this matter is a heavy one. Belief in something meant by the "uniformity of nature" is, I think, as natural to us as belief in an absolute up and down, and is supported by many habits of thought which are fundamental and pervasive. And so far as I know, it has never up till now been questioned, except by those who willingly faced a skeptical alternative. In a sense, this belief is not to be questioned here, but rather whether it has any alternative at all; the precise problem is, perhaps, just what is involved in the necessary "uniformity." In this difficult situation, instead of proceeding directly to the center of the problem, I wish to begin with a variety of more peripheral considerations. Perhaps if a sufficient number of external buttresses are removed, the false conception will fall of its own weight.

Two points which are immediately relevant to the question of order in reality can be brought forward from what precedes; first, that reality and the content of experience are not directly synonymous, and second, that our categories are so divided that always we play a sort of game of "animal, vegetable, or mineral" with the given. It is reality, not experience, which must be orderly. Failure of a certain type of order is the criterion which excludes the given from reality (of a certain type). Thus so far as any one category is in question, our method of understanding experience is to segregate, as "reality," that part which is orderly in the required fashion; the rest is understood by being labelled "unreal." With this in mind, our rational demand that reality shall be orderly somewhat reminds one of the silly

old story we used to tell as boys of the man who
made a list of those he could whip: when a neigh-
bor whose name was included belligerently affirmed, "You can't whip me," the maker of the
list replied, "All right; then I'll just rub your
name off." Experience has not much chance to
thwart our demand for order when the failure to
be orderly in certain ways merely results in its
being rubbed off the list of that which it is demanded shall be thus orderly.

To be sure, what is excluded from one category
must be brought under some other if it is to be
intelligible. But any set of coördinate categories
is simply a method for exhausting the possibilities. The "unreal" is a temporary pigeon-hole for
what requires to be sorted or analyzed in some
further fashion. The unsatisfactoriness of such a
scrap-basket category merely reflects this desira-
bility of a further understanding of its content.
But to be able to classify what is presented as
"unreal" or "illusion," though it may represent
only superficial understanding, means nevertheless a very important understanding, precisely because it means that this content of experience is
not relevant in the present connection, that it cannot figure as a negative instance of an empirical
generalization and so on. So far, then, the reality
presented to us in experience is certain to be intelligible and orderly, because the failure to make
a certain kind of sense merely results in its being

relegated to the box we keep for pi. The only question is, *how much* of experience will be reality, and how much illusion. It will be obvious that this depends, in part, at least, upon the intellectual ingenuity of the knower—his power, when some expected order fails, to discover some other which is definite to like degree. It is further clear that to the question, "How much of given experience will be illusory?" there can be no a priori answer.

In this connection it is well to remark that our understanding of the given is always a matter of degree, and that the order demanded of reality is, similarly, more or less specific. If there is any sense in which the real must be "through and through" orderly, at least such through and through order is an ideal correlated with that "complete understanding" which is impossible to any but an absolute mind. And there must be some other sense in which predictable order is *not* demanded of the real. The reasons for this will bear a little investigation.

I find this morning on my study window a number of apparently random grayish smudges. The explanation promptly comes to mind; small children played here yesterday. Just this pattern of smudges probably never occurred before and never will again. But this failure to exhibit any definitely anticipatable arrangement excites no surprise; it is just what one expects of children's finger marks. This superficiality of our demand for order reflects, in part, the lack of any further cognitive problem. If my choicest possessions were all missing this morning, I should ask for something more. The detective would come in and, starting from a system which exhausts in certain ways the possibilities of finger-marks, would seek to establish a correlation identifying a thief. But even so, these finger marks would still fail to be uniform with anything else in *some* ways in which order could exist and might be expected. The phrase "through and through" as applied to the uniformity or order demanded of reality is rather vague.

It also suggests itself that, in the process of our learning the nature of the real, what we do is to look for *some* order of a certain general type and, if we do not find that, to look for some *other*. The first attempt at uniformity may be, for example, that sparks fly upward, water runs down hill and "Everything seeks its natural level." Balked in this, a second attempt is, "Bodies fall in proportion to their weight." Finally we have $v = g\ t$. The point here is not simply that one attempted generalization having failed, we seek another. It is that the type of uniformity first sought—a correlation between gravitational behavior and physical kinds—does not exist. Nor is there any correlation with weight. The correlation found between velocity and time is of an entirely different sort. Not order "through and through" but *some* order is what is requisite to intelligibility. And in the light of the nature of our learning process, the dictum "There must be some order in any given area of reality" takes on the character of a regulative principle, not particularly different in significance from, "If at first you don't succeed; try, try again." More explicitly and accurately, the situation may be stated thus: A certain minimal order is prescribed a priori in the recognition of the real. It is a regulative maxim of reason to seek further uniformities which may be stated in principles finally of maximal comprehensiveness and simplicity. But there neither is nor can be any prescription of the specific type of uniformity or correlation which is demanded in this interest of further intelligibility. Moreover, the particular kind of order discoverable in one segment of the real may be definitely absent in some other segment in which it might with equal reasonableness be anticipated.

The situation is entirely comparable if we turn from the kind of uniformity necessary for generalization to the kind which is essential for the recognition of objects. A certain minimal uniformity is prescribed by the categorial classification as reality of a certain type. Further uniformity may be sought for the purpose of further classification. But the manner in which such further uniformity shall be found is not determinable —unless by some schème of subordinate cate-

gories, exhausting the possibilities in a particular
way—in advance of familiarity with the area of
reality which is in question. Nor can it rationally
be "demanded" that any particular degree or kind
of such uniformity shall be always exhibited by
experience which is intelligible. What the recognition of objects requires is some correlation between given appearance and that sequence with
further experience which is requisite to identification and to discrimination of veridical from
mistaken apprehension. But it cannot be required for the intelligibility of experience that
within the limits of the *given* there must be that
which affords the basis of such uniform correlation. If within every empirical content merely as
given there were that which possessed absolute uniform correlation with that further sequence which
is essential to a correct apprehension, then illusion
and mistake would be possible only to the inex-
perienced and the fool. It is true that only the
irrational need be, in the strictest sense, deceived
by appearances; but this is because the rational
must realize that mistaken apprehension is always possible and identifications in general are
only probable. The possibilities of sequence between the appearance and further experience
must be at least dual wherever the experienced
and intelligent observer finds even the slightest
possibility of mistaken apprehension. Obviously
it is not the case that every given quale or every

complex of such has some uniform correlation with something else, sufficient to render it intelligible in the manner knowledge seeks, else we should all of us stand convicted of stupidity to a degree which is quite implausible.

There is another way in which it can be made evident that we cannot require that experience, in order to be intelligible, must be such that something in the given content of any experience is uniformly followed by something else in further experience. If this were the case, then within every experience merely as given must be something which determines absolutely this further experience which is predictable from it. This further experience, in turn, would likewise dictate some future experience, and so on. Thus any given experience would uniquely determine the course of future experience, or at least of some endless chain of further experiences. It may seem that this is precisely what *is* required for knowledge and prediction. But it is not: in a world so constituted whatever could be learned would not be worth knowing, because nothing could be done about it. It is worth learning that hot stoves burn precisely because the feeling of radiated heat does *not* inevitably determine that further sequence which we first investigated to our cost, but only determines it *under certain further conditions* which we take care not to allow. There *is* a uniformity in *reality*—hot things burn—which is

definable as a uniformity of *possible experience*.
But the antecedent in terms of which the consequent, being burned, is determined, is something
much more complex than what is confined within
the given experience of radiated heat. Otherwise
we should fatally go on to be burned every time
we felt it, just as we did at first. Now *some* things,
which are predictable, are doubtless unavoidable
in experience. But even in these cases; it does not
necessarily follow that they are determined consequents of given experience. It is possible—and
much more likely—that here too the antecedent
of which they are uniform consequents is something much larger and more complex than any
previous given experience. Often our inability to
avoid them is due to our ignorance of the further conditions, beyond our experience, upon
which these consequents follow. If we knew
enough, we could still avoid them, and that is the
agony of our situation. And often also—if not
universally—where some future experience is beyond our power to avoid, and would still be beyond our power even if our knowledge should be
greater, it is nevertheless the case that the determining antecedent is not wholly within our experience but contains further conditions outside it
but also outside our capacity to change. If it were
not for these further conditions, we might still
have precisely this experience and yet escape the
dénouement. Quite clearly then, knowledge does

not require that kind of uniformity which would mean that something given in experience is uniformly followed by something further in experience. If this were so, then life—so far as we could know and understand—would be merely a fatal unfolding of the inevitable, and our knowledge would be a worthless revelation of that fate. Even those who read life and reality in terms of such inevitable unfolding, do not condemn us to foresee it step by step merely through intelligent inspection of our given experience. As has been pointed out, those predictions which are the primary constituents of our useful knowledge of nature are of the form: Since X is given, if condition Y should be supplied, then Z would accrue. Where Y is a condition which I myself fulfill, or refrain from fulfilling, my knowledge serves to guide my action to desired ends. The sweetness of the apple, the hotness of the stove, etc., are known by means of such truth of hypothetical propositions: this round, ruddy somewhat being given, if I should bite, it would taste sweet; this visual presentation and feeling of warmth being given, if I should touch, I should be burned. As has been pointed out, if I could *do* nothing about experience, then since such hypotheticals would be meaningless, reality would be no thicker than an inevitable stream of consciousness—that is, I should not confront *reality* but at most only a fatally determined life. Knowledge of *reality* serves for the control of *experience:* without the possibility of control, not only would knowledge be worthless; there would be for us no reality to know. Both the usefulness of knowledge and the meaningfulness of reality require that the uniformity apprehended by knowledge should not be such that the determining antecedent is completely contained in the experience now fixed by being given. It is required for the significance of knowledge and the real that uniformities be specifiable—as probable at least—in terms of *possible* experience. But between possible and actual experience is the whole of that which differentiates reality from mere immediacy. Whatever the uniformity of reality required for knowledge may mean, it *cannot* mean a fixed and uniform sequence in which given experience is one complete term.

It is further to the point that the whole effort of intelligence and those habits of action which are presumably its genetic antecedents, are bent to the apprehension of whatever in the given may constitute a distinguishing mark and serve the purpose of prediction. The instant mental reaction to experience, the manner in which we approach it and the way in which we abstract from it the presentation of objects, reflect millennia of nature's work to the end that we may grasp whatever in experience is clue to some uniformity of the sort which intelligibility requires. Such characters of the given arrest the attention and are for us *something*, while that which does not thus possess meaning slides off the surface of the mind; it requires a reversal of all that is natural and habitual for us to catch it, and there is no word by which it may be held. Hence it is almost inevitable that the extent to which actually given experience is uniform or contains clues to uniformity, should be exaggerated to our casual inspection.

There is another consideration which should be added to this. It is a rational demand, of at least as good standing as the demand for uniformity, that every individual object shall be unique. Such uniqueness cannot reside in the given appearance of the thing: the number of sensory qualia we can distinguish is finite, and the number of combinations and arrangements possible within the mental field of a single experience, though large, is totally inadequate to uniqueness. This uniqueness can only reside in the further specifiability of the object in possible experience continuous with the appearance of it; that is, in something which is true about the object, though it is not at this moment apparent, and something which, by appropriately directed investigation, we could learn. Hence this demand for uniqueness requires that every recognizable appearance must be correlated with some further verifiable specification of the object, in a way which is different in at least some one respect from each and every other. When the multiplicity of objects, actual and conceivable, is contemplated, it becomes clear that the extent to which experience is thus required to be non-uniform is indefinitely large.

I do not here defend the theoretical consistency of such conception of uniqueness, and I do not accuse any one of holding to it in this form; any more than I would attribute the theory of "through and through" uniformity to anybody in particular. My object is to let one shibboleth fight another, to the end that certain vague and unexamined modes of thought may be dragged into the light and certain superstitious and equally vague beliefs about experience may be destroyed. The most that can reasonably be believed is that experience when caught in the net of our categories, will always afford *some* clue to an actually existent further uniformity of some sort. Identifiable or recognizable appearances in their continuity with further experience, must be at least as much *non*-uniform as uniform.

A further simple illustration of the way in which non-uniformity may be remarked and yet have no significance for knowledge, may be of service. There is a popular superstition that no two snow crystals ever exhibit precisely the same pattern. I have no idea what warrant there is for it, and perhaps the reader has not either. We can see that the number of possibilities of such crystalline forms is indefinitely large, but within the limits of size and of the smallest discernible element, it would be finite. Suppose that neither general uniformity nor uniqueness should obtain. Nothing in this would be baffling to our recognition of snow or our knowledge about it. Whether this illustration really serves or not, at least nature is full of such—frost-patterns, the leaves of trees, the structure of growing plants, etc. Yet those relatively slight and superficial ways in which two oak-leaves or two frost-patterns are alike, suffice for our recognition of them and our generalizations about them. A non-uniformity, to be significant for knowledge, must be very specific —it must be a negative instance of our predictive recognition or attempted generalization. And even when we are thus thwarted, we simply give up our previously held specific mark or law, and proceed to understand that kind of object *in some other way*.

Quite frequently that order which intelligibility and law require has to be sought at some one level and escapes us at other levels. A general illustration is the whole body of those phenomena recognized by science in which macroscopic uniformity is superimposed upon microscopic multifariousness. That law at the macroscopic level may even be based upon an assumed randomness of the microscopic, is instanced by the kinetic theory of gases. As is well known, it may be held that law in general has this character. Whether this theory of law as statistical generalization of random distribution at some lower level is defensible or not, at least it is of great importance that the absence of observable order which is called "chance" itself becomes a kind of uniformity and may give rise to law.

This type of consideration is, it seems to me, an observation about our modes of dealing with phenomena rather than about nature or experience. There are other types of illustration also of the fact that certain kinds of order are imposed where none is directly observable. The outstanding example is, of course, arithmetical order, which presumes nothing more than some kind of identifiability. I do not refer here to the counting of assemblages; important though that may be, still it is less important than the serial arrangements imposed upon intensive (that is, qualitative) differences. At least I believe that this is what examination of our categories would reveal. The multiple types of such "arrangements" of what is in no sense arranged in nature or experience—either before or after—will need no comment; nor will the fact that such imposed order quite generally provides the basis in terms of which other types of order are expressed.

At the risk of going beyond what could be clear without detailed examination of our categories, I would draw attention to two character-

istics of such imposed order.* In the first place, it
allows an infinite multiplicity to be brought under a finite simplicity of rule. It may seem trivial
to remark that ten characters and a rule of adding 1 give us command of infinity, but without
that, or something similar, there would be no point
in counting—though there might be in serial arrangement. And second, correlation between numerical order and an imposed serial arrangement
of qualities extends the power of this type of order to what is in no sense countable. Such imposed
order, which demands no sort of uniformity of
nature beyond the persistence of identifiable characters, is at least a prime constituent of intelligibility, though without some sort of correlation
between it and that further kind of order which
means determinable sequence of experience, it
would not possess the significance which it does.

This type of correlation can be illustrated by
the case of color. The distinguishable color-qualia
are not unlimited in number but are confusingly
numerous, and also they are subject to the accident of indiscernible difference; B may be indistinguishable both from A and from C, through A
and C are recognizedly different. We make a vir-
tue of this difficulty by translating the A–B–C
qualia as a continuous series. The manner in
which this procedure is systematically carried out,

*It will occur to the reader that, according to Cassirer, such dimen-
sional and serial arrangement is the *universal type* of conceptual order.

in the color-pyramid, needs no exposition here. It should be noted that this arrangement would permit of algebraic treatment, quite independent of any correlation between color and harmonic motions, which is a *further* order, of the type of discovered generalization.

Color also illustrates another common method of achieving simplicity; that is, by dividing a whole field of qualia into classes by the use of names with a qualitative range of denotation. "Red" or "blue" represents no single quale, but instead a considerable variety of such. That the mind could hardly make a beginning of bringing order into given experience without this device, should be evident. It is made use of wherever it is the case that no imaginable instance can completely contain or illustrate the essential denotation of the concept—as there can be no image of triangle in general or dog in general. This assignment to a name of a range of denotation should be sharply distinguished from that abstraction of the essential and ignoring of other characters which is represented by many theories as the universal basis of general names. Such theories are, of course, inadequate in several ways.*

---

*The real basis of classification of the kind in question is, of course, similarity. Similarity is of two types, partial identity and resemblance proper. A spatial or temporal whole, like a contour or a melody, may be divisible into parts some of which may be qualitatively identical. But similar color-qualities are an instance of the other type. Resemblance means the possibility of confusion. It is apprehended by con-

The substitution of simple classification based on resemblance for an indeterminately large number of distinguished qualia, is of considerable importance in connection with probability-judgments. For instance, there is a finite probability that this book will be bound in red, because it must be bound in red, orange, yellow, green, blue, purple, black, white, or gray, if it is bound at all. The determinable probability arises through the fact (among others) that, within the universe of discourse in question, the possibilities are exhausted by a definite number of categories.

It is evident that the last few pages have touched superficially upon a variety of topics relative to the categories, each of which is worthy of extended examination. But as has been said, these matters are not of central importance to the main issue. The points which I hope have been suggested, if not established, are the following: Reality is more orderly than experience, because reality is experience categorized. Lack of certain types of anticipated order leads to repudiation of the given content as "unreal." The "unreal" must be capable of being understood—in some other way—but understanding is always a mat-

scious or unconscious recognition of this possibility. A man "looks like" my brother if, at a quick glance or at a distance, I might mistake him for my brother. Things are more or less similar according as optimimum conditions must be more or less nearly approached for distinction to be made. Partial identity may also be included under this rubric. It should be noted that recognition of similarity is a kind of latent generalization.

ter of degree, and the designation "unreal" ordinarily marks that type of superficial understanding which characterizes the situation in which it is
important only that a particular given experience be excluded from the field or what is relevant
to the problem in hand. All generalizations are
based upon reality, not upon uncategorized experience. Neither reality, or nature, nor experience
is orderly in the sense that what is presented may
be taken in any way we please and found to exhibit uniformity with other instances. Intelligibility does not require such "through and through"
uniformity but only *some* uniformity. What such
uniformity shall be, we do not dictate to experience, save that specific kinds are requisite to subsumption in particular categories. Beyond that,
the rational demand for uniformity wears somewhat the appearance of regulative ideal, or maxim
for the conduct of investigation. Intelligibility
and understanding are not incompatible with irre-
ducible variety; such lack of uniformity may be
irrelevant to the particular mode of cognition.
Further, we seem to have a theoretical interest in
unlimited variety, as is evidenced by our requirement of uniqueness in the individual thing. Again,
much of the basic uniformity of various areas of
experience is not discovered but imposed by categorial procedures which argue nothing intrinsically orderly in what is given. Outstanding examples are the serial and dimensional orderings of

qualitative variety, as well as schematic classifications, on the basis of similarity, by which an indefinitely large range of possible variety is brought within a definitely limited number of alternatives.

If now, I may suppose that this inadequate examination will be sufficient to guard against the commoner misapprehensions about the "uniformity of nature," I should like to proceed to those considerations which I believe to be really central for our problem. What is required in the way of order if experience is to be intelligible and knowledge possible is only that there should be apprehensible things and objective facts—and to this we can conceive no alternative whatever, unless it be the non-existence of everything.

As should now be evident, the existence of an apprehensible thing is not assured by the mere givenness of experience, though if there were no things for us, there would be, in an obvious sense, no experience. Things exist for our apprehension as certain sequences of possible experience, of which given presentations are probable indices. For this, the sole necessity is that, certain presentations being given, the possibilities of further experience should not be unlimited; that is, that it should not be the case that every recognizable appearance is equally associated with, or followed by, every other. Let us give this fundamental requirement of knowledge formal statement: *Prin-*

ciple A; It must be false, that every identifiable entity in experience is equally associated with every other. This principle is what Mr. Keynes has called the "limitation of independent variety,"* except that it is here applied to the identifiable constituents in experience, particularly with reference to their sequence, instead of to the qualities of objects with reference to their correlation in reality.

What I wish to point out is, first, that this single requirement satisfies everything which is necessary, in the way of order in experience or reality, for the validity of empirical generalizations, based on past experience and applicable to the future; and second, that although this has the appearance of a limitation of the possibilities of experience it has in the end no alternative. To put it in paradox; every possible experience is *ipso facto* a possibility of experience, but it is not possible that all possibilities should be actual. Any possibility is a possible actuality, but it is not possible that all possibilities should be concomitantly real. The coincident actuality of all possibilities is impossible. Thus the requirement that actuality be a limitation of the all-possible, is not itself a limitation of the possibilities. Instead, it is something which could not conceivably fail to be the case; there is no alternative.

Let us turn first to the requirement that there

*A Treatise on Probability. Ch. XXII.

should be apprehensible things and objective facts. As has been pointed out, the existence of things and the possibility of our knowing them—in the only sense in which we *can* know them—does not require that what we attempt to regard as things should be in each and every case objective realities. Given appearance is no more than a probable index of the existence of such a particular reality. Furthermore, any particular substantive concept, even though it should be current for a thousand years, may eventually turn out to represent, not an objective thing, but a mistaken reification. The concatenation in experience which the applicability of the concept requires may not, in fact, obtain. There may be no unicorns; there may be no disease entities; there may be no such thing as the soul. If the reality of knowledge required that every uniformity which we seek, by the invention of a concept to designate it, should be present in possible experience, or if it required that every given appearance should be an index to some uniformity which could be predicated with certainty, then it would not be plausible that there is any such thing as knowledge. All that is required is that given appearances should be probable indices to such uniformities as may be designated by concepts. This in turn means that statistical generalizations from the past sequences of experience must establish in some measure their probability for the future. And this, again, de-

pends, as has been stated, upon the limitation of
independent variety in the correlation between
given appearances and further possibilities of experience.

The point may be made clear by an analogy
which, as the reader should be warned, is incomplete but may nevertheless be useful. Suppose that
we observe a certain sequence in cards, dealt from
a pack, to be repeated several times. Will this establish a probability of its future repetition? If
we may suppose some limitation of the possibilities, such as adhering of the cards or trickery in
the deal, it may. But if we suppose no such limitation upon those ideal conditions which packs of
cards and their shuffling are meant to approximate, then even numerous repetitions of an observed run will not in the least increase the antecedent probability of its future occurrence. If,
then, we may compare identifiable qualia and complexes of such (recognizable appearances) to the
cards, and experience in general to an ideal pack
under ideal conditions, a statistical generalization of past sequences in experience could not establish that in future one such sequence should be
probable as against others in which the given appearance should be the same. That is, no appearance would be probable index to further possible
experience. Since what any substantive concept
denotes in experience is some definite sequence or
set of such, there could be, in an experience which

was subject to no limitation upon the all-possible sequence of given presentations, no recognition of things by their appearances as even probable.

But—to continue our analogy—if we can suppose the pack from which cards are dealt to be defective or the dealing subject to trickery, then a statistical generalization as to past runs will establish a genuine probability for the future, and the continued verification of such a generalization will continually increase its probability. It will still be the case that any *particular* generalization of this sort may represent "mere coincidence" in the past and fail in future. But the point which it is especially important to observe is that if the assumption that there *are* limitations which some uniformity of sequence *might* reflect is a warranted assumption, then this fact of itself is sufficient to establish the validity of the argument, in any particular case, from past uniformity to its probability for the future. If, however, it should be positively known that the runs of cards are ideally governed and subject to *no* such limitation, then there would be *no* such probability. The especial point here is that the validity of arguing from any past coincidence to its probability in the future does not depend upon our knowing any *particular* ground for this *particular* uniformity (other than its past occurrence), but does depend upon our knowing—as at least possible—a ground for such uniformities *in general*.

So far the point of our analogy is, that the validity of arguing from the correlation between a given presentation and that further experience which means a particular kind of object denoted by a particular concept, does not require us to know any particular reason for that particular correlation or for the existence of just that sort of thing (other than the past experience itself). It requires us to know—as possible at least—that such correlations, things *in general*, exist. If this assumption is valid, then the prediction (as probable) of that future experience which means the verification of the presence of an object corresponding to a particular concept, from a given presentation with which such further experience has been associated in the past, is valid; and the probability is equally genuine when, as a fact, the past conjunction is a "mere coincidence" which future experience will prove not to be valid as a generalization. That is, mistaken apprehensions, as *probable judgments*, will, if there has been no logical error in the judgment, be valid, as much as those which are actually verified by the future.

It is also to be noted that, if the assumption that things in general exist should be valid, then the probability for the future of the correlation between a given presentation and certain further experience will be increased with each successive verification of that correlation. The particular principles of probability upon which this rests need not be examined here;* the reader will perhaps be satisfied upon the point by consideration of the analogy: if we have ground for assuming poor shuffling or interference or some such limitation, the probability for the future of a particular run which has been repeated will increase with each repetition of it. At least this will be so after a certain number of repetitions have already occurred, if we suppose the conditions unaltered.

This assumption of the existence of things, that is, of certain recurrent correlations in the sequence of possible experience, is all that is required for the validity, as probable, of empirical generalizations or "laws," and of the argument from past to future with respect to these. It will be evident from previous chapters that the existence of objective properties is conditional upon precisely this same type of uniform sequence in experience. The verification of such properties requires precisely the same connection between given appearances and further possible experience, and requires nothing more. Obviously the assumption of objective properties is involved in the assumption of things. Furthermore, if things exist, which are cognizable and therefore the objects of possible concepts, it is evident that there must be laws. Laws prescribe, or describe, precisely such uniform sequences. In fact, although laws or em-

*On this point, see Keynes, "A Treatise on Probability." Ch. XX.

pirical generalizations formulate relations of objects, or properties of objects, which are non-essential rather than essential, this difference is irrelevant to the possibility of knowledge. What is essential in a thing is determined by the particular concept which it serves our interest to apply, rather than by anything else. The properties essential to "a stone" do not include its being "a freely-falling body," and the essential properties of a "freely-falling body" do not include its being a stone. But certain laws or generalizations must hold of an object in order that it be a stone and certain others must hold in order that it be a freely-falling body. The laws which characterize or constitute essential properties of freely-falling bodies are non-essential or merely empirical generalizations about stones under certain circumstances. Moreover, not only are all essential properties capable of representation as laws, but every empirical generalization is such that some substantive concept is capable of being framed so as to require conformity to it as the distinguishing or essential property of a particular kind of thing. Scientific concepts especially have this character explicitly; they define or classify objects on the basis of their conformity to certain laws, prescribing modes of behavior. Indeed, any objective fact—meaning by this any state of affairs which is describable in conceptual terms—is a property of objects and may be denoted by a substantive concept marking it as essential. In fact, unless the whole point of the last two chapters has been lost, it will be clear that the difference between essential and non-essential properties, and between prescriptive laws and empirical generalizations, is one determined by pragmatic considerations of the particular interests our knowledge is to serve which dictate particular modes of analysis, rather than by any difference in the objective state of affairs upon which these are directed. *What* laws *must be* valid, would depend upon what things exist; but the general assumption that there are things (of some sort) includes the assumption that there are valid generalizations of the type of law. If there could not be a world without the uniformities of possible experience requisite to the existence of things, then there could not be a world without uniformities of the type of law.

As is the case with things, so too with law, the validity of the prediction that a particular generalization which has held in the past will likewise hold in future, depends upon the general assumption that *there are* laws. If there are such uniform sequences as laws describe, then the occurrence of one such in the past establishes a probability of it in future, and each successive verification increases that probability. And here, too, the probability-judgment, if logically drawn, will be valid even in those particular cases in which future experience will prove past instances to have been "mere coincidences" and the generalization to be false.

Thus the assumption that things exist—that there are (some) such recurrent sequences as substantive concepts require for their application— is sufficient to secure the validity of knowledge in general, when the nature of empirical knowledge is correctly interpreted as probable judgment. As has been remarked previously, the form which skepticism has often taken, of doubting the validity of all empirical generalizations while leaving unquestioned the existence of apprehensible things, in terms of which such dubious generalizations could at least be intelligibly phrased, represents a totally impossible position. It could only *seem* self-consistent on the assumption that the validity of knowledge requires the *certainty* of empirical generalization and of prediction. Since any reasonable examination of knowledge must conclude that the pretense to such certainty is unwarranted and the ascription of it is a misreading of the actual nature of science and of common-sense attitudes, what such skepticism has slain is a man of straw, though to be sure it is just this scarecrow which has frightened philosophers out of their wits for a considerable period.

Before passing on, we should remind ourselves once more at this point that the assumption of the existence of apprehensible things does not mean the assumption that experience is uniform in the sense that certain determined sequences *universally* follow upon a given first term (the presentation). If it meant that, then no apprehension of a thing would be valid unless the given presentation should be such as to render mistaken apprehension absolutely impossible. Since errors of apprehension are possible and identification of objects are probable, it follows that the prescribed sequences, requisite to the existence of things, are such as would be predictable, with certainty, only in terms of some larger whole of experience than can be included in a single presentation. Our actual predictions—our actual knowledge of things, predicated upon given presentations—is in terms of such sequences of experience as admit of exceptions such as mistake and illusion. Hence as generalizations about actual experience, the existence of apprehensible things means only such uniformity as can be formulated in generalizations of the statistical type, which admit of exception. *No absolute uniformities* of actual experience are required either for the existence of things or for the objective character of law. Laws too, of course, are exempt from being proved false by mistaken apprehensions of the things or objective facts with which we suppose ourselves to be dealing.

The examination of the categories, "thing," "event," "property," "relation," "law," is a most difficult and complex matter. I make no pretense to have exhausted even the essential considerations for any one of these. In particular, I should not like to seem to assert that there is no difference between what is requisite to the nature of a thing and to the objectivity of law. The attempt is only to show that there could not be a world of apprehensible things in which empirical generalizations should fail of valid foundation; that if there are things then laws of the type which empirical generalization seeks to grasp must hold; and hence that such generalizations may be genuinely probable and that empirical knowledge, as the only sort of thing it can reasonably be supposed to be, is genuinely possible.

If this point is established, then the only alternative to the conception that our knowledge in general is valid, is the conception that there are no things; that nothing exists to be known and no mind exists to know it. The nearest approximation we can make to such a conception is, perhaps, that there might be an experience which is a mere flitting of meaningless presentations. But for such experience, if we can conceive it, the distinction of "real" and "unreal" could have no meaning. This being so, it is a little obscure just what we suppose ourselves to be talking about when we try to frame such a conception; perhaps about the experience of an oyster with the oyster left out.

I do not mean to take advantage of the fact

that skepticism can only make itself intelligible in terms which render it not self-consistent. This is a fact, and a most important one. But it might be claimed—though I do not know that it ever has been—that skepticism intends only to exhibit a *reductico ad absurdum* of the pretense to knowledge, by beginning with definite assumptions about the mind, etc., and on that basis proving the invalidity of these assumptions along with every other.

This possible intent of skepticism seems the more important to examine because it would appear, in the above, that the account of knowledge here given avoids skepticism only by an assumption which has a conceivable alternative; and that this alternative is precisely the absence from experience of all order of the kind which means significance and intelligibility. In this situation, it might be said: "It is not humanly possible to divest ourselves of assumptions—such as the existence of definitely conceivable things—which have no rational foundation, and still talk or think, but it is possible to be sufficiently self-critical to realize that such unavoidable assumptions are non-rational and mere 'animal faith.'"

I believe this to be demonstrably false, and shall attempt to make this fact clear. But before approaching that topic, there are two points about skepticism, with the above meaning, which it may be well to observe.

Historically there have been two main grounds of skeptical conceptions, the relativity of sense-perception and the absence of "necessary connections" in experience. Quite often these are confused together and results appropriate only to the first are added to the second. It is the first of these only which gives plausibility to the conception that there is a reality which is unknowable to us because we are separated from it by the manner of our apprehension. This ground of skepticism has, I hope, been dispelled by the considerations of previous chapters. It neglects the fact that "real" is systematically ambiguous; that "appearances" themselves must constitute one kind of reality. It also neglects the further facts that reality of any sort is definable and meaningful only in terms of *some* experience, actual or hypothetical, and that regardless of the relativity of perception, appearances inevitably are, for a rational understanding, a ground of *true* knowledge of the reality which appears even though that knowledge should be incomplete. As a result, it is impossible to conceive "reality" as completely unknowable; and since it is not plausible that, under actual or realizable conditions, reality can be *completely* known to us, the significance of the "unknowable" dwindles to the commonplace fact that humans are not omniscient. Nothing in the train of thought which starts from the relativity of perception can in any way vitiate such knowledge as we *have* or seem to have. The ground of this sort of skepticism is the false conception of knowledge as representation.

The other type of skepticism turns upon a correct conception of knowledge as predictive judgment. Its particular ground is the absence of "necessary connections of matters of fact." This may well be equivalent to the falsity of the assumption which has here been shown requisite to the existence of apprehensible things. Actually, of course, Hume supposed that necessary connections must mean such iron-clad uniformities in experience as would enable certainty of prediction, whereas it is only genuine probability which is requisite. But I hope it will be clear that if this is the ground of skepticism, it is quite unwarranted to supplement this conception by a notion of a reality somehow concealed from us by the chaotic character of experience. The *logical* conclusion would be that of Gorgias, "Nothing is," or at least the admission that we can have no rational ground for asserting a reality of any sort. If we cannot humanly avoid this, that is merely to observe the fundamentally irrational character of our "animal faith" and the *reductio ad absurdum* of all attempts at consistent belief.

The second point to be observed before we pass on, is that we must not confuse such irrational "animal faith" with that wholly rational attitude of him who, acting on the basis of a *probable* judgment, confronts the future he predicts with the realization that the possibility of his being disappointed is a real one. In both cases, one would face the future with an attitude determined by past experience but one which, in the particular instance, the future might prove to be fruitless. But in the one case, this attitude has no rational ground and incorporates no truth; in the other, it represents a knowledge—of probability—which is not only rational but absolutely true, whatever the dénouement. If one should ask, "But what, practically, would be the difference?" that is a point which we shall reach shortly.

We come now to the main point: it is impossible to imagine any sort of experience which would not present such statistical stabilities as would validate probable prediction, and such as would represent the experience of things. Our analogy of experience to runs of cards is, on this point, as unfavorable as could easily be devised, because packs of cards and their manipulation are intelligently directed to the end of minimizing the possibilities of prediction in those respects which determine the outcome of the game. But it is worth remarking at the outset that the point of card-games, except for children, is to pit our wits against this maximal uncertainty and determine a long-run outcome favorable to ourselves in spite of it. If the sequence in experience should be as independent and lacking in "necessary connection" as the sequence of cards, that could not frustrate prediction or destroy the practical value of probability-judgments. Indeed if cards should represent, in the analogy, recognizable qualia or complexes of such in presentations, our attention should be drawn to the fact that, on this point, the analogy is better than might be supposed. There are no sequences in experience which are determinable with certainty by a given presentation alone. Real things represent stabilities of a type which enormously transcend what can be given in any one experience. If the reality of things required the presence in experience of sequences absolutely determined by a first term, then we should have no reason to believe in their existence. As has been pointed out too often already, what is required is only that a given presentation determine a probability of future possible experience.

The reason why Principle A imposes no actual limitation upon the possibilities of experience may be formulated in a second dictum: *Principle B;* In any situation (if sufficiently extended) in which there are identifiable entities which fail to satisfy Principle A—*i. e.*, whose association is "random" —there will be other entities, systematically connected with the former or specifiable in terms of them, which do satisfy Principle A. The principal methods by which we determine "orderly" constituents of experience in terms of "random" ones are by proceeding to simpler elements through analysis, by taking a larger whole into which the primary constituents may be organized, or by confining attention to *abstracted* elements, and disregarding the remainder of the given as irrelevant.

To revert to our analogy, if the sequences of cards are purely random or subject to no laws but those of chance, then the stable entities of card-games, comparable to things, will be something such as tricks-taken, or suits, or kinds of hands such as full-houses, straights, etc. Or they will be entities of a lower order such as the pips on the cards. As is obvious, the chance character in the sequence of dealt cards does not frustrate the attempt at statistical generalizations which give guidance for successful play. Even with entities thus deliberately devised to approximate pure chance in certain ways, there are certain wholes which, neglecting the "non-essential," give rise to generalizations. In fact, no better basis for statistical generalization could be devised than the known fact that certain constituents of the situation are distributed in genuinely "random" fashion. Since any departure from "pure chance" is itself subject to generalization of some sort, a statistical basis for probable judgment cannot conceivably fail to be afforded.*

What particular stabilities, and what types, are

---

*In this connection, the analogy will be improved if we think of our predictions about runs of cards as based on past runs (as they might be), not upon prior knowledge of the constitution of the pack.

to be found, cannot be prescribed to experience or reality. The *particular* order discoverable in reality, the extent of it, and the degree of its conceptual simplicity, are of course, absolute data. The supposition that we may always find law in terms of any experimental entities we please and with predetermination of the type of the uniformity to be found, is totally unwarranted and is unnecessary to the validity of knowledge. Our concepts are devised with purpose to catch the significant, the subject of meaningful generalization, at whatever level and in whatever way we may. When particular concepts fail, we merely abandon them—through analysis or organization or abstraction, and so on—in favor of corrected ones, which take cognizance of, and include the ground of, our previous failure. That conception *in general* should be invalid, is quite impossible. The attempt to envisage an experience or state of affairs such that *every* attempt to discover stabilities must fail, is the attempt to conceive the inconceivable —to conceive what would not be things or objective facts nor subject to any generalization which makes what is denoted conformable to concepts. The experience or reality which should be incompatible with conception, *ipso facto* cannot be conceived.

It may seem that there is one aspect of the matter not yet covered; the validity of the argument from past to future. It may appear that it would be possible, not only that *particular* predictions based upon the past should be useless as anticipation of the future—which their character as probable allows—but that *in general* the anticipation of the future in the light of the past is without theoretical warrant. This point really is covered by Principle A, when we remember that the kind of association of constituents in experience which is essential to their comprehension in things is sequence in possible experience. But when we remember that it is the validity of *probable* prediction only which is required, the matter can be more explicitly stated, and quite simply: *Principle C;* the statistical prediction of the future from the past cannot be generally invalid, because whatever is future to any given past, is in turn past for some future. That is, whoever continually revises his judgment of the probability of a statistical generalization by its successively observed verifications and failures, cannot fail to make more successful predictions than if he should disregard the past in his anticipations of the future. This might be called the "Principle of statistical accumulation." It is quite evident that it holds even with respect to what is determined only by "pure chance"—in the only sense that we can conceive anything such. This is what is meant by saying that probability or chance is measured by that fraction which is approximated "in the long run."

Though the attempt to envisage what would

frustrate conception and knowledge is, in the nature of the case, futile, it may be worth while to conceive the worst possible experience, from that point of view, by a somewhat fantastic illustration. Let us think of our experience as constituted by complexes or patterns of qualia which come to us in sequence, and let us suppose that this experience is given to us, not by a Berkeleian God who in his goodness preserves certain uniform sequences in order that we may predict experience according to natural law, but by a perverse demon whose sole purpose is to mislead us and render knowledge impossible. If the distinguishable sensory qualia should be finite in number, as they are in actual experience, this demon must necessarily repeat, but he might repeat identifiable complexes and previous sequences to as small a degree as possible. However, if, as a result, these presented patterns did not afford a sufficiently good basis for conception, we should analyze them into sub-patterns or other constituents which would be of more frequent appearance, or should classify them according to some simplified schematism based on similarity, or give them dimensional or serial arrangement approximating to an ideal continuum, or in some other fashion proceed by abstraction or reorganization or a combination of the two to circumvent the multifarious variety of the given. For the rest, the character of it would be relegated to the "non-essential" and merely mark the relative uniqueness of particular moments of experience; it would be non-significant, like the particular character of frost-patterns and snow crystals. We should be inattentive to such non-significant features of the given; and if any one should call our attention to their comparative frequency, we might regard his observation as a foolish remark about the obvious but unimportant. If the demon should likewise minimize the extent to which particular *sequences* should be repeated, he might make knowledge difficult to a degree. But at least we should presumably come to possess the very important generalization that the maximum of novelty may confidently be expected. We should organize all our conduct on the principle that "lightning seldom strikes twice in the same place" and "history never repeats," with consequent advantage to ourselves. As a fact, however, we should circumvent the demon on this point at the same time that we attained relative simplicity of recognition, and should carry out similar procedures with reference to sequence. We should analyze, abstract, and relegate what we could not find somehow significant to the status of "irrelevant concomitants of significant 'causal' sequences." By ignoring a sufficient proportion of the characteristics of experience as it came to us, we should arrive at such simplicity that, in terms of it, even the most disadvantageous sequence of the primary constituents—*e. g.*, a "random" order—must afford some repetition and uniformity. Knowledge might be made difficult, but could not be made impossible.

This would be something as if we were required to play a game with cards dealt from a pack we never saw and could only infer from the hands dealt us, and as if these cards were dealt with trickery and malice—something worse than a good decent game of chance. But even in such circumstances, the principle of statistical accumulation would operate. If we were required to bet on this game, we might be unequal to our demon antagonist to any degree you please; our ignorance might be great, and our failures and loss correspondingly large. But by nothing which he could do could be so devise it that we should not lose *less* of our money if we intelligently observed past dealings and continually revised our betting on the basis of accumulated experience.

Indeed we need only to prod our imaginations to remark that this actual experience of ours fits the illustration better than one might suppose. Most of the pattern and sequence of our experience is non-significant; those characters which by our practical attitude we single out and remark and make prediction in terms of, are inordinately meager as compared with the total of presented distinguishable pattern and sequence of qualia. Most of experience is as non-significant as the intricate pattern of the rug I have been gazing at is to me now. Beyond a few details which suffice for recognition, this intricacy does not even draw attention, and if attended, it hardly functions as knowledge. It neither verifies anything nor baffles knowledge, because it arouses no anticipatory attitude. Confronting any given experience, the first act of intelligent cognition is to discard all but a few items of what is presented as excess mental baggage irrelevant from the point of view of our predictive purpose. It is the relatively meager remainder which constitutes the clue to expected uniformity.

Even if the hypothetical demon should have an infinite number of qualia and complexities at his disposal, instead of a finite number, it is doubtful if we should be worse off. We should merely discard more of our experience, as marking that uniqueness of each moment and each thing which is irrelevant to knowledge; we should frame our concepts and make our predictions in terms of the remainder, or of abstractions and other such imposed simplifications. On any hypothesis which can be framed about experience, however perverse, I think it will be clear that a similar thing would hold, or else that the fantasy is not even imaginable but would merely mean the elimination of reality, of significance, of all questions and the mind itself.

In any experience such as we can, even at the worst, suppose our own to be, conception will be valid and knowledge will be possible. The three principles which have been stated will hold, and generalization will be subject to genuine probability. No further and avoidable metaphysical assumption is required. The mind will always be capable of discovering that order which is requisite to knowledge, because a mind such as ours, set down in any chaos that can be conjured up, would proceed to elicit significance by abstraction, analysis and organization, to introduce order by conceptual classification and categorial delimitation of the real, and would, through learning from accumulated experience, anticipate the future in ways which increasingly satisfy its practical intent.

APPENDIX A

NATURAL SCIENCE AND ABSTRACT CONCEPTS

In his introductory chapter to "Einstein's Theory of Relativity," Max Born has written:* "The development of the exact sciences leads along a path to a goal which, even if far from being attained, yet lies clearly exposed before us: it is that of creating a picture of nature which, confined within no limits of possible perception or intuition, represents a pure structure of conception, conceived for the purpose of depicting the sum of all experiences uniformly and without inconsistencies." And he goes on to characterize this world of "inaudible tones, invisible light, imperceptible heat," in which the limited range of the human senses is ignored, as a "sum of abstractions" and "subtle logical configurations."

It may well be that the inevitable movement of the exact sciences is in this direction in which mathematics has preceded them; toward the deductive mode of development and toward concepts which are laid down less in terms of those sense-qualities by which we directly identify empirical objects and more in terms of those systematic correlations which figure in natural law. The physical definition of sound or color in terms of wave-lengths or rates of vibration, serve as simple illustrations of the sort which Born has in mind. Concepts which are abstract to a degree, and remote from the merely apparent or directly discriminable, are dictated by interest in that uniformity and comprehensiveness which are essential to intellectual economy and ex-

*English translation, p. 2.

actness. And the deductive method of presentation
—as we are beginning to understand—is not a
method of proof at all (since the "first principles"
are as much corroborated by their consequences as
the consequences are by their deducibility) but is
simply the most compendious and economical method
of tying up an enormous multiplicity of facts in a
relatively small number of bundles. It is a method
which becomes possible only when a high degree of
precision has been attained and the interrelations
of different classes of phenomena are quite thoroughly understood. But when these requirements are
met, the power of deductive order to summarize
great masses of facts, while still preserving their
relations to one another, is an advantage almost
compelling.

Abstractness in the concepts, and that systematic
order which reaches its highest degree in the deductive system, go hand in hand. The reason is one
which is inherent in the nature of the problem which
science undertakes to solve. The conceived "things"
of the unsophisticated consciousness are, relatively
speaking, coagulations of sense-qualities; they are
such as are identifiable, with a minimum of risk, by
their momentary appearance. But thinghood must
also include objective change, since the purpose of
such abstractions, or excisions, from the immediately
presented is the possibility of prediction. Science
but seeks to raise to a higher power this possibility
of correlating identifiable "thing" and predictable
change. In so doing, however, it is obliged to abandon, in some measure, the things of common sense,
relatively identifiable by their appearances, and to
substitute therefor things which are conceived in
terms of correlations less directly observable. In its
basic and defining concepts, it moves away from
sense-appearance and in the direction of *law*. Those
systematic correlations, for example, which are first
painfully established as the uniform behavior of

gravitating objects—a law of change—later become the defining characteristics of "mass," which in turn becomes the essential property of matter. Or those uniformities which chemistry pursues are finally attained in terms of atoms or electrons (which are essentially imperceptible, and in that sense purely conceptual entities). Such ultimate things, identifiable by sense only through uniformity of behavior and correlation, displace the tastes and odors and other sensible qualities by which salts and acids, gold and air and water, are identified. And then, perhaps, we mystify ourselves because we have a world of "inaudible tones, invisible light," and matter that we cannot imagine!

This regress of science from the directly perceptible may be phrased in another way. Any "thing" is a bridge between given experience and predictable change. A thing of any sort must always be such that it is identifiable—directly or indirectly, with easy assurance or with difficulty—by something which is the "appearance" of it. Else the concept would meet with no clue to its application, and the purpose of it would be lost. But thinghood must also include objective change; otherwise the identification of it in direct experience would enable no prediction and, once again, the purpose of the concept would be lost. The difference between the concepts of unsophisticated common sense and those of science is that common-sense things are relatively easy to identify but relatively unreliable guides to prediction, whereas the things of science are relatively safe guides to prediction but correspondingly difficult of immediate identification. This is because the scientific concept takes that correlation and uniformity which may be formulated as law and makes it the *essence* of the thing.

I should not like to become entangled with the ancient and honorable notion of "substance," but it is evident that we may find here a clue to some of the problems concerning this. Since a concept of that which is merely momentary would serve no purpose, the "thing itself" (for any grade of thing) is always conceived by means of those properties which persist through the process of experience or objective change. These are its *essential* properties. Whenever this relatively stable complex of properties is altered, the thing in question goes out of existence —*e. g.*, the wood is burned, leaving ashes. But the extreme antithesis of being a "thing" is not being an objective change which is subject to law—since what is predictable may be brought within the concept and made essential—but is merely such change as should be unpredictable, uncontrollable, and hence baffling to the understanding. Thus when the change is predictable or controllable, it is not a "disappearance" but a "transformation," internal to the nature of some conceivable "thing." The predictable transformation from liquid to solid at 32° F. is an essential property of water. It is not a property of that potable liquid which precedes the freezing, and is annihilated and replaced by ice. (At least it is not such for an unsophisticated tropic-dweller, whose concept cannot include prediction of it.) It is a property of that thing whose concept is satisfied both before and after the freezing; hence of that which persists and is the subject of the transformation.

Thus in every transformation—that is, in every process of objective change which is predictable and hence intelligible—there are two layers of things. The lumber disappears, the desk comes into being; but it is the same wood. Some of the essential properties of lumber have disappeared, some of the essential properties of a desk have come into being; but all those of wood have persisted. When our last word is "It disappeared" or "It came into being," we cannot predict or control change, which is what we mean when we say that we cannot understand it.

Destruction and creation are, thus, unscientific categories. The methodological postulate of all science is that the problem of understanding the process of reality, to which it addresses itself, is essentially capable of solution; and hence, that all change is transformation. Thus the ultimate things of science must, in the nature of its ideal, be eternal; and it cannot stop until it has disclosed them. That in its attempt to conceive what is eternally persistent, it must import into its concept as essential the law which anticipates transformation in general, and that the ideatum of such a concept will be remote from what can be directly identified in sense-experience, and perhaps will not be imaginable at all, belongs to the nature of the case.

Nevertheless it remains true that the difference between the substantive concepts of science and those of common sense can only be one of degree. As has been pointed out, *all* conception of things is predictive; and on the other hand no concept of science would be significant if the thing denoted could not be indirectly identified in experience through its manifestations, correlations, or effects. The point to be noted is only that the relative abstractness of scientific concepts is an inevitable concomitant of its greater comprehensiveness and power of accurate prediction. Increasing abstractness and an increased satisfaction of the ends projected by "exactness," "order," "system," go together. Both are consequences of that formulation of comprehensive key-conceptions in which basic things and fundamental laws are no longer distinct ideas, because the substantive concepts are themselves framed in terms of those correlations of phenomena exhibited in law.

In the march toward these ideals, there comes a stage when it is no longer easily possible to say whether concepts are devised, and laws discovered, to fit phenomenal facts, or whether the conceptual system itself rules and facts are reconceived in conformity to it. At least the give and take between these two is on approximately equal terms. Whether, for example, the devising of such concepts as "energy of position" and "curvature of space" represents a modification of system or law to fit facts, or an alteration in the manner of conceiving facts so as to fit an a priori comprehensive schema of interterpretation, seems to be a question only of that aspect of the procedure which shall be emphasized.

With exact natural science, as with mathematics, a stage is possible, if it is not already reached, in which the problem of scientific truth can be phrased equally well as the discovery of empirical laws sufficiently comprehensive to constitute a systematic whole, or as the selection of an abstract system which will be applicable to the facts. Just as the problem of space may be envisaged either as that of discovering the system of laws governing certain relations of ideally rigid bodies, or as that of selecting an abstract geometry which accords with observed phenomena, so perhaps the issues between a Newtonian and a relativity kinematics may be phrased equally well as questions of the correct generalization of certain physical phenomena or as the question of choice in application between the two abstract systems, both of which have that logical integrity which comes from strict adherence to their fundamental concepts. It would be but a short step, if it is not already possible, to viewing such alternative systems as strictly deductive elaborations of purely abstract concepts and postulated relations. So viewed, such systems would have the same kind of truth, and be objects of the same kind of knowledge, which characterize a pure geometry apart from its applications.

But if we thus extrapolate along the line of development which exact science seems to follow, and assign to it the highest degree of independence of

directly given data of sense, it still remains true that
the *truth about nature* cannot have such independence. When we inquire upon what ground the selection of an abstract system to be applied to concrete physical phenomena would be determined, it
becomes clear that, directly or indirectly, sense-data
must necessarily figure in such a decision. The logical integrity of an abstract system is no guarantee
of applicability. Let the connection between what is
presented in sense and the idealized abstractions of
the system be as remote as you please, this connection is of the essence of any truth about phenomenal
nature.

Scientific concepts import into themselves, and
make essential to the scientific thing, more of what
belongs to the systematic interconnections of phenomena; and by way of compensation, they extrude,
as non-essential, something of what is more apparent
or easily observed. Now whatever is of the essence
of a thing need not be established by induction or
vested in empirical generalization. If, for example,
possible resolution into hydrogen and oxygen is of
the essense of water, there is no problem of induction to establish this property. That something
which, in ancient Greece, would have been classified
under water, as one of the four elements, might not
be thus decomposable, has nothing to do with the
matter, except as it marks the fact that we repudiate
this ancient concept.

If we reflect a little upon the history of chemistry, or any other of the older sciences, will it not be
obvious that the determination of what belongs to
the deductive elaboration of concepts and what to
empirical generalization from experience, depends
rather simply upon our modes of conception themselves? And further, that the manner in which science departs from common sense is characteris-
tically one which enlarges the scope of deduction by
the direction in which it modifies its concepts? That

such scientific concepts are built upon inductive generalization in earlier stages, is obvious enough. And that we cannot lift ourselves by our scientific bootstraps and enlarge our understanding of nature by altering definitions, will likewise need no comment. But it would be a misunderstanding to suppose that established principles of science begin as hypotheses or tentative generalizations and are, by continued inductive verification, finally made certain, so that we dare embody them in definitions. More accurately, the process is one in which what we call induction enlarges the scope of experience, so that those correlations which are most useful for knitting together the facts of nature in a comprehensive network are gradually revealed and confirmed. Thus a more judicious ground of conception is reached. But the principles made definitive by such pragmatically superior conception neither wait upon any novel certainty to be established by induction nor do they acquire such certainty when made definitive. As applicable to certain phenomena of nature, they are not completely certain either before or after. When this potable liquid called water has been decomposed into hydrogen and oxygen a certain number of times without exception, the probability that this will always happen reaches such a pitch that this property may reasonably be adopted as the essential mark of a new concept. That another such experiment still might fail, is as possible after that as before. But it is now the possibility that the (new) concept water will prove inapplicable to some tasteless liquid, instead of the possibility that water (as previously conceived) may fail to have this property universally.

If we follow this process to the limit, we find that by gradual transition that stage of systematic correlation may be reached in which we have all the major principles of some science embraced in a deductive system. But this means no absolute certainty about nature which did not previously exist. The problem now becomes whether, or how far, this deductive system is applicable to empirical facts.

Appendix B

ESTHESIS AND ESTHETICS

The nearest approach to pure givenness is doubtless the esthetic experience. Cognition is always in part instrumental or pragmatic, but so far as an experience is esthetic, it constitutes an end in itself. Or if we use the word "esthetic" more widely, so as to include negative as well as positive values, at least the esthetic aspect of experience concerns its quality as end.

There are any number of questions of esthetic theory which might be raised here: whether intrinsic value is always a dimension of the immediate; whether esthetic "form" is given or is in part construction; whether the value-quality of the experience should be regarded as intrinsic to the content or as a function of the mind or as a relation of the two. I beg leave to avoid such controversial questions, so far as possible. It would seem that the facts with which we are concerned are fairly clear, and that such questions are, in part at least, such as will be settled by determining the field of esthetics rather than by answering questions about the nature of experience. It is obvious that the instrumental sign-function of a presentation and its significance as immediate felt quale are cognate aspects of experience. These two cannot be separated in their temporal existence; every presentation has both at once. But the value of it as a cognitive sign and its value as esthetic are (presumably) independent. The former is extrinsic; the latter intrinsic. Not only does all experience possess an intrinsic value-aspect—a positive or negative value as an end in itself—but "there is one glory of the sun and another glory of the moon": esthetic apprehension is not exhausted by placing the experience in a one-dimensional scale of immediate values.

There is such a thing as direct appreciation of the given, and such immediate apprehension of the quality of what is presented must figure in all empirical cognition. Nevertheless the object of esthetic *judgment* must always transcend the merely given. Given experience would need no appraisal, nor could the assessment of value exercise any helpful function, if the object of it were simply and solely this experience itself. Experience wears its own intrinsic value-aspect on its face, and no appraisal of it as just this unique and given experience is necessary. The object of appraisal is (usually at least) to connect this quality with something or context as a matrix of *further* such experience.* A judgment of value has direct relation to our action. That whose value is positive is to be sought; that whose value is negative is to be avoided. But experiences having a certain quality can be sought or avoided only through just such prediction as is involved in empirical cognition in general.

The most primitive of esthetic apprehensions are those expansive movements and approaches toward the stimulus, or that quiescence, which mark our hope that the present enjoyment will continue, and those contractions, withdrawals, or merely random movements, by which we attempt to avoid or alter the unpleasant experience. Such primitive attitudes are hardly judgments; they are, rather, unconsidered responses. Yet already they concern relation of the present to a possible future as much as the quality of the present itself. Such primitive attitudes are replaced by more complex ones, deliberate seeking and intelligent avoiding, only when the immediate apprehension of value is coupled with an instrumental cognition which penetrates the temporal

*See p. 212, footnote.

processus of experience and consciously predicts. It is the residence of value in certain experiential contexts, and the relation between the supervenience of such experiences and the modes of our possible activity, which is the object of the judgment.

It may be said that there are two questions: What is the value of the experience? and How is such experience to be got or avoided? But if it be claimed that only the former is a question of esthetics, I shall beg leave to differ. The former question is hardly a real one, because it answers itself. For *given* experience, there can be no doubt about it; and for any *other* experience the question of value is the question whether some immediately apprehensible (value) quale will accrue in a certain empirical context. The object of appraisal is some *thing* or situation as a matrix for experience of a certain quality. It is only so that the esthetic judgment can have significance for practice, and become a guide to art or life.

In the end, of course, all judgments of value must depend on some direct intuition of value. And I should suppose that judgments of comparative value —of better and worse—must depend at bottom upon some direct comparison of quality as immediate. We are here at a point where discussion might easily degenerate into a quarrel about words. All I wish to point out is that when what is evaluated is precisely and solely what is immediately intuited—some aspect of this experience itself, or some two items of experience, both directly given—then this evaluation is not a *judgment* in the sense of being something which needs verification or could be verified; it is no object of learning or of reasonable discussion. Direct valuing and direct preferring, of the immediately given as such, are not, I should suppose, matters concerning which there could be either mistake or argument, though certainly they are essential.

It may be objected that certain experiences pall

while others are likely to become increasingly satisfactory or valuable. But, of course, given unique experience never becomes anything but past. It is the
continuing object, or certain empirical contexts as
designated by other qualities than value, which may
become altered in their value-aspect, in ways which
the esthetician and the artist are concerned to study.
Esthetics seeks to disclose the *enduring* values in
terms of those things or contexts in which positive
esthetic quality resides.

Thus so far as esthetic experience is a *judgment*,
or gives rise to knowledge, in the sense in which the
content of knowledge can be learned or verified, that
judgment is concerned with the same sort of relations between different "givens" in the process of experience which figure also in other types of empirical
cognition. There is knowledge here, not so far as the
esthetic experience is pure esthesis or coalesces with
the given, but precisely so far as it transcends the
given and reaches out to further possible experience
related to the present in certain ways.

Nevertheless, the *terminus ad quem* of the esthetic
judgment is different from that of merely instrumental or practical judgments, of the type which
figure in natural science, etc., which are what is more
frequently meant by the word "knowledge." *All* empirical judgment concerns the processus of experience. But—if I may be permitted the expressions—
the practical judgment asks, "Where do we go from
here?" while the esthetic judgment asks, "What is
the use of going?" There is no such thing as "esthetic experience," since all experience has both the
aspect of value and the aspect of sign: it is at once
esthesis and cognitively significant. But there are,
for any presentation, these two questions: "What is
the object which is here presented, and how is it related to others?" and "What is the value of this
presented object as an enduring matrix of experience?" So far as these concern some temporal span

which runs beyond the present, both are questions the answer to which will be knowledge. For neither, is this answer to be discovered merely by sinking ourselves in the presentation itself and putting thought to sleep. And for neither is it possible to make an answer without reference to the specific quality of the given experience as pure esthesis. But so far as the contrast is between such pure esthesis and construction or relation by thought with what transcends the given, pure esthesis is not knowledge or judgment. The *given* as such need not be *judged*.

If the mystic and the intuitionist are outraged by the appropriation of the term "knowledge" to such narrow use, one would gladly give them back their beloved word, if only they will provide us with some other which will mark the distinction which is it necessary to make here—the distinction between the immediately apprehended and incommunicable "feel" or sensuous quality, which may have intrinsic value and be an end in itself, and the instrumental or pragmatic significance of other-than-itself which attaches to this given, and whose importance lies in its extrinsic or leading character (its meaning as a sign) and in its connection with our possible action.

CONCEPTS AND "IDEAS"

It has been pointed out in Chapter III that the concept, as that term is here used, represents an abstraction from the cognitive mental state, which includes also an element of esthesis representing, for the individual mind, the denotation or application of this concept in terms of the given.

It will appear, from Appendix B, that for the significance of a particular mental state as apprehension of *value*, this element of esthesis may be decisive. So far as experience can have the aspect of end in itself, the determination of value cannot be independent of the immediately apprehended quality of the given. But also it will be evident that for evaluative apprehension of what is objective—of objects, situations, and typical configurations of possible experience—the conceptual element is likewise indispensable. If, for example, I wish so to direct my conduct as to secure a maximum realization of the positively esthetic, then I must be regardful not only of the immediate qualities of such experiences as will be possible to me, but also of those connections of one experience with another which constitute the essence of conceptual understanding and make it predictive and hence a guide to action.

There are, moreover, interests which transcend those of knowledge with regard to other people. So far as I am interested in other persons only to secure their coöperative behavior for purposes of my own, my interest is purely cognitive. It ends in their behavior and is regardless of the quality with which I suppose our common experiences are felt by them. But so far as I desire, or feel it my duty, to treat other persons not only as behaving objects present in my environment but also as ends in themselves, I have an interest, which cannot be abstracted from, in the absolute quality of their immediate experience. The importance of such interests is commensurate with the significance of love and duty in human life.

So far as we have such social ends and purposes, in distinction from aims which are exclusively individual, we are under the necessity to frame notions, and to seek truths, with respect to which the quality of experience in another mind is determinative. The ethical conception of the good, and the esthetic conception of the beautiful, are such notions, if we take these to be social categories and suppose that individual appreciations ought to be subordinated to, or at least regardful of, prevailing or general apprehensions of the valuable. For instance, it will be of the essence of the "good" as a predicate of objects in general that it be a possible matrix of satisfactory experience, not only to me but to the generality of persons. In this, it stands in contrast to a purely conceptual community of meaning. As was pointed out in Chapter II, if I should, by some idiosyncrasy of sense, apprehend "red" by immediately given qualia peculiar to me, but should, on account of the social origins of language, apply this term to the same objects as other persons—that is, find it in the same patterns of relation—then my cognitive *concept* of red would be identical with that of other persons, regardless of its peculiar quality as immediately given. But if my meaning of the "good" should represent a similar idiosyncrasy, then the purposes for the sake of which I have framed and use this term would be defeated, whether I should know it or not. I do not *mean* to designate as "good" what other persons merely behave toward in the same way I do or find in the same contexts as I do: I intend by it that which affects them with the same, or similar, qualities of experience with which I am affected in the presence of it. Notions so framed may appropriately be termed "ideas." Such ideas are basic for the sciences of values; for ethics, esthetics, and the philosophy of religion. In terms of them all truths of (social or objective) appreciation must be framed.

The directly given quality of experience, however, can never be conveyed or expressed; it is ineffable and incommunicable. I seek to interpret other minds by empathy or *einfühlung*, and inference from behavior. That such sympathetic comprehension is not pathetic fallacy, there is—so far as I can see—no theoretical assurance. It transcends the possibility of verifiable knowledge, and can be founded only on a postulate.

If the taxi-man has a proper *concept* of an hour and can meet me at the end of that time, we achieve a perfect practical understanding regardless of the tedium or vivacity with which the passing time may differently affect us. The hour we are concerned about, in our interests of coöperative behavior, is a purely relational thing, which may be the same for both of us regardless of the fact that, if I could put myself inside his experience, this hour might feel twice as long as to me now. For me to disregard this immediate quale which the time has for the taxi-man, is to treat him as a thing and not as a fellow creature. But I cannot literally *know* his experience: I can only *postulate* that his behavior is a clue to it. Upon such postulate, ethics must be founded.

There are many motives—among them a powerful and perhaps central motive of religion—which move us to extend such postulation to reality as a whole. We are interested not only to manipulate things and predict their behavior, but to question whether reality is stable in a fashion which is *not* merely the reliability of obedience to natural law. Has reality on the whole a stable relation to our values? Does it conserve the humanly ideal, or does it inevitably frustrate us in the end, or is it "indifferent" to our valuings? We inevitably raise this question. To suppose that it means anything or has an answer, is inevitably to attribute to what we regard as ultimate reality one essential character of persons—determination by relation to value. But if "ultimate reality" means anything; if, further, ultimate reality has an "attitude" toward human ends—if it be "personal"; still I can only read this mind of God by a postulate, however much the vehemence of faith and the yearning to break through that loneliness which is the fate of self-conscious beings may move me to affirm it as knowledge.

Apparently it is a native longing of humanity to transcend the bounds of subjectivity; to know our object not only in the pragmatic sense of successful prediction and control but in a deeper sense of somehow coinciding with its nature. To represent this coincidence of subject and object as genuinely possible and as true knowledge, is characteristic of mysticism, of intuitionism, and of that type of idealism represented by Schopenhauer and Bergson. The world is my idea—says Schopenhauer—but the notion that it is nothing more than my idea is incredible. That would be the solipsism which is maintained only in mad-houses. But what more than my idea can it be, consistently with my genuine knowledge of it? If it is something more than what it means for me, something in itself, then it must mean something *for* itself; it must, in this respect, be of a nature fundamentally like my own. Insight into the true nature of a reality which is independent of me—which has more than a "for me" character—is possible only if that nature is spiritual. My immediate experience is clue to it only because, in its character of will, my nature coincides with the nature of all reality. The parallel, for other and similar conceptions, the reader will be able to draw for himself.

In brief, such idealism, as distinguished from other types by its admission that reality is independent of the mind which knows it, rests upon a dilemma which is real and is, by such idealism, correctly understood: Either knowledge does not mean identity of quality or nature between subject and object, or the only intelligible fashion in which reality in general can be conceived is on some analogy to mind or life, as spiritual. Such idealism chooses the latter alternative. As I have tried to argue, the other is the true one. In the case of other conscious beings, empathy has a meaning. In the case of the inanimate, it is dubious whether such meaning is possible at all. But in any case, *knowledge* is independent of any supposed identity of quality between subjective knowing state and objective thing. *Other* interests may concern such identity, but knowledge does not. Genuinely verifiable knowledge cannot, thus, interpret things on any analogy to spirits. On the contrary, it can grasp other minds only as things, revealed in the patterns of behavior of certain physical beings. The rest is postulate.

MIND'S KNOWLEDGE OF ITSELF

It will very likely appear to the reader of Chapter II that the analysis of the cognitive experience there given leads to a difficulty about our knowledge of the mind itself. This difficulty is, I think, more apparent than real, and is mainly due to that background of our thought for which the history of modern epistemological developments is responsible. Perhaps the matter may be briefly put as follows: Compatible with conceptions here presented, the ascription of reality to anything as an object of knowledge must represent an interpretation put upon some presentation in experience. But the mind, too, must be knowable. Either that, or it must be accepted as transcendent of experience, which would make of it just that kind of dubious and metaphysical assumption which has here been declared against in the theory of knowledge. Apparently, then, the mind itself must somehow be given. Mind, however, is exactly that to which the element in experience which is *not* given has been ascribed. If, then, the mind and its activity are given, then everything in cognition is given, and the distinction fails. But if mind is not given, then how can it be known; how can it be other than a meaningless fiction of the transcendent?

The nature of mind in general is a fundamental and complex problem of metaphysics, including much with which we are not here concerned. While it is not possible to avoid such metaphysical problems altogether, the attempt will be to restrict discussion directly to the point in hand—that is, to explain the possibility of the mind's knowledge of itself, compatible with the conception that the knowledge of a real object is through interpretation of something given in experience, and that the element of interpretation in knowledge is due to mind.

The key to this problem may be discovered, I think, by a slightly critical examination of what is involved in our ordinary ascriptions of reality and our usual attributions of "responsibility." As was pointed out in Chapter I, a proper method in philosophy will take it to consist in just such critical clarification of common modes of predication. What follows, then, attempts merely to draw attention to those phases of experience which are what we *mean* when we say that thinking qualifies the object of knowledge, and when we say that the mind itself is known.

My experience of the pen with which I am writing has been analyzed into a presentation now before me and an intellectual construction or interpretation put upon it. When I say that this given cylindrical appearance is *due to* the real fountain pen in my hand, I *mean that*, as I feel assured from past experience, there are various continuities of this given presentation with other actual and possible experience in ways which are characteristic of just this kind of real physical object. The givenness of just this kind of appearance, together with just these specific continuities, *constitute the meaning of* "*a physically real fountain pen now in my hand.*" Similarly when I say that the taking of it as "pen" and not as "plaything" or merely "cylinder" is *due to my mind*, I mean that, as I feel assured from past experience, if my attitude and purpose were other than they are, the significant cognitive context of this presentation would be other than it is. The elucidation of just this correlation between different mental attitudes and interests, on the one hand, and different significant contexts of the given on the other, would be the explication (or partial explication) of *the meaning of "my thinking mind conditioning the content of experience."*

It might be said that this is roughly comparable to a more naïve pronouncement, which might be attributed to common sense: There is a brute-fact element in knowledge which is distinguished as that which is due to the presence of the object; and there is an element of relation, association, or construction which is distinguished as being due to the mind. If, however, we should suppose that actually being "due to the object" and being "due to the mind" are the *criteria* which mark this distinction between elements in cognition, then we should have the cart before the horse. We should then be committing the error, which is frequent in naïve realism, of supposing that a distinction *within* knowledge can depend on a prior one *outside* it. To be sure, any plausible analysis of knowledge must be *consistent with* the statement that the veridical perception of the object *in* the mind is due (in part) to the presence of the object *to* the mind. Even idealism must find some eventually valid meaning for ordinary pronouncements about the causation of perceptive states. Still, being due to the object is no *criterion* of givenness, because the recognition of the presence is itself dependent on this givenness of the presentation. The presentation is due to, or caused by, the object; but *knowledge* of the object is due to the presentation.

An exactly similar difficulty would hold for any theory which should attempt to delimit or explain the "formal" element of interpretation by the criterion of its being due to the mind. That such construction *is* thus due to mind may be accepted as a fact; obviously *something* in knowledge will be due to mind if there is any such thing as a mind. But just as the object can be known only through or by means of that presentation which is due to it, so mind (as cognitive) can only be known through that "formal" element in experience to which it gives rise. If we did not find both the given and interpretation *in* experience, we should have no epistemological ground for the distinction of subject and object. Hence to rest the division of cognitive experience into "matter" and "form" upon a supposedly prior distinction of mind and independent object, is to commit an obvious and vicious circle.

It is necessary—however undesirable—to pause upon this methodological point, because it is precisely what lies at the root of the supposed difficulty about conceiving that a mind which is one of the conditions of experience in general should be itself knowable and empirical. The alternative is transcendentalism, which explains knowledge by reference to a conditioning mind and—to avoid the paradox of mind conditioning itself—posits this mind as beyond or behind all experience. Such transcendentalism vitiates both epistemology and metaphysics. It vitiates epistemology because to suppose that the content of knowledge is informed or determined by some transcendent agent or principle, which is not to be found *in* experience, is to substitute a creation-myth for the analysis of knowledge. And it vitiates metaphysics by this invention of a transcendent agent which, on the very account of knowledge which such a theory gives, it would be impossible to know. The ascription of the categories to a transcendent mind and of the matter of knowledge to transcendent things in themselves, are precisely similar fallacies. Those who hope to avoid the latter must, in all consistency, give up the former.

It may be said that mind, as that which supplies the categorial conditions of experience, is something which, in the nature of the case, must be beyond or behind experience and cannot be in it, but that the existence of such a mind is "presupposed" by experience in general. If this vague word "presuppose" has any real and pertinent meaning, I should suppose its connotation would be of an hypothesis or assumption which is logically necessary to explain the facts in question. But the difference between an hypothesis which is absolutely required in order to explain a fact, and direct experience of the thing hypostatized, is a wholly imaginary difference. To see this, we should begin, not with hypotheses which are required or necessary but with such as are only more or less probable. That which *explains* experience is always something which the experience in question gives us *some* reason (some partial ground) for assuming. So put, this may seem a commonplace. But if this point be fully grasped, it will throw much light upon the connection between the probability of hypotheses and the "perception" of "empirical facts." It will also do much to resolve such difficulties in the theory of knowledge as the one with which we are here concerned.

Let us return to our illustration. At the moment, the content of this present experience leads me to say that I have a fountain pen in my hand. That is, I explain or interpret certain data of sense by the hypothesis of the fountain pen. This hypothesis is partially verified by the presented data of sense themselves. For the rest, it depends upon the verifiable truth of certain implicit predictions which constitute my interpretation or explanation of these sense-data. For instance, I expect it to continue to write at my will, or if it does not, then I expect it to begin again after I dip it in the ink-bottle and manipulate the lever. These implicit predictions— too numerous and complex to mention—are all of them about further possible experience. If experience could exhaust *all* such prediction, what I mean by "the fountain pen in my hand" would *completely coincide with what this totality of experience would include*. When I say that this present content of my experience is "due to" the fountain pen, I state a

highly probable fact. When I say that the fountain
pen as a real and knowable object is an interpretation that I put upon my present experience—by
framing this supposedly verifiable hypothesis about
further possible experience—I state the same fact
in another way.

Between the fountain pen in my hand, the distant star, and an alpha-particle or electron, there
is no difference in type, from the point of view of
my knowledge, but only a difference of degree in
the probability of my interpretation, or the possible
discrepancy between it and what further experience
might disclose. And whatever, in my interpretation,
is thus probable only, is intrinsically capable of
being verified or falsified in such possible experience. There is nothing in it which is beyond the possibility of experience altogether. If there were, it
would also be beyond all meaning. The difference of
these examples is in the extent to which what is
meant by "the pen," "the star," "the electron," is
verified in the presently given sense-data, or conversely, in the degree to which what is meant is not
thus immediately verified and hence is only more or
less probable. The pen is "directly," though only
partially, given at the moment. The star of alpha-
particle is "indirectly" given; that is to say, between the immediately presented point of light or
the track in the photograph and the full meaning
of "a star" or "an alpha-particle," there is a more
obvious or greater interval. The electron, I may be
tempted to say, nobody can perceive. But in experi-
encing those laboratory phenomena which oblige us
—if they do—to believe in the existence of electrons, the electron is partially given. This behavior
of the oil droplet, or whatever, requires the existence of electrons to explain or interpret it. And the
only kind of reality I can ascribe to the electron, is
the nature I attribute to it in explaining this and
other pertinent experience. As Charles Peirce has

phrased it: "Consider what effects that might conceivably have practical bearings you conceive the objects of your conception to have. Then, your conception of those effects is the whole of your conception of the object."*

Apply these considerations to the conception of a supposedly transcendent mind or agent which categorizes experience. If there were nothing in experience which was the datum of mind, there would be no possible ground for assuming the existence of any. If, on the other hand, the only rational explanation of certain features of experience is the hypothesis of mind having a certain character or exercising certain functions, then this logically necessitated explanation of such experience would constitute our knowledge of such mind. A mind which is "presupposed" or necessarily assumed in order to account for experience is partially revealed in every experience which thus "presupposes" it, and the whole meaning of it would be exhausted in the totality of such experience. There is nothing in the nature of it which can be meaningfully asserted beyond what such experience, actual and possible, would exhibit. So far as it is beyond all possible experience, it is not a conceivable explanation of anything. So far as it is even a possible explanation of experience, it is not transcendent of experience in general. The possible transcendence of mind, exactly like the transcendence of the real object, is the interval between what—in our conception of this mind—present experience verifies and what nothing short of the totality of pertinent experience would verify.

We are now in position to approach the heart of the difficulty about the "givenness" of mind. Two elements have been distinguished in the cognitive experience; the given, which is characterized by our inability to remove or alter it merely by an activity

*"Chance, Love, and Logic," p. 45.

of thought, and a construction or interpretation which is attributed to the activity of mind. But this mind must be identifiable through some sort of datum of experience and must have its meaning in the empirical in general.

The activity of mind is evidenced, first, in the *feeling* of such activity. We should most of us have difficulty in describing this feeling, because we are normally inattentive to those correlates of it which can be stated otherwise than in terms of its effects outside the body. Thus we may be quite unable to say whether what we call the feeling of thinking is a feeling of innervation or certain specific conations or only a warmth of the jaw. But though we are not here concerned with the psychological description of the thought process, it may be well to point out that the *possibility* of such description, or even of the problem, depends upon the identification *first* of that whose correlations, or "description" or "analysis," is to be given. If, then, the traditional difficulty of this psychological problem should tempt any one to deny the existence of any mental phenomenon truly describable as thinking, it may be that he commits a fallacy of oversophistication, and is looking under the table for what is on it. Let him describe what happens when we *think* we think, and if his description is a true one, then what he describes is what *ought* to be called thinking. But whoever should be unacquainted with the *feeling* of thinking would automatically be precluded from attaching any meaning to the term at all.

The *effect* of thinking, we learn as we learn the effect of flexing our muscles or of any other activity. When I interpret this thing in my hand as "a cylinder," its shape forthwith stands out in the field of attention and other aspects of it relatively fall away; the relation of it to one set of other things (seen or imaged) rise before me, and other such relations may lapse. The image of it rolling off my desk may come into consciousness, whereas the memory of paying money on receiving it probably will not. I learn that what is thus classed under the head of construction or interpretation is due to my activity much as I learn that the shape of these scratches on the paper is due to my activity. If I purpose to write, the scratches come; if I purpose to wait until I am clearer what I want to say, then for a time no more scratches. In general, I learn my own activity through the correlation between certain directly observable feelings, classed by common sense as desire, interest, purpose, etc., and certain externally observable happenings. (These feelings are as much given items of experience as the feeling of presented red or soft. The correlation of them with such further items as the externally observable happenings is not, in the same sense, given but is a generalization the truth of which we learn by an induction from many such experiences. The feelings are conceived or *named*, as things in general are conceived and named, in the light of such learned stable relationships. Thus such a category as "purpose" or even "attention" may be psychologically inept, because it may be the case that a correlation between these feelings and sufficiently specific or fundamental neuroses is difficulty or impossible to discover. But if this should be so, still it would be no criticism of common sense nor of the use of such categories in epistemology, because both common sense and the analysis of cognition are relatively little concerned with brain and nervous processes, or even with those relatively slight and subtle bodily happenings frequently connoted in psychology by "behavior." For example, I am familiar with the feeling of intending to write. The correlation between this and the scratches on the paper is likewise familiar. But I do not know what muscles I use when I write, to say nothing of intervening processes less easily observed. Nor does

an interest in epistemology dictate that I should become specially interested in them.)

In the course of experience, I learn the correlation which exists between such feelings as attending,
concentrating on a given item, being interested, and
the further associations or configurations which
then accrue or stand out in consciousness. If it be
asked, "How do I know that it is the *mind* to which
such characteristic alterations are due?" the answer is that I learn what is due to the mind by the
difference which it makes if I refuse to attend or
am differently interested in the given. For the rest,
the answer is indicated by the above observations
concerning the relation between the phenomena explained and that which they are explained as "due
to." What I *mean* by the mind is partially revealed
in just such feelings of purpose, desire, interest, and
the like, and these other alterations in the process of experience which are attendant upon them.
Whether this mind is an immaterial agent, or a
Democritean complexus of smooth round atoms, is
simply a further question with which we are not
here concerned. "The mind" in general includes very
many other kinds of phenomena beside those of cognition. To characterize the mind as a whole is a
metaphysical problem of the first magnitude. But
on any metaphysical account which should be even
conceivably correct, what we mean by mind must
be just what is revealed in the totality of those
phenomena which are *ascribed to* mind. To try to
find the mind in any other sense, is the counterpart
of the fallacy of attempting to discover the substance of the physical object apart from all its
qualities, relations, and effects. What is meant by
"the activity of thinking" is precisely such correlation between attending, reflecting, etc., and those
alterations of context of the thing attended which
experience shows will ordinarily and normally be
induced by these. We learn the existence and nature

of thought, as we learn the nature and existence of
anything else, through the difference that it makes
in experience. The mind and its activity transcend,
of course, what is revealed in any *particular* case.
Ascribing the particular phenomenon to mind is an
interpretation; the significance of what is predicated is not exhausted by this phenomenon itself
but includes a relation of this to a multitude of
others, which the predication implicitly asserts to
be intrinsically possible of experience. Such a predication, being interpretive, can be mistaken in the
particular instance. But the totality of such *valid*
interpretations or attributions, exhibit the meaning of "the cognitive activity of mind."

I believe that we may now remove the last major
difficulty about our knowledge of the mind if we
observe that although the activity of mind is a
datum of experience, it is not the kind of datum to
which the word "given" has been applied in the preceding. A comparison may be helpful here. It is a
datum of experience that I can move my arm, or
that I can twitch a certain muscle at will. But this
fact is something which I have learned; it represents a generalization from experience, not the mere
givenness of the twitch. This fact or generalization
is the *correlation* between the twitch and my intention. That this correlation exists, is a datum of experience—an unalterable fact—but this general or
stable fact is not given with the twitch. It is because
of this reliable correlation, which I have learned,
that I call the muscle-twitch something that I *do*.

Similarly, the ascription of certain phases of the
cognitive experience, here called "interpretation," to
the mind, represents the empirical generalization
that between this element in experience and our attitudes of attending and reflecting there is a reliable
correlation. The existence of this correlation is an
absolute datum; but it is not the kind of datum
which "given" is defined to mean. This datum is the

fact *that* when we thus think, then certain contexts
of the thing thought about accrue, in ways in which
they do not accrue when we think to some different
purpose or fail to attend or reflect. When I think
this in my hand as "cylinder," the image of rolling
adds itself: when I think it as "a poor buy," or
when I am thinking what I want to write and so
ignore this item in my field of vision, the image of
rolling is absent. This image, taken by itself, would
be homogeneous with "the given," just as a voluntary
muscle-twitch, by itself, is homogeneous with an in-
voluntary twitch. But the one twitch—as I have
learned—is correlated with my intention, while the
other is independent of it. Similarly, the visual pattern of the pen in my hand and the image of it rolling are both data of experience, under certain circumstances. But it is the circumstances which matter. Whether I choose to find this visual pattern as
it now is or some other shape, it remains just this.
That item answers to the criterion of givenness: it
is independent of my attitude of thought. But the
accrual or non-accrual of the image of rolling and
other such context is—as I have also learned—*not*
thus independent, but is correlated with my attitude
of thought. This context, then, answers to the criterion of construction or interpretation, of being
"due to the mind." To say that the activity of mind
is "given," would thus be subtly incorrect. But to
say that the activity of mind is something known
through certain data of experience—data which
are in one sense homogeneous with those designated
as "given"—is no paradox but, I should suppose, a
more or less obvious fact. The mind, as known, represents our interpretation of such data; their projected relation to a multitude of other such instances
and to further experience which we take to be intrinsically possible.

The paradox of mind knowing itself is merely one
of language. If it appears to be comparable to the

puppy. trying to turn around fast enough to catch his own tail, that is because it is falsely supposed that the thing to be known is identical with this act of knowing. The mind which is known transcends the momentary knowing just as the external object known transcends its instantaneous phenomenal appearance. I know my mind by means of generalization from certain phases and aspects of past experience which are, by construction, added as context to similar phases of my present experience; just as I know the object by means of generalization from past experience which, by interpretation, is added as context to the present phenomenal appearance of it. And that present datum of experience which is interpreted as "activity of thought" is just as objective and intrinsically observable a kind of datum as is the phenomenal appearance of an external object.

The mind—and particularly its purpose and activity—is, of course, ultimately mysterious, just as concentration upon the presentation of the starry heaven reveals it as something ultimately mysterious, when all those prosaic and familiar correlations of this and that, which constitute its explanation, are shorn away, and we stand before it in its pristine glory. But the mind is mysterious in no specially different sense than this one in which reality altogether is ultimately mysterious.

The conception of any esoteric or peculiar type of knowledge by which we grasp the nature of our own minds, is both implausible and unnecessary. That the mind is at once that to which interpretation of the given in experience is due, and something itself known by interpretation of certain characteristics or data of experience, is—as has often been observed—no more paradoxical than that we should be able to change our own position as well as the position of other things, or direct any other activity upon ourselves.

The feeling of paradox which may persist here is a legacy of the transcendentalist mode of thought. If mind be conceived as an ultimate reality, while that which results from the interpretation or construction by mind is conceived to have a merely apparent or lower order of existence, then obviously the real mind cannot know itself. It is for just this reason that the transcendentalist's elaborate story of the categorizing of experience by the mind is inconsistent with itself, since if this account of knowledge should be true it could not be known to be true. Similarly if what is "known as" an interpretation by the mind is created by or "constituted" by that interpretation, then the mind cannot know itself, since we can hardly imagine what we should mean by saying that it created itself or constituted itself. Fichte, of course, is driven to just this desperate strait; the mind "posits itself, and this is the first act of positing." Thus mind becomes the ultimate and hopelessly esoteric mystery.

In any discussion of mind in the theory of knowledge, it is particularly desirable to observe that there are two characteristic modes of "explanation" —by the *ratio essendi* and by the *ratio cognoscendi* —and that these two run in opposite directions. In the case of the external object, this is clear enough and prosaic enough. The *ratio essendi* of the sense-data is the presence of the real object; and the *ratio cognoscendi* of the object is the sense-data themselves. Likewise in the case of the mind; the real mind is the *ratio essendi* (the cause of) the interpretational or "formal" aspects of cognitive experience, and these aspects are themselves the *ratio cognoscendi* (the clue to) the cognizing mind. The case is not fundamentally different than for real things and their appearances or phenomenal effects in general. The star is the cause of the light and the light is evidence of the star; the electron is cause of the motion of the oil-droplet and this motion is evidence of the electron. At the limit, the nature of the real cause coincides with the totality of its conceivably experienceable effects. But this does not remove the disparity between the real nature of the cause and the presently observed and meager revelation of it. Nor does it invalidate the different significance of the two opposed directions which our characteristic modes of understanding may take. The causal or "cosmic" explanation, of science and common sense, runs from cause to effect, from hypostatized thing to observable evidence. The analysis and verification of knowledge runs from effect to cause, from evidence to the thing evidenced. Perhaps it needs to be emphasized that one type of explanation or analysis, satisfying certain purposes, does not exclude or make superfluous other types of explanation, instigated by a different interest or made from some other point of view—that one analysis may be wholly true without being the whole of the truth.

Epistemological investigation is, naturally, by way of the *ratio cognoscendi:* that is its peculiar task. Those "theories of knowledge" which reverse the direction of explanation and give a causal, natural-scientific account, merely substitute a more or less uncritical and psychological methodology, based upon dubious assumptions, for their proper business.

Transcendentalism is, in general, the result of the opposite fallacy of attempting to base everything on the theory of knowledge. It tries to suppress, as superfluous or merely secondary, all natural-scientific explanation of those phenomena of which it takes cognizance, and to substitute for it an analysis of our *knowledge* of these phemonena. Thus it ends by identifying cognition and creation, by affirming that there is no *ratio essendi* save the *ratio cognoscendi*, the content of knowledge or the mind. The characteristic result is the reduction of the reality which appears to the appearance itself, and the elevation of the mind above appearance to a realm in which it is not knowable as other things are known.

THE APPLICABILITY OF ABSTRACT CONCEPTUAL SYSTEMS TO EXPERIENCE

There is one problem about the application of abstract conceptual systems to experience, not mentioned in Chapter IX, which merits a little attention. That is the question: How far does the character of given experience determine the applicability or inapplicability of concepts, when these concepts are first envisaged as abstract patterns of purely logical relations? In the first place, it is obvious that if we take a conceptual system completely in the abstract, as is done in the case of pure mathematics, there is no indication in the system itself of its applicability or inapplicability to anything. It may be remarked, however, that the very fact of its being developed at all is evidence of its applicability to *something*. I do not mean by this that such systems of mathematics originate as applied or empirical truth, and are later abstracted from such application. That is true, in general, though there are such exceptions as quaternions and the non-Euclidean geometries. What I mean is, that whether "imageless thought" is psychologically possible at all or not, no human being has, or ever will have, logical powers sufficient to enable him to elaborate the analysis of concepts in systematic fashion without reliance upon imagery. If the mathematical system applies to nothing else, it will apply to a set of distinguishable arrangements of symbols used according to certain rules. This is a relatively trivial application to experience, but it *is* an application to something empirical nevertheless. In fact, we might well ask if the designation "abstract" as applied to

mathematics is not a figure of speech, since no system is to be discovered, in the mathematician's mind
or elsewhere, in complete isolation from denotations.
The point is, however, that such denotations may be
"accidental"; and there is *no* such denotation from
which the system cannot be separated (and trans-
ferred to some other) while retaining its intended
identity as a system of abstract concepts.

The well-known practices of mathematics, in devising tests of consistency and independence, will at
once confirm in the reader's mind the fact that any
abstract conceptual system, however elaborate, will
be such that more than one empirical denotation
could be found for it. It represents a type of order
which is exhibited by more than one kind of empirical things. Since this is true of mathematical systems, which are relatively complex, it is fairly
evident without further corroboration that it will
also be true of concepts in general.

It is not quite so clear whether the *same* empirical
content may be denoted by *different* conceptual systems—different not in name simply but in that pattern of logical order which is the essence of the abstract concept. Out of hand, one might suppose that
this will not be possible unless—comparing two systems of concepts to be applied to the same content
—the application of one set of concepts neglects
certain items of the empirical which the other set includes in its denotation. In general, that is probably
true. If two conceptual interpretations should both
be applicable to the same content, the one will be
more abstract or general than the other, or will be
abstract in a different way. In *that* sense, the applicability of different concepts to the same empirical
thing or situation is a commonplace, since there is
nothing which can be named by one name which can
not also be named by some other—desk, furniture,
convenience, wood, antique, expensive, ugly! It is
more to the point to observe that different abstract

conceptual systems which are quite complex and are of the same order of structural complication may be applied to the same empirical content and include in their denotation the same empirical characters, though they are quite different conceptual systems as types of logical order. A good illustration is that kind of point-for-point correlation in denotation by which it may be proved that if Euclidean geometry is free from inconsistency, then some non-Euclidean system—say Riemann's—is so also. One may apply Riemannian plane geometry to the surface of a hemisphere by letting Riemannian "straight" denote Euclidean "great-circle cut orthogonally by a plane," etc. An even more illuminating illustration would be the systematic reinterpretation of Newtonian-Euclidean facts in the kinematics of relativity theory.

Envisaging the abstractly conceptual as a type of order or pure pattern of logical relationships, one might say that at least the given character of the empirical imposes certain limits upon the concepts which can be applied to it; that a conceptual system cannot be imposed if it requires distinction where no distinction in the given can be marked, or relation where no conjunction in the given can be found. Such a statement would at least draw attention to an important consideration which seems to limit the *usefulness* of applying a conceptual interpretation to a given content. In general, a conceptual interpretation which makes distinctions or relations where, in experience, none are to be discovered, will be a poor intellectual instrument for dealing with that phenomenal content. And yet, there is abundant evidence that we not only can but do apply concepts to the given where this involves making distinctions and relations which empirically cannot be discovered. Not only that, but often such interpretation serves a useful purpose and is highly scientific. For instance, the array of color-qualities is interpreted as a continuum, by correlation with vibration-frequencies, etc., although the directly discriminable color-qualities are certainly neither infinite in number nor such that between any two another can be found. The same is true of pitches; and exactly this procedure is frequent in the scientific interpretation of sense-qualities. In fact, one might say that arrangement in a one-, two-, or *n*-dimensional continuum is *the* scientific way of attacking all sorts of areas of experience, though *no* type of the empirical, as given, is genuinely continuous in the sense required by such mathematico-scientific analysis. Absolutely never is it capable of direct differentiation into the infinity of distinct gradations which characterize the order of the mathematical continuum. It is for this reason (amongst others) that Bergson repudiates such scientific interpretation as misrepresentative of reality. And Professor Whitehead, by his "method of extensive abstraction," has shown us how situations of this sort can (ideally) be reinterpreted so as to disclose the order which is conceptually required as genuinely present, not as an order of the directly given but as an order of our own *ways of ordering* it. In fact, although consideration of space and of the reader's interest forbid extended illustration, a little attention to scientific procedure makes it clear that one could pile Ossa upon Pelion of evidence that conceptual systems may usefully and validly be applied to given content although they involve making distinctions which are not given and establishing relations where none are found.

To the question, "What abstract concepts or systems could be applied to what given content?" the only answer which seems possible is: It is unsafe to say that *any* concept *could not* be applied to *any* empirical content. In this, as in other respects, it is hazardous to set bounds to human ingenuity, or even to delimit a priori what could be made useful.

To the question, "What will determine such application?" the answer seems to be: Complex considerations, in which the purposes to be served, the type of order of the concepts, and the general character of the given, will all be important, but in which, apparently, no one of these factors by itself is capable of being decisive. This, as it seems to me, but serves to emphasize the fact that the conceptual interpretation of experience is, at bottom, something concerning which rationalistic accounts and empiricistic theories are, in their opposite ways, both false, and the pragmatic is the true one.

APPENDIX F

THE LOGICAL CORRELATES OF THE A
PRIORI AND THE A POSTERIORI

The theory of the a priori set forth in Chapter VIII contains two main theses: (1) All a priori truths are definitive; they explicate criteria of classification, including the criteria of reality in its various categories; and conversely, all criteria of reality are a priori and independent of experience because they concern the classification or interpretation of empirical given content and do not indicate or determine that content itself. (2) The choice of concepts and systems of such for application to experience is pragmatically determined.

Another way of expressing the first of these two would be to say that a priori propositions coincide with the class of truths which are analytically determined and with propositions true in intension; what is a posteriori coincides with the logically synthetic and with propositions true in extension. The equivalence of the a priori, the analytic, and the intensional, on the one hand, of the a posteriori, the synthetic, and the extensional, on the other, has frequently been denied. Failure to observe these equivalences has led to extreme confusion in logic, much of which persists at the present time. The most important topic in this connection would be the meaning of implication and the nature of inference. But examination of that question would of necessity be too long and complex for inclusion here. What can be offered in brief space is a sketch of the distinction between propositions in intension and in extension.

433

The a priori proposition and the empirical generalization are usually indistinguishable by their form. Both are universal in intent, and are normally expressed by an "all" proposition or by one in which the "all" though unexpressed is obviously understood. The difference between these two is that between the intensional and the extensional "all." If I say, "Parrots are birds," I am correctly understood as meaning that any creature not a bird could not be a parrot. But if I assert, "Parrots have a raucous cry," I should not be correctly interpreted if I were taken to mean that a bird with a melodious note could not belong to the genus "parrot." The first proposition is a priori; the second, an empirical generalization.

The difference between the two may be expressed in various equivalent ways. The first explicates the intension or essence of the subject-term "parrot"; the second asserts only the inclusion of the class of actually existing creatures which come under the definition of "parrot" in another class, "creatures with a raucous cry." The first expresses in the predicate something logically contained in the subject; the subject-concept implies the predicate-concept. The second states a factual connection of two classes of objects. The first can be transformed into a strict hypothetical proposition, "For any X you please, if X is a parrot, then necessarily X is a bird." But if we similarly transform the second, "If X is a parrot, then X has a raucous cry," we must recognize that we have here a different meaning of "If . . ., then . . ."; that it does not state a logically necessary but only a material or factual relation—what is called by Mr. Russell a "formal implication," which holds only of the materially existent, not of the all-possible. (Incidentally, this name is highly inappropriate.) Finally, we can exhibit this difference in unambiguous and decisive fashion if we express the meaning of each of these propositions as a negation. The first means, "A parrot which is not a bird is logically inconceivable"; the second means only, "A parrot without a raucous cry does not exist." Propositions in intension concern what is possible, impossible, or necessary; an affirmative universal in intension states a necessity and negates a possibility. Propositions in extension concern only what does or does not exist. It is obvious that a universal in intension implies the corresponding universal in extension: what is impossible cannot exist. But the reverse does not hold. Knowledge a priori is knowledge applicable to existence; but knowledge of the existent merely as such is not a priori.

The significance of the theory of the a priori here presented may be brought out by considering the different ground of our knowledge in these two cases. We know that all parrots are birds without any extended examination of parrots, or without any experience of them at all, provided only we are clear about the concept which the term expresses. A parrot which is not a bird is impossible because no matter what characteristics any living creature might present, if it lacked the essential properties of a bird it would not properly be classifiable as a parrot. This a priori knowledge of parrots does not preclude the existence of any imaginable creature or limit in any way the possibilities of future experience. Living creatures not yet discovered, or not yet evolved, may be anything you please; but they cannot be parrots if they are not birds. It is for this reason and—as is here maintained—for this reason alone, that the proposition can be known true a priori. The illustration chosen is trivial; but it will nevertheless be typical provided only we remember that the distinction of real from unreal is a classification, and that what is designated as "unreal" as well as the "real" is given in experience. Knowledge a priori is knowledge of our own concepts. It is also knowledge of reality in the sense that certain kinds of realities must exhibit certain categorial characteristics; their failure to do so rules them out of the category in question.

Since adequate examination of the distinction between propositions in intension and propositions in extension is nowhere to be found in the literature of logic, it may be of assistance to present here briefly the application of this distinction to the traditional forms.

The universal "All X is Y" in intension means, "If anything is an X, then necessarily it is a Y; all *possible* X's are Y's." The universal in extension means, "All *actual* X's are Y's." It is particularly illuminating to consider the special case in which no X's exist. Contrast "All trespassers on this property are liable to arrest" with "All trespassers on this property are minors." Suppose that nobody trespasses. The truth of the former is unaffected. If certain conditions designated by law have been met, trespass *implies* liability to arrest. The latter proposition, one might say, becomes insignificant. But every proposition ought to be true or false under all circumstances; and logicians have had to be precise about this matter because of certain problems, some of which will be mentioned in what follows. According to the dictum now commonly accepted, if nobody trespasses, then the proposition, "All trespassers are Y" is true, whatever Y may be; or in general, if the subject-term denotes an empty class, every universal proposition about that subject is true *in extension*. (Many logicians neglect the distinction of extension and intension, and so apply this dictum to *all* universal propositions, with consequent difficulties to their theories.) If nobody trespasses, then *in extension* any proposition whatever is true about all trespassers; all the trespassers that *exist* are minors, red devils, pink elephants, or what you will.

The case of the universal negative is somewhat

more obvious. In intension, "No X is Y" means,
"The concept X excludes the concept Y; no possible X is a Y." In extension, it means simply, "The
class of things which are both X and Y is an empty
class; no such exist." Thus if nobody trespasses,
"No trespasser is liable to arrest" would be true if
meant in extension; but it is false in intension. In
extension, no trespasser is anything, because there
are none. In intension, the question is whether the
concept of trespass excludes liability to arrest, and
that question is entirely independent of the existence or non-existence of trespassers.

Though the distinction of extensional from intensional meanings commonly passes unnoticed, it may
be remarked for universal propositions in the case of
definitions and legal principles. For particular
propsitions, the distinction is even less familiar. But
the ground of it is the same. In extension, "Some X
is Y" means, "Members of the class 'both X and Y'
exist." In intension it means the contradiction of the
universal negative, "The concept X does not exclude the concept Y; the logical species 'both X and
Y' is possible or conceivable." Similarly, the particular negative, "Some X is not Y," means in extension, "Members of the class 'X but not Y' exist";
while in intension it means, "The concept X does not
imply the concept Y; the logical species 'X but not
Y' is conceivable."

Though as has been said, particular propositions
which are intensional in meaning are relatively infrequent, still examples may be found. For instance,
if a professor of jurisprudence should say, "Some
grounds of civil suit are torts and some are not,"
and should be asked for demonstration, he might
give it without any recourse to actual breaches of
contract, conspiracies to defraud, etc., merely by
pointing out the implications of legal concepts. His
meaning is that, under the law, there are two species
of possible action for which a remedy may be sought

by civil suit. Or again, he might prove his point by
purely hypothetical cases; that they never occurred
would be irrelevant.

The case of the singular proposition is especially
interesting. Mr. Russell has propounded the theory
that a proposition about a singular subject (described by some phrase) is true if and only if (1)
everything to which the subject-term applies has
the predicated character, (2) the subject-term applies to one existent thing, (3) it applies to only
one. This has gained wide currency among logicians.
It is a doubtful interpretation of the singular proposition in extension, and a perfectly impossible one
of the singular in intension.

The doubt as to its correctness in extension is unimportant for us but may be noted in passing.* If
a boastful friend asserts, "All the fish I catch will
be big ones," we might rally him by rejoining, "All
the fish you catch you can put in your eye." This
answer, in the form of a universal proposition, is
meant in extension. The point of making it is that
we assert, by implication, that he will not catch any
fish, because otherwise our proposition would be
false. Thus we illustrate the fact that common-sense
recognizes that the universal proposition in extension is true when the subject denotes an empty class.
But if our friend should say instead, "The first fish
I catch will be a big one" (a singular proposition),
we might similarly rejoin, "The first fish you catch
will be a whale," meaning that this is true because
there will not be any first fish. Thus if the interpretation of the singular proposition is to accord
with *some* current usages, it must, like the universal, be *true* whenever the subject denotes the non-
existent, instead of false as Mr. Russell's theory requires.

The singular in intension, while infrequent, is of
pretty clear interpretation. If I say, "The President

*I mention only one ground of doubt; others have been put forward.

of the United States must be native-born," my obvious meaning is to assert that the concept "President," as delimited by the Constitution, has this implication. If it should happen that the incumbent of the office had died and no successor had been inducted, that would be irrelevant to my intended assertion. Similarly, a lawyer might state, "The residuary legatee under this will, is entitled to . . .," meaning to explicate the terms of the will under the law, and meaning nothing whatever about the existence or non-existence of a party answering to the designation of residuary legatee under the will. The singular proposition in intension, like the universal, states that the subject-concept implies (or does not imply) the predicate. The difference is only that the subject of the singular in intension is a concept such that it applies to one, and to only one, possible object.

Thus, throughout, the proposition in intension is true if it correctly states a relation of concepts, and is entirely independent of considerations of existence or non-existence. Propositions in extension, on the contrary, are dependent on facts of existence. Thus propositions in intension are analytically determinable and a priori; propositions in extension are synthetic and a posteriori.

In conclusion, some of the logical difficulties which traditional logical precepts encounter in the case of extensional propositions the subject of which denotes an empty class, may be briefly noted. According to tradition, the relations of the four typical propositions, (A) "All X is Y," (E) "No X is Y," (I) "Some X is Y," and (O) "Some X is not Y," are as follows: A and E are contraries, that is, such that they cannot both be true but both may be false. I and O are subcontraries, that is, they may both be true but cannot both be false. A and O, E and I, are contradictories, that is, they cannot both be true and cannot both be false. *I* follows from *A*, and *O* from *E*, but the reverse implications do not hold. Let "*X* is *Y*" be "trespassers will be prosecuted," and suppose nobody trespasses. "Some trespassers will be prosecuted" and "Some trespassers will not be prosecuted" are then both false. If it should be said that "All trespassers will be prosecuted" is false because there are none, then *A* and *O* will not be contradictory, since *O* is false also. *E* is obviously true; hence *E* and *I* may be contradictory. But *O* does not follow from *E*, since *E* is true but *O* is false. For uniformity of relation between universals and particulars, it is necessary to accept the current dictum, that *A*, like *E*, is true when the subject denotes an empty class. This makes *A* and *O*, *E* and *I*, contradictory. But *A* and *E* are not contrary, being both true; *I* and *O* are not subcontrary, both being false. And *I* does not follow from *A*, nor *O* from *E*, because *A* and *E* are both true, *I* and *O* both false.

The traditional relations of the "square of opposition" hold of propositions in intension, that is, of propositions about the all-possible. The relation of contradiction holds in extension on the current interpretation of *A* as always true when the subject denotes an empty class. The other traditional relations all fail concerning propositions in extension.

Traditional logical doctrines will uniformly be found to have been worked out for intension, and to be commonly applied as if all propositions stated relations of intension. Current revisions of tradition will all too frequently be found to have been formulated with an opposite oversight—as if all propositions had their meaning in extension.

INDEX

INDEX

(Where references under an entry are numerous, the most important or decisive is sometimes indicated by "esp.")

443

CATALOG OF DOVER BOOKS

The more difficult books are indicated by an asterisk (*)

Books Explaining Science and Mathematics

WHAT IS SCIENCE?, N. Campbell. The role of experiment and measurement, the function of mathematics, the nature of scientific laws, the difference between laws and theories, the limitations of science, and many similarly provocative topics are treated clearly and without technicalities by an eminent scientist. "Still an excellent introduction to scientific philosophy," H. Margenau in PHYSICS TODAY. "A first-rate primer . . . deserves a wide audience," SCIENTIFIC AMERICAN. 192pp. 5⅜ x 8.   S43 Paperbound **$1.25**

THE NATURE OF PHYSICAL THEORY, P. W. Bridgman. A Nobel Laureate's clear, non-technical lectures on difficulties and paradoxes connected with frontier research on the physical sciences. Concerned with such central concepts as thought, logic, mathematics, relativity, probability, wave mechanics, etc. he analyzes the contributions of such men as Newton, Einstein, Bohr, Heisenberg, and many others. "Lucid and entertaining . . . recommended to anyone who wants to get some insight into current philosophies of science," THE NEW PHILOSOPHY. Index. xi + 138pp. 5⅜ x 8.   S33 Paperbound **$1.25**

EXPERIMENT AND THEORY IN PHYSICS, Max Born. A Nobel Laureate examines the nature of experiment and theory in theoretical physics and analyzes the advances made by the great physicists of our day: Heisenberg, Einstein, Bohr, Planck, Dirac, and others. The actual process of creation is detailed step-by-step by one who participated. A fine examination of the scientific method at work. 44pp. 5⅜ x 8.   S308 Paperbound **75¢**

THE PSYCHOLOGY OF INVENTION IN THE MATHEMATICAL FIELD, J. Hadamard. The reports of such men as Descartes, Pascal, Einstein, Poincaré, and others are considered in this investigation of the method of idea-creation in mathematics and other sciences and the thinking process in general. How do ideas originate? What is the role of the unconscious? What is Poincaré's forgetting hypothesis? are some of the fascinating questions treated. A penetrating analysis of Einstein's thought processes concludes the book. xiii + 145pp. 5⅜ x 8.   T107 Paperbound **$1.25**

THE NATURE OF LIGHT AND COLOUR IN THE OPEN AIR, M. Minnaert. Why are shadows sometimes blue, sometimes green, or other colors depending on the light and surroundings? What causes mirages? Why do multiple suns and moons appear in the sky? Professor Minnaert explains these unusual phenomena and hundreds of others in simple, easy-to-understand terms based on optical laws and the properties of light and color. No mathematics is required but artists, scientists, students, and everyone fascinated by these "tricks" of nature will find thousands of useful and amazing pieces of information. Hundreds of observational experiments are suggested which require no special equipment. 200 illustrations; 42 photos. xvi + 362pp. 5⅜ x 8.   T196 Paperbound **$1.95**

THE UNIVERSE OF LIGHT, W. Bragg. Sir William Bragg, Nobel Laureate and great modern physicist, is also well known for his powers of clear exposition. Here he analyzes all aspects of light for the layman: lenses, reflection, refraction, the optics of vision, x-rays, the photoelectric effect, etc. He tells you what causes the color of spectra, rainbows, and soap bubbles, how magic mirrors work, and much more. Dozens of simple experiments are described. Preface. Index. 199 line drawings and photographs, including 2 full-page color plates. x + 283pp. 5⅜ x 8.   T538 Paperbound **$1.85**

SOAP-BUBBLES: THEIR COLOURS AND THE FORCES THAT MOULD THEM, C. V. Boys. For continuing popularity and validity as scientific primer, few books can match this volume of easily-followed experiments, explanations. Lucid exposition of complexities of liquid films, surface tension and related phenomena, bubbles' reaction to heat, motion, music, magnetic fields. Experiments with capillary attraction, soap bubbles on frames, composite bubbles, liquid cylinders and jets, bubbles other than soap, etc. Wonderful introduction to scientific method, natural laws that have many ramifications in areas of modern physics. Only complete edition in print. New Introduction by S. Z. Lewin, New York University. 83 illustrations; 1 full-page color plate. xii + 190pp. 5⅜ x 8½.   T542 Paperbound **95¢**

CATALOGUE OF DOVER BOOKS

*THE EVOLUTION OF SCIENTIFIC THOUGHT FROM NEWTON TO EINSTEIN, A. d'Abro. A detailed account of the evolution of classical physics into modern relativistic theory and the concommitant changes in scientific methodology. The breakdown of classical physics in the face of non-Euclidean geometry and the electromagnetic equations is carefully discussed and then an exhaustive analysis of Einstein's special and general theories of relativity and their implications is given. Newton, Riemann, Weyl, Lorentz, Planck, Maxwell, and many others are considered. A non-technical explanation of space, time, electromagnetic waves, etc. as understood today. "Model of semi-popular exposition," NEW REPUBLIC. 21 diagrams. 482pp. 5⅜ x 8.
T2 Paperbound **$2.00**

EINSTEIN'S THEORY OF RELATIVITY, Max Born. Nobel Laureate explains Einstein's special and general theories of relativity, beginning with a thorough review of classical physics in simple, non-technical language. Exposition of Einstein's work discusses concept of simultaneity, kinematics, relativity of arbitrary motions, the space-time continuum, geometry of curved surfaces, etc., steering middle course between vague popularizations and complex scientific presentations. 1962 edition revised by author takes into account latest findings, predictions of theory and implications for cosmology, indicates what is being sought in unified field theory. Mathematics very elementary, illustrative diagrams and experiments informative but simple. Revised 1962 edition. Revised by Max Born, assisted by Gunther Leibfried and Walter Biem. Index. 143 illustrations. vii + 376pp. 5⅜ x 8.
S769 Paperbound **$2.00**

PHILOSOPHY AND THE PHYSICISTS, L. Susan Stebbing. A philosopher examines the philosophical aspects of modern science, in terms of a lively critical attack on the ideas of Jeans and Eddington. Such basic questions are treated as the task of science, causality, determinism, probability, consciousness, the relation of the world of physics to the world of everyday experience. The author probes the concepts of man's smallness before an inscrutable universe, the tendency to idealize mathematical construction, unpredictability theorems and human freedom, the supposed opposition between 19th century determinism and modern science, and many others. Introduces many thought-stimulating ideas about the implications of modern physical concepts. xvi + 295pp. 5⅜ x 8.
T480 Paperbound **$1.65**

THE RESTLESS UNIVERSE, Max Born. A remarkably lucid account by a Nobel Laureate of recent theories of wave mechanics, behavior of gases, electrons and ions, waves and particles, electronic structure of the atom, nuclear physics, and similar topics. "Much more thorough and deeper than most attempts . . . easy and delightful," CHEMICAL AND ENGINEERING NEWS. Special feature: 7 animated sequences of 60 figures each showing such phenomena as gas molecules in motion, the scattering of alpha particles, etc. 11 full-page plates of photographs. Total of nearly 600 illustrations. 351pp. 6⅛ x 9¼.
T412 Paperbound **$2.00**

THE COMMON SENSE OF THE EXACT SCIENCES, W. K. Clifford. For 70 years a guide to the basic concepts of scientific and mathematical thought. Acclaimed by scientists and laymen alike, it offers a wonderful insight into concepts such as the extension of meaning of symbols, characteristics of surface boundaries, properties of plane figures, measurement of quantities, vectors, the nature of position, bending of space, motion, mass and force, and many others. Prefaces by Bertrand Russell and Karl Pearson. Critical introduction by James Newman. 130 figures. 249pp. 5⅜ x 8.
T61 Paperbound **$1.60**

MATTER AND LIGHT, THE NEW PHYSICS, Louis de Broglie. Non-technical explanations by a Nobel Laureate of electro-magnetic theory, relativity, matter, light and radiation, wave mechanics, quantum physics, philosophy of science, and similar topics. This is one of the simplest yet most accurate introductions to the work of men like Planck, Einstein, Bohr, and others. Only 2 of the 21 chapters require a knowledge of mathematics. 300pp. 5⅜ x 8.
T35 Paperbound **$1.75**

SCIENCE, THEORY AND MAN, Erwin Schrödinger. This is a complete and unabridged reissue of SCIENCE AND THE HUMAN TEMPERAMENT plus an additional essay: "What Is an Elementary Particle?" Nobel Laureate Schrödinger discusses such topics as nature of scientific method, tne nature of science, chance and determinism, science and society, conceptual models for physical entities, elementary particles and wave mechanics. Presentation is popular and may be followed by most people with little or no scientific training. "Fine practical preparation for a time when laws of nature, human institutions . . . are undergoing a critical examination without parallel," Waldemar Kaempffert, N. Y. TIMES. 192pp. 5⅜ x 8.
T428 Paperbound **$1.35**

CONCERNING THE NATURE OF THINGS, Sir William Bragg. The Nobel Laureate physicist in his Royal Institute Christmas Lectures explains such diverse phenomena as the formation of crystals, how uranium is transmuted to lead, the way X-rays work, why a spinning ball travels in a curved path, the reason why bubbles bounce from each other, and many other scientific topics that are seldom explained in simple terms. No scientific background needed—book is easy enough that any intelligent adult or youngster can understand it. Unabridged. 32pp. of photos; 57 figures. xii + 232pp. 5⅜ x 8.
T31 Paperbound **$1.35**

*THE RISE OF THE NEW PHYSICS (formerly THE DECLINE OF MECHANISM), A. d'Abro. This authoritative and comprehensive 2 volume exposition is unique · in scientific publishing. Written for intelligent readers not familiar with higher mathematics, it is the only thorough explanation in non-technical language of modern mathematical-physical theory. Combining both history and exposition, it ranges from classical Newtonian concepts up through the electronic theories of Dirac and Heisenberg, the statistical mechanics of Fermi, and Einstein's relativity theories. "A must for anyone doing serious study in the physical sciences," J. OF FRANKLIN INST. 97 illustrations. 991pp. 2 volumes.
T3 Vol. 1, Paperbound **$2.00**
T4 Vol. 2, Paperbound **$2.00**

History of Science and Mathematics

THE STUDY OF THE HISTORY OF MATHEMATICS, THE STUDY OF THE HISTORY OF SCIENCE, G. Sarton. Two books bound as one. Each volume contains a long introduction to the methods and philosophy of each of these historical fields, covering the skills and sympathies of the historian, concepts of history of science, psychology of idea-creation, and the purpose of history of science. Prof. Sarton also provides more than 80 pages of classified bibliography. Complete and unabridged. Indexed. 10 illustrations. 188pp. 5⅜ x 8.   T240 Paperbound **$1.25**

A HISTORY OF PHYSICS, Florian Cajori, Ph.D. First written in 1899, thoroughly revised in 1929, this is still best entry into antecedents of modern theories. Precise non-mathematical discussion of ideas, theories, techniques, apparatus of each period from Greeks to 1920's, analyzing within each period basic topics of matter, mechanics, light, electricity and magnetism, sound, atomic theory, etc. Stress on modern developments, from early 19th century to present. Written with critical eye on historical development, significance. Provides most of needed historical background for student of physics. Reprint of second (1929) edition. Index. Bibliography in footnotes. 16 figures. xv + 424pp. 5⅜ x 8.   T970 Paperbound **$2.00**

A HISTORY OF ASTRONOMY FROM THALES TO KEPLER, J. L. E. Dreyer. Formerly titled A HISTORY OF PLANETARY SYSTEMS FROM THALES TO KEPLER. This is the only work in English which provides a detailed history of man's cosmological views from prehistoric times up through the Renaissance. It covers Egypt, Babylonia, early Greece, Alexandria, the Middle Ages, Copernicus, Tycho Brahe, Kepler, and many others. Epicycles and other complex theories of positional astronomy are explained in terms nearly everyone will find clear and easy to understand. "Standard reference on Greek astronomy and the Copernican revolution," SKY AND TELESCOPE. Bibliography. 21 diagrams. Index. xvii + 430pp. 5⅜ x 8.   S79 Paperbound **$1.98**

A SHORT HISTORY OF ASTRONOMY, A. Berry. A popular standard work for over 50 years, this thorough and accurate volume covers the science from primitive times to the end of the 19th century. After the Greeks and Middle Ages, individual chapters analyze Copernicus, Brahe, Galileo, Kepler, and Newton, and the mixed reception of their startling discoveries. Post-Newtonian achievements are then discussed in unusual detail: Halley, Bradley, Lagrange, Laplace, Herschel, Bessel, etc. 2 indexes. 104 illustrations, 9 portraits. xxxi + 440pp. 5⅜ x 8.   T210 Paperbound **$2.00**

PIONEERS OF SCIENCE, Sir Oliver Lodge. An authoritative, yet elementary history of science by a leading scientist and expositor. Concentrating on individuals—Copernicus, Brahe, Kepler, Galileo, Descartes, Newton, Laplace, Herschel, Lord Kelvin, and other scientists—the author presents their discoveries in historical order, adding biographical material on each man and full, specific explanations of their achievements. The full, clear discussions of the accomplishments of post-Newtonian astronomers are features seldom found in other books on the subject. Index. 120 illustrations. xv + 404pp. 5⅜ x 8.   T716 Paperbound **$1.65**

THE BIRTH AND DEVELOPMENT OF THE GEOLOGICAL SCIENCES, F. D. Adams. The most complete and thorough history of the earth sciences in print. Geological thought from earliest recorded times to the end of the 19th century—covers over 300 early thinkers and systems: fossils and hypothetical explanations of them, vulcanists vs. neptunists, figured stones and paleontology, generation of stones, and similar topics. 91 illustrations, including medieval, renaissance woodcuts, etc. 632 footnotes and bibliographic notes. Index. 511pp. 5⅜ x 8.   T5 Paperbound **$2.00**

THE STORY OF ALCHEMY AND EARLY CHEMISTRY, J. M. Stillman. "Add the blood of a red-haired man"—a recipe typical of the many quoted in this authoritative and readable history of the strange beliefs and practices of the alchemists. Concise studies of every leading figure in alchemy and early chemistry through Lavoisier, in this curious epic of superstition and true science, constructed from scores of rare and difficult Greek, Latin, German, and French texts. Foreword by S. W. Young. 246-item bibliography. Index. xiii + 566pp. 5⅜ x 8.   S628 Paperbound **$2.45**

HISTORY OF MATHEMATICS, D. E. Smith. Most comprehensive non-technical history of math in English. Discusses the lives and works of over a thousand major and minor figures, from Euclid to Descartes, Gauss, and Riemann. Vol. I: A chronological examination, from primitive concepts through Egypt, Babylonia, Greece, the Orient, Rome, the Middle Ages, the Renaissance, and up to 1900. Vol. 2: The development of ideas in specific fields and problems, up through elementary calculus. Two volumes, total of 510 illustrations, 1355pp. 5⅜ x 8. Set boxed in attractive container.   T429,430 Paperbound the set **$5.00**

Classics of Science

THE DIDEROT PICTORIAL ENCYCLOPEDIA OF TRADES AND INDUSTRY, MANUFACTURING AND THE TECHNICAL ARTS IN PLATES SELECTED FROM "L'ENCYCLOPEDIE OU DICTIONNAIRE RAISONNE DES SCIENCES, DES ARTS, ET DES METIERS" OF DENIS DIDEROT, edited with text by C. Gillispie. The first modern selection of plates from the high point of 18th century French engraving, Diderot's famous Encyclopedia. Over 2000 illustrations on 485 full page plates, most of them original size, illustrating the trades and industries of one of the most fascinating periods of modern history, 18th century France. These magnificent engravings provide an invaluable glimpse into the past for the student of early technology, a lively and accurate social document to students of cultures, an outstanding find to the lover of fine engravings. The plates teem with life, with men, women, and children performing all of the thousands of operations necessary to the trades before and during the early stages of the industrial revolution. Plates are in sequence, and show general operations, closeups of difficult operations, and details of complex machinery. Such important and interesting trades and industries are illustrated as sowing, harvesting, beekeeping, cheesemaking, operating windmills, milling flour, charcoal burning, tobacco processing, indigo, fishing, arts of war, salt extraction, mining, smelting iron, casting iron, steel, extracting mercury, zinc, sulphur, copper, etc., slating, tinning, silverplating, gilding, making gunpowder, cannons, bells, shoeing horses, tanning, papermaking, printing, dying, and more than 40 other categories. 920pp. 9 x 12. Heavy library cloth. T421 Two volume set **$18.50**

THE PRINCIPLES OF SCIENCE, A TREATISE ON LOGIC AND THE SCIENTIFIC METHOD, W. Stanley Jevons. Treating such topics as Inductive and Deductive Logic, the Theory of Number, Probability, and the Limits of Scientific Method, this milestone in the development of symbolic logic remains a stimulating contribution to the investigation of inferential validity in the natural and social sciences. It significantly advances Boole's logic, and describes a machine which is a foundation of modern electronic calculators. In his introduction, Ernest Nagel of Columbia University says, "(Jevons) . . . continues to be of interest as an attempt to articulate the logic of scientific inquiry." Index. liii + 786pp. 5⅜ x 8. S446 Paperbound **$2.98**

***DIALOGUES CONCERNING TWO NEW SCIENCES, Galileo Galilei.** A classic of experimental science which has had a profound and enduring influence on the entire history of mechanics and engineering. Galileo based this, his finest work, on 30 years of experimentation. It offers a fascinating and vivid exposition of dynamics, elasticity, sound, ballistics, strength of materials, and the scientific method. Translated by H. Crew and A. de Salvio. 126 diagrams. Index. xxi + 288pp. 5⅜ x 8. S99 Paperbound **$1.75**

DE MAGNETE, William Gilbert. This classic work on magnetism founded a new science. Gilbert was the first to use the word "electricity," to recognize mass as distinct from weight, to discover the effect of heat on magnetic bodies; invented an electroscope, differentiated between static electricity and magnetism, conceived of the earth as a magnet. Written by the first great experimental scientist, this lively work is valuable not only as an historical landmark, but as the delightfully easy-to-follow record of a perpetually searching, ingenious mind. Translated by P. F. Mottelay. 25 page biographical memoir. 90 fix. lix + 368pp. 5⅜ x 8. S470 Paperbound **$2.00**

***OPTICKS, Sir Isaac Newton.** An enormous storehouse of insights and discoveries on light, reflection, color, refraction, theories of wave and corpuscular propagation of light, optical apparatus, and mathematical devices which have recently been reevaluated in terms of modern physics and placed in the top-most ranks of Newton's work! Foreword by Albert Einstein. Preface by I. B. Cohen of Harvard U. 7 pages of portraits, facsimile pages, letters, etc. cxvi + 412pp. 5⅜ x 8. S205 Paperbound **$2.25**

A SURVEY OF PHYSICAL THEORY, M. Planck. Lucid essays on modern physics for the general reader by the Nobel Laureate and creator of the quantum revolution. Planck explains how the new concepts came into being; explores the clash between theories of mechanics, electro-dynamics, and thermodynamics; and traces the evolution of the concept of light through Newton, Huygens, Maxwell, and his own quantum theory, providing unparalleled insights into his development of this momentous modern concept. Bibliography. Index. vii + 121pp. 5⅜ x 8. S650 Paperbound **$1.15**

A SOURCE BOOK IN MATHEMATICS, D. E. Smith. English translations of the original papers that announced the great discoveries in mathematics from the Renaissance to the end of the 19th century: succinct selections from 125 different treatises and articles, most of them unavailable elsewhere in English—Newton, Leibniz, Pascal, Riemann, Bernoulli, etc. 24 articles trace developments in the field of number, 18 cover algebra, 36 are on geometry, and 13 on calculus. Biographical-historical introductions to each article. Two volume set. Index in each. Total of 115 illustrations. Total of xxviii + 742pp. 5⅜ x 8. S552 Vol I Paperbound **$1.85** / S553 Vol II Paperbound **$1.85** / The set, boxed **$3.50**

CATALOGUE OF DOVER BOOKS

*THE THIRTEEN BOOKS OF EUCLID'S ELEMENTS, edited by T. L. Heath. This is the complete EUCLID — the definitive edition of one of the greatest classics of the western world. Complete English translation of the Heiberg text with spurious Book XIV. Detailed 150-page introduction discusses aspects of Greek and medieval mathematics: Euclid, texts, commentators, etc. Paralleling the text is an elaborate critical exposition analyzing each definition, proposition, postulate, etc., and covering textual matters, mathematical analyses, refutations, extensions, etc. Unabridged reproduction of the Cambridge 2nd edition. 3 volumes. Total of 995 figures, 1426pp. 5⅜ x 8.   S88, 89, 90 — 3 vol. set, Paperbound **$6.00**

*THE GEOMETRY OF RENE DESCARTES. The great work which founded analytic geometry. The renowned Smith-Latham translation faced with the original French text containing all of Descartes' own diagrams! Contains: Problems the Construction of Which Requires Only Straight Lines and Circles; On the Nature of Curved Lines; On the Construction of Solid or Supersolid Problems. Notes. Diagrams. 258pp.   S68 Paperbound **$1.50**

*A PHILOSOPHICAL ESSAY ON PROBABILITIES, P. Laplace. Without recourse to any mathematics above grammar school, Laplace develops a philosophically, mathematically and historically classical exposition of the nature of probability: its functions and limitations, operations in practical affairs, calculations in games of chance, insurance, government, astronomy, and countless other fields. New introduction by E. T. Bell. viii + 196pp.   S166 Paperbound **$1.35**

DE RE METALLICA, Georgius Agricola. Written over 400 years ago, for 200 years the most authoritative first-hand account of the production of metals, translated in 1912 by former President Herbert Hoover and his wife, and today still one of the most beautiful and fascinating volumes ever produced in the history of science! 12 books, exhaustively annotated, give a wonderfully lucid and vivid picture of the history of mining, selection of sites, types of deposits, excavating pits, sinking shafts, ventilating, pumps, crushing machinery, assaying, smelting, refining metals, making salt, alum, nitre, glass, and many other topics. This definitive edition contains all 289 of the 16th century woodcuts which made the original an artistic masterpiece. It makes a superb gift for geologists, engineers, libraries, artists, historians, and everyone interested in science and early illustrative art. Biographical, historical introductions. Bibliography, survey of ancient authors. Indices. 289 illustrations. 672pp. 6¾ x 10¾. Deluxe library edition.   S6 Clothbound **$10.00**

GEOGRAPHICAL ESSAYS, W. M. Davis. Modern geography and geomorphology rest on the fundamental work of this scientist. His new concepts of earth-processes revolutionized science and his broad interpretation of the scope of geography created a deeper understanding of the interrelation of the landscape and the forces that mold it. This first inexpensive unabridged edition covers theory of geography, methods of advanced geographic teaching, descriptions of geographic areas, analyses of land-shaping processes, and much besides. Not only a factual and historical classic, it is still widely read for its reflections of modern scientific thought. Introduction. 130 figures. Index. vi + 777pp. 5⅜ x 8.
S383 Paperbound **$2.95**

CHARLES BABBAGE AND HIS CALCULATING ENGINES, edited by P. Morrison and E. Morrison. Friend of Darwin, Humboldt, and Laplace, Babbage was a leading pioneer in large-scale mathematical machines and a prophetic herald of modern operational research—true father of Harvard's relay computer Mark I. His Difference Engine and Analytical Engine were the first successful machines in the field. This volume contains a valuable introduction on his life and work; major excerpts from his fascinating autobiography, revealing his eccentric and unusual personality; and extensive selections from "Babbage's Calculating Engines," a compilation of hard-to-find journal articles, both by Babbage and by such eminent contributors as the Countess of Lovelace, L. F. Menabrea, and Dionysius Lardner. 11 illustrations. Appendix of miscellaneous papers. Index. Bibliography. xxxviii + 400pp. 5⅜ x 8.   T12 Paperbound **$2.00**

*THE WORKS OF ARCHIMEDES WITH THE METHOD OF ARCHIMEDES, edited by T. L. Heath. All the known works of the greatest mathematician of antiquity including the recently discovered METHOD OF ARCHIMEDES. This last is the only work we have which shows exactly how early mathematicians discovered their proofs before setting them down in their final perfection. A 186 page study by the eminent scholar Heath discusses Archimedes and the history of Greek mathematics. Bibliography. 563pp. 5⅜ x 8.   S9 Paperbound **$2.00**

Puzzles, Mathematical Recreations

SYMBOLIC LOGIC and THE GAME OF LOGIC, Lewis Carroll. "Symbolic Logic" is not concerned with modern symbolic logic, but is instead a collection of over 380 problems posed with charm and imagination, using the syllogism, and a fascinating diagrammatic method of drawing conclusions. In "The Game of Logic" Carroll's whimsical imagination devises a logical game played with 2 diagrams and counters (included) to manipulate hundreds of tricky syllogisms. The final section, "Hit or Miss" is a lagniappe of 101 additional puzzles in the delightful Carroll manner. Until this reprint edition, both of these books were rarities costing up to $15 each. Symbolic Logic: Index. xxxi + 199pp. The Game of Logic: 96pp. 2 vols. bound as one. 5⅜ x 8.   T492 Paperbound **$1.50**

PILLOW PROBLEMS and A TANGLED TALE, Lewis Carroll. One of the rarest of all Carroll's works, "Pillow Problems" contains 72 original math puzzles, all typically ingenious. Particularly fascinating are Carroll's answers which remain exactly as he thought them out, reflecting his actual mental process. The problems in "A Tangled Tale" are in story form, originally appearing as a monthly magazine serial. Carroll not only gives the solutions, but uses answers sent in by readers to discuss wrong approaches and misleading paths, and grades them for insight. Both of these books were rarities until this edition, "Pillow Problems" costing up to $25, and "A Tangled Tale" $15. Pillow Problems: Preface and Introduction by Lewis Carroll. xx + 109pp. A Tangled Tale: 6 illustrations. 152pp. Two vols. bound as one. 5⅜ x 8.   T493 Paperbound **$1.50**

AMUSEMENTS IN MATHEMATICS, Henry Ernest Dudeney. The foremost British originator of mathematical puzzles is always intriguing, witty, and paradoxical in this classic, one of the largest collections of mathematical amusements. More than 430 puzzles, problems, and paradoxes. Mazes and games, problems on number manipulation, unicursal and other route problems, puzzles on measuring, weighing, packing, age, kinship, chessboards, joiners', crossing river, plane figure dissection, and many others. Solutions. More than 450 illustrations. vii + 258pp. 5⅜ x 8.   T473 Paperbound **$1.25**

THE CANTERBURY PUZZLES, Henry Dudeney. Chaucer's pilgrims set one another problems in story form. Also Adventures of the Puzzle Club, the Strange Escape of the King's Jester, the Monks of Riddlewell, the Squire's Christmas Puzzle Party, and others. All puzzles are original, based on dissecting plane figures, arithmetic, algebra, elementary calculus and other branches of mathematics, and purely logical ingenuity. "The limit of ingenuity and intricacy," The Observer. Over 110 puzzles. Full Solutions. 150 illustrations. vii + 225pp. 5⅜ x 8.   T474 Paperbound **$1.25**

MATHEMATICAL EXCURSIONS, H. A. Merrill. Even if you hardly remember your high school math, you'll enjoy the 90 stimulating problems contained in this book and you will come to understand a great many mathematical principles with surprisingly little effort. Many useful shortcuts and diversions not generally known are included: division by inspection, Russian peasant multiplication, memory systems for pi, building odd and even magic squares, square roots by geometry, dyadic systems, and many more. Solutions to difficult problems. 50 illustrations. 145pp. 5⅜ x 8.   T350 Paperbound **$1.00**

MAGIC SQUARES AND CUBES, W. S. Andrews. Only book-length treatment in English, a thorough non-technical description and analysis. Here are nasik, overlapping, pandiagonal, serrated squares; magic circles, cubes, spheres, rhombuses. Try your hand at 4-dimensional magical figures! Much unusual folklore and tradition included. High school algebra is sufficient. 754 diagrams and illustrations. viii + 419pp. 5⅜ x 8.   T658 Paperbound **$1.85**

CALIBAN'S PROBLEM BOOK: MATHEMATICAL, INFERENTIAL AND CRYPTOGRAPHIC PUZZLES, H. Phillips (Caliban), S. T. Shovelton, G. S. Marshall. 105 ingenious problems by the greatest living creator of puzzles based on logic and inference. Rigorous, modern, piquant; reflecting their author's unusual personality, these intermediate and advanced puzzles all involve the ability to reason clearly through complex situations; some call for mathematical knowledge, ranging from algebra to number theory. Solutions. xi + 180pp. 5⅜ x 8.
T736 Paperbound **$1.25**

MATHEMATICAL PUZZLES FOR BEGINNERS AND ENTHUSIASTS, G. Mott-Smith. 188 mathematical puzzles based on algebra, dissection of plane figures, permutations, and probability, that will test and improve your powers of inference and interpretation. The Odic Force, The Spider's Cousin, Ellipse Drawing, theory and strategy of card and board games like tit-tat-toe, go moku, salvo, and many others. 100 pages of detailed mathematical explanations. Appendix of primes, square roots, etc. 135 illustrations. 2nd revised edition. 248pp. 5⅜ x 8.
T198 Paperbound **$1.00**

MATHEMAGIC, MAGIC PUZZLES, AND GAMES WITH NUMBERS, R. V. Heath. More than 60 new puzzles and stunts based on the properties of numbers. Easy techniques for multiplying large numbers mentally, revealing hidden numbers magically, finding the date of any day in any year, and dozens more. Over 30 pages devoted to magic squares, triangles, cubes, circles, etc. Edited by J. S. Meyer. 76 illustrations. 128pp. 5⅜ x 8.   T110 Paperbound **$1.00**

Entertainments, Humor

ODDITIES AND CURIOSITIES OF WORDS AND LITERATURE, C. Bombaugh, edited by M. Gardner. The largest collection of idiosyncratic prose and poetry techniques in English, a legendary work in the curious and amusing bypaths of literary recreations and the play technique in literature—so important in modern works. Contains alphabetic poetry, acrostics, palindromes, scissors verse, centos, emblematic poetry, famous literary puns, hoaxes, notorious slips of the press, hilarious mistranslations, and much more. Revised and enlarged with modern material by Martin Gardner. 368pp. 5⅜ x 8. T759 Paperbound **$1.50**

A NONSENSE ANTHOLOGY, collected by Carolyn Wells. 245 of the best nonsense verses ever written, including nonsense puns, absurd arguments, mock epics and sagas, nonsense ballads, odes, "sick" verses, dog-Latin verses, French nonsense verses, songs. By Edward Lear, Lewis Carroll, Gelett Burgess, W. S. Gilbert, Hilaire Belloc, Peter Newell, Oliver Herford, etc., 83 writers in all plus over four score anonymous nonsense verses. A special section of limericks, plus famous nonsense such as Carroll's "Jabberwocky" and Lear's "The Jumblies" and much excellent verse virtually impossible to locate elsewhere. For 50 years considered the best anthology available. Index of first lines specially prepared for this edition. Introduction by Carolyn Wells. 3 indexes: Title, Author, First lines. xxxiii + 279pp. T499 Paperbound **$1.25**

THE BAD CHILD'S BOOK OF BEASTS, MORE BEASTS FOR WORSE CHILDREN, and A MORAL ALPHA-BET, H. Belloc. Hardly an anthology of humorous verse has appeared in the last 50 years without at least a couple of these famous nonsense verses. But one must see the entire volumes—with all the delightful original illustrations by Sir Basil Blackwood—to appreciate fully Belloc's charming and witty verses that play so subacidly on the platitudes of life and morals that beset his day—and ours. A great humor classic. Three books in one. Total of 157pp. 5⅜ x 8. T749 Paperbound **$1.00**

THE DEVIL'S DICTIONARY, Ambrose Bierce. Sardonic and irreverent barbs puncturing the pomposities and absurdities of American politics, business, religion, literature, and arts, by the country's greatest satirist in the classic tradition. Epigrammatic as Shaw, piercing as Swift, American as Mark Twain, Will Rogers, and Fred Allen, Bierce will always remain the favorite of a small coterie of enthusiasts, and of writers and speakers whom he supplies with "some of the most gorgeous witticisms of the English language" (H. L. Mencken). Over 1000 entries in alphabetical order. 144pp. 5⅜ x 8. T487 Paperbound **$1.00**

THE PURPLE COW AND OTHER NONSENSE, Gelett Burgess. The best of Burgess's early nonsense, selected from the first edition of the "Burgess Nonsense Book." Contains many of his most unusual and truly awe-inspiring pieces: 36 nonsense quatrains, the Poems of Patagonia, Alpha-bet of Famous Goops, and the other hilarious (and rare) adult nonsense that place him in the forefront of American humorists. All pieces are accompanied by the original Burgess illustrations. 123 illustrations. xiii + 113pp. 5⅜ x 8. T772 Paperbound **$1.00**

MY PIOUS FRIENDS AND DRUNKEN COMPANIONS and MORE PIOUS FRIENDS AND DRUNKEN COMPANIONS, Frank Shay. Folksingers, amateur and professional, and everyone who loves singing: here, available for the first time in 30 years, is this valued collection of 132 ballads, blues, vaudeville numbers, drinking songs, sea chanties, comedy songs. Songs of pre-Beatnik Bohemia; songs from all over America, England, France, Australia; the great songs of the Naughty Nineties and early twentieth-century America. Over a third with music. Woodcuts by John Held, Jr. convey perfectly the brash insouciance of an era of rollicking unabashed song. 12 illustrations by John Held, Jr. Two indexes (Titles and First lines and Choruses). Introductions by the author. Two volumes bound as one. Total of xvi + 235pp. 5⅜ x 8½. T946 Paperbound **$1.00**

HOW TO TELL THE BIRDS FROM THE FLOWERS, R. W. Wood. How not to confuse a carrot with a parrot, a grape with an ape, a puffin with nuffin. Delightful drawings, clever puns, absurd little poems point out far-fetched resemblances in nature. The author was a leading physicist. Introduction by Margaret Wood White. 106 illus. 60pp. 5⅜ x 8. T523 Paperbound **75¢**

PECK'S BAD BOY AND HIS PA, George W. Peck. The complete edition, containing both volumes, of one of the most widely read American humor books. The endless ingenious pranks played by bad boy "Hennery" on his pa and the grocery man, the outraged pomposity of Pa, the perpetual ridiculing of middle class institutions, are as entertaining today as they were in 1883. No pale sophistications or subtleties, but rather humor vigorous, raw, earthy, imaginative, and, as folk humor often is, sadistic. This peculiarly fascinating book is also valuable to historians and students of American culture as a portrait of an age. 100 original illustrations by True Williams. Introduction by E. F. Bleiler. 347pp. 5⅜ x 8. T497 Paperbound **$1.35**

Americana

THE EYES OF DISCOVERY, J. Bakeless. A vivid reconstruction of how unspoiled America appeared to the first white men. Authentic and enlightening accounts of Hudson's landing in New York, Coronado's trek through the Southwest; scores of explorers, settlers, trappers, soldiers. America's pristine flora, fauna, and Indians in every region and state in fresh and unusual new aspects. "A fascinating view of what the land was like before the first highway went through," Time. 68 contemporary illustrations, 39 newly added in this edition. Index. Bibliography. x + 500pp. 5⅜ x 8.   T761 Paperbound **$2.00**

AUDUBON AND HIS JOURNALS, J. J. Audubon. A collection of fascinating accounts of Europe and America in the early 1800's through Audubon's own eyes. Includes the Missouri River Journals —an eventful trip through America's untouched heartland, the Labrador Journals, the European Journals, the famous "Episodes", and other rare Audubon material, including the descriptive chapters from the original letterpress edition of the "Ornithological Studies", omitted in all later editions. Indispensable for ornithologists, naturalists, and all lovers of Americana and adventure. 70-page biography by Audubon's granddaughter. 38 illustrations. Index. Total of 1106pp. 5⅜ x 8.
T675 Vol I Paperbound **$2.00**
T676 Vol II Paperbound **$2.00**
The set **$4.00**

TRAVELS OF WILLIAM BARTRAM, edited by Mark Van Doren. The first inexpensive illustrated edition of one of the 18th century's most delightful books is an excellent source of first-hand material on American geography, anthropology, and natural history. Many descriptions of early Indian tribes are our only source of information on them prior to the infiltration of the white man. "The mind of a scientist with the soul of a poet," John Livingston Lowes. 13 original illustrations and maps. Edited with an introduction by Mark Van Doren. 448pp. 5⅜ x 8.
T13 Paperbound **$2.00**

GARRETS AND PRETENDERS: A HISTORY OF BOHEMIANISM IN AMERICA, A. Parry. The colorful and fantastic history of American Bohemianism from Poe to Kerouac. This is the only complete record of hoboes, cranks, starving poets, and suicides. Here are Pfaff, Whitman, Crane, Bierce, Pound, and many others. New chapters by the author and by H. T. Moore bring this thorough and well-documented history down to the Beatniks. "An excellent account," N. Y. Times. Scores of cartoons, drawings, and caricatures. Bibliography. Index. xxviii + 421pp. 5⅝ x 8⅜.   T708 Paperbound **$1.95**

THE EXPLORATION OF THE COLORADO RIVER AND ITS CANYONS, J. W. Powell. The thrilling first-hand account of the expedition that filled in the last white space on the map of the United States. Rapids, famine, hostile Indians, and mutiny are among the perils encountered as the unknown Colorado Valley reveals its secrets. This is the only uncut version of Major Powell's classic of exploration that has been printed in the last 60 years. Includes later reflections and subsequent expedition. 250 illustrations, new map. 400pp. 5⅝ x 8⅜.
T94 Paperbound **$2.00**

THE JOURNAL OF HENRY D. THOREAU, Edited by Bradford Torrey and Francis H. Allen. Henry Thoreau is not only one of the most important figures in American literature and social thought; his voluminous journals (from which his books emerged as selections and crystalliza-tions) constitute both the longest, most sensitive record of personal internal development and a most penetrating description of a historical moment in American culture. This present set, which was first issued in fourteen volumes, contains Thoreau's entire journals from 1837 to 1862, with the exception of the lost years which were found only recently. We are reissuing it, complete and unabridged, with a new introduction by Walter Harding, Secretary of the Thoreau Society. Fourteen volumes reissued in two volumes. Foreword by Henry Seidel Canby. Total of 1888pp. 8⅜ x 12¼.   T312-3 Two volume set, Clothbound **$20.00**

GAMES AND SONGS OF AMERICAN CHILDREN, collected by William Wells Newell. A remarkable collection of 190 games with songs that accompany many of them; cross references to show similarities, differences among them; variations; musical notation for 38 songs. Textual dis-cussions show relations with folk-drama and other aspects of folk tradition. Grouped into categories for ready comparative study: Love-games, histories, playing at work, human life, bird and beast, mythology, guessing-games, etc. New introduction covers relations of songs and dances to timeless heritage of folklore, biographical sketch of Newell, other pertinent data. A good source of inspiration for those in charge of groups of children and a valuable reference for anthropologists, sociologists, psychiatrists. Introduction by Carl Withers. New indexes of first lines, games. 5⅜ x 8½. xii + 242pp.   T354 Paperbound **$1.65**

Philosophy, Religion

GUIDE TO PHILOSOPHY, C. E. M. Joad. A modern classic which examines many crucial problems which man has pondered through the ages: Does free will exist? Is there plan in the universe? How do we know and validate our knowledge? Such opposed solutions as subjective idealism and realism, chance and teleology, vitalism and logical positivism, are evaluated and the contributions of the great philosophers from the Greeks to moderns like Russell, Whitehead, and others, are considered in the context of each problem. "The finest introduction," BOSTON TRANSCRIPT. Index. Classified bibliography. 592pp. 5⅜ x 8.
T297 Paperbound **$2.00**

HISTORY OF ANCIENT PHILOSOPHY, W. Windelband. One of the clearest, most accurate comprehensive surveys of Greek and Roman philosophy. Discusses ancient philosophy in general, intellectual life in Greece in the 7th and 6th centuries B.C., Thales, Anaximander, Anaximenes, Heraclitus, the Eleatics, Empedocles, Anaxagoras, Leucippus, the Pythagoreans, the Sophists, Socrates, Democritus (20 pages), Plato (50 pages), Aristotle (70 pages), the Peripatetics, Stoics, Epicureans, Sceptics, Neo-platonists, Christian Apologists, etc. 2nd German edition translated by H. E. Cushman. xv + 393pp. 5⅜ x 8.
T357 Paperbound **$1.85**

ILLUSTRATIONS OF THE HISTORY OF MEDIEVAL THOUGHT AND LEARNING, R. L. Poole. Basic analysis of the thought and lives of the leading philosophers and ecclesiastics from the 8th to the 14th century—Abailard, Ockham, Wycliffe, Marsiglio of Padua, and many other great thinkers who carried the torch of Western culture and learning through the "Dark Ages": political, religious, and metaphysical views. Long a standard work for scholars and one of the best introductions to medieval thought for beginners. Index. 10 Appendices. xiii + 327pp. 5⅜ x 8.
T674 Paperbound **$1.85**

PHILOSOPHY AND CIVILIZATION IN THE MIDDLE AGES, M. de Wulf. This semi-popular survey covers aspects of medieval intellectual life such as religion, philosophy, science, the arts, etc. It also covers feudalism vs. Catholicism, rise of the universities, mendicant orders, monastic centers, and similar topics. Unabridged. Bibliography. Index. viii + 320pp. 5⅜ x 8.
T284 Paperbound **$1.75**

AN INTRODUCTION TO SCHOLASTIC PHILOSOPHY, Prof. M. de Wulf. Formerly entitled SCHOLASTICISM OLD AND NEW, this volume examines the central scholastic tradition from St. Anselm, Albertus Magnus, Thomas Aquinas, up to Suarez in the 17th century. The relation of scholasticism to ancient and medieval philosophy and science in general is clear and easily followed. The second part of the book considers the modern revival of scholasticism, the Louvain position, relations with Kantianism and Positivism. Unabridged. xvi + 271pp. 5⅜ x 8.
T296 Clothbound **$3.50**
T283 Paperbound **$1.75**

A HISTORY OF MODERN PHILOSOPHY, H. Höffding. An exceptionally clear and detailed coverage of western philosophy from the Renaissance to the end of the 19th century. Major and minor men such as Pomponazzi, Bodin, Boehme, Telesius, Bruno, Copernicus, da Vinci, Kepler, Galileo, Bacon, Descartes, Hobbes, Spinoza, Leibniz, Wolff, Locke, Newton, Berkeley, Hume, Erasmus, Montesquieu, Voltaire, Diderot, Rousseau, Lessing, Kant, Herder, Fichte, Schelling, Hegel, Schopenhauer, Comte, Mill, Darwin, Spencer, Hartmann, Lange, and many others, are discussed in terms of theory of knowledge, logic, cosmology, and psychology. Index. 2 volumes, total of 1159pp. 5⅜ x 8.
T117 Vol. 1, Paperbound **$2.00**
T118 Vol. 2, Paperbound **$2.00**

ARISTOTLE, A. E. Taylor. A brilliant, searching non-technical account of Aristotle and his thought written by a foremost Platonist. It covers the life and works of Aristotle; classification of the sciences; logic; first philosophy; matter and form; causes; motion and eternity; God; physics; metaphysics; and similar topics. Bibliography. New Index compiled for this edition. 128pp. 5⅜ x 8.
T280 Paperbound **$1.00**

THE SYSTEM OF THOMAS AQUINAS, M. de Wulf. Leading Neo-Thomist, one of founders of University of Louvain, gives concise exposition to central doctrines of Aquinas, as a means toward determining his value to modern philosophy, religion. Formerly "Medieval Philosophy Illustrated from the System of Thomas Aquinas." Trans. by E. Messenger. Introduction. 151pp. 5⅜ x 8.
T568 Paperbound **$1.25**

LEIBNIZ, H. W. Carr. Most stimulating middle-level coverage of basic philosophical thought of Leibniz. Easily understood discussion, analysis of major works: "Theodicy," "Principles of Nature and Grace," "Monadology"; Leibniz's influence; intellectual growth; correspondence; disputes with Bayle, Malebranche, Newton; importance of his thought today, with reinterpretation in modern terminology. "Power and mastery," London Times. Bibliography. Index. 226pp. 5⅜ x 8.
T624 Paperbound **$1.35**

CATALOGUE OF DOVER BOOKS

AN ESSAY CONCERNING HUMAN UNDERSTANDING, John Locke. Edited by A. C. Fraser. Unabridged reprinting of definitive edition; only complete edition of "Essay" in print. Marginal analyses of almost every paragraph; hundreds of footnotes; authoritative 140-page biographical, critical, historical prolegomena. Indexes. 1170pp. 5⅜ x 8.
T530 Vol. 1 (Books 1, 2) Paperbound **$2.25**
T531 Vol. 2 (Books 3, 4) Paperbound **$2.25**
2 volume set **$4.50**

THE PHILOSOPHY OF HISTORY, G. W. F. Hegel. One of the great classics of western thought which reveals Hegel's basic principle: that history is not chance but a rational process, the realization of the Spirit of Freedom. Ranges from the oriental cultures of subjective thought to the classical subjective cultures, to the modern absolute synthesis where spiritual and secular may be reconciled. Translation and introduction by J. Sibree. Introduction by C. Hegel. Special introduction for this edition by Prof. Carl Friedrich. xxxix + 447pp. 5⅜ x 8.
T112 Paperbound **$1.85**

THE PHILOSOPHY OF HEGEL, W. T. Stace. The first detailed analysis of Hegel's thought in English, this is especially valuable since so many of Hegel's works are out of print. Dr. Stace examines Hegel's debt to Greek idealists and the 18th century and then proceeds to a careful description and analysis of Hegel's first principles, categories, reason, dialectic method, his logic, philosophy of nature and spirit, etc. Index. Special 14 x 20 chart of Hegelian system. x + 526pp. 5⅜ x 8.
T254 Paperbound **$2.25**

THE WILL TO BELIEVE and HUMAN IMMORTALITY, W. James. Two complete books bound as one. THE WILL TO BELIEVE discusses the interrelations of belief, will, and intellect in man; chance vs. determinism, free will vs. determinism, free will vs. fate, pluralism vs. monism; the philosophies of Hegel and Spencer, and more. HUMAN IMMORTALITY examines the question of survival after death and develops an unusual and powerful argument for immortality. Two prefaces. Index. Total of 429pp. 5⅜ x 8.
T291 Paperbound **$1.75**

THE WORLD AND THE INDIVIDUAL, Josiah Royce. Only major effort by an American philosopher to interpret order of things in systematic, comprehensive manner. Royce's formulation of an absolute voluntarism remains one of the original and profound solutions to the problems involved. Part One, Four Historical Conceptions of Being, inquires into first principles, true meaning and place of individuality. Part Two, Nature, Man, and the Moral Order, is application of first principles to problems concerning religion, evil, moral order. Introduction by J. E. Smith, Yale Univ. Index. 1070pp. 5⅜ x 8.
T561 Vol. 1 Paperbound **$2.25**
T562 Vol. 2 Paperbound **$2.25**
Two volume set **$4.50**

THE PHILOSOPHICAL WRITINGS OF PEIRCE, edited by J. Buchler. This book (formerly THE PHILOSOPHY OF PEIRCE) is a carefully integrated exposition of Peirce's complete system composed of selections from his own work. Symbolic logic, scientific method, theory of signs, pragmatism, epistemology, chance, cosmology, ethics, and many other topics are treated by one of the greatest philosophers of modern times. This is the only inexpensive compilation of his key ideas. xvi + 386pp. 5⅜ x 8.
T217 Paperbound **$2.00**

EXPERIENCE AND NATURE, John Dewey. An enlarged, revised edition of the Paul Carus lectures which Dewey delivered in 1925. It covers Dewey's basic formulation of the problem of knowledge, with a full discussion of other systems, and a detailing of his own concepts of the relationship of external world, mind, and knowledge. Starts with a thorough examination of the philosophical method; examines the interrelationship of experience and nature; analyzes experience on basis of empirical naturalism, the formulation of law, role of language and social factors in knowledge; etc. Dewey's treatment of central problems in philosophy is profound but extremely easy to follow. ix + 448pp. 5⅜ x 8.
T471 Paperbound **$1.85**

THE PHILOSOPHICAL WORKS OF DESCARTES. The definitive English edition of all the major philosophical works and letters of René Descartes. All of his revolutionary insights, from his famous "Cogito ergo sum" to his detailed account of contemporary science and his astonishingly fruitful concept that all phenomena of the universe (except mind) could be reduced to clear laws by the use of mathematics. An excellent source for the thought of men like Hobbes, Arnauld, Gassendi, etc., who were Descarte's contemporaries. Translated by E. S. Haldane and G. Ross. Introductory notes. Index. Total of 842pp. 5⅜ x 8.
T71 Vol. 1, Paperbound **$2.00**
T72 Vol. 2, Paperbound **$2.00**

THE CHIEF WORKS OF SPINOZA. An unabridged reprint of the famous Bohn edition containing all of Spinoza's most important works: Vol. I: The Theologico-Political Treatise and the Political Treatise. Vol. II: On The Improvement Of Understanding, The Ethics, Selected Letters. Profound and enduring ideas on God, the universe, pantheism, society, religion, the state, democracy, the mind, emotions, freedom and the nature of man, which influenced Goethe, Hegel, Schelling, Coleridge, Whitehead, and many others. Introduction. 2 volumes. 826pp. 5⅜ x 8.
T249 Vol. I, Paperbound **$1.50**
T250 Vol. II, Paperbound **$1.50**

CATALOGUE OF DOVER BOOKS

THE SENSE OF BEAUTY, G. Santayana. A revelation of the beauty of language as well as an important philosophic treatise, this work studies the "why, when, and how beauty appears, what conditions an object must fulfill to be beautiful, what elements of our nature make us sensible of beauty, and what the relation is between the constitution of the object and the excitement of our susceptibility." "It is doubtful if a better treatment of the subject has since been published," PEABODY JOURNAL. Index. ix + 275pp. 5⅜ x 8.
T238 Paperbound **$1.00**

PROBLEMS OF ETHICS, Moritz Schlick. The renowned leader of the "Vienna Circle" applies the logical positivist approach to a wide variety of ethical problems: the source and means of attaining knowledge, the formal and material characteristics of the good, moral norms and principles, absolute vs. relative values, free will and responsibility, comparative importance of pleasure and suffering as ethical values, etc. Disarmingly simple and straightforward despite complexity of subject. First English translation, authorized by author before his death, of a thirty-year old classic. Translated and with an introduction by David Rynin. Index. Foreword by Prof. George P. Adams. xxi + 209pp. 5⅜ x 8. T946 Paperbound **$1.45**

AN INTRODUCTION TO EXISTENTIALISM, Robert G. Olson. A new and indispensable guide to one of the major thought systems of our century, the movement that is central to the thinking of some of the most creative figures of the past hundred years. Stresses Heidegger and Sartre, with careful and objective examination of the existentialist position, values—freedom of choice, individual dignity, personal love, creative effort—and answers to the eternal questions of the human condition. Scholarly, unbiased, analytic, unlike most studies of this difficult subject, Prof. Olson's book is aimed at the student of philosophy as well as at the reader with no formal training who is looking for an absorbing, accessible, and thorough introduction to the basic texts. Index. xv + 221pp. 5⅜ x 8½. T55 Paperbound **$1.45**

SYMBOLIC LOGIC, C. I. Lewis and C. H. Langford. Since first publication in 1932, this has been among most frequently cited works on symbolic logic. Still one of the best introductions both for beginners and for mathematicians, philosophers. First part covers basic topics which easily lend themselves to beginning study. Second part is rigorous, thorough development of logistic method, examination of some of most difficult and abstract aspects of symbolic logic, including modal logic, logical paradoxes, many-valued logic, with Prof. Lewis' own contributions. 2nd revised (corrected) edition. 3 appendixes, one new to this edition. 524pp. 5⅜ x 8.
S170 Paperbound **$2.00**

WHITEHEAD'S PHILOSOPHY OF CIVILIZATION, A. H. Johnson. A leading authority on Alfred North Whitehead synthesizes the great philosopher's thought on civilization, scattered throughout various writings, into unified whole. Analysis of Whitehead's general definition of civilization, his reflections on history and influences on its development, his religion, including his analysis of Christianity, concept of solitariness as first requirement of personal religion, and so on. Other chapters cover views on minority groups, society, civil liberties, education. Also critical comments on Whitehead's philosophy. Written with general reader in mind. A perceptive introduction to important area of the thought of a leading philosopher of our century. Revised index and bibliography. xii + 211pp. 5⅜ x 8½.
T996 Paperbound **$1.50**

WHITEHEAD'S THEORY OF REALITY, A. H. Johnson. Introductory outline of Whitehead's theory of actual entities, the heart of his philosophy of reality, followed by his views on nature of God, philosophy of mind, theory of value (truth, beauty, goodness and their opposites), analyses of other philosophers, attitude toward science. A perspicacious lucid introduction by author of dissertation on Whitehead, written under the subject's supervision at Harvard. Good basic view for beginning students of philosophy and for those who are simply interested in important contemporary ideas. Revised index and bibliography. xiii + 267pp. 5⅜ x 8½.
T989 Paperbound **$1.50**

MIND AND THE WORLD-ORDER, C. I. Lewis. Building upon the work of Peirce, James, and Dewey, Professor Lewis outlines a theory of knowledge in terms of "conceptual pragmatism." Dividing truth into abstract mathematical certainty and empirical truth, the author demonstrates that the traditional understanding of the a priori must be abandoned. Detailed analyses of philosophy, metaphysics, method, the "given" in experience, knowledge of objects, nature of the a priori, experience and order, and many others. Appendices. xiv + 446pp. 5⅜ x 8.
T359 Paperbound **$1.95**

SCEPTICISM AND ANIMAL FAITH, G. Santayana. To eliminate difficulties in the traditional theory of knowledge, Santayana distinguishes between the independent existence of objects and the essence our mind attributes to them. Scepticism is thereby established as a form of belief, and animal faith is shown to be a necessary condition of knowledge. Belief, classical idealism, intuition, memory, symbols, literary psychology, and much more, discussed with unusual clarity and depth. Index. xii + 314pp. 5⅜ x 8. T235 Clothbound **$3.50**
T236 Paperbound **$1.50**

LANGUAGE AND MYTH, E. Cassirer. Analyzing the non-rational thought processes which go to make up culture, Cassirer demonstrates that beneath both language and myth there lies a dominant unconscious "grammar" of experience whose categories and canons are not those of logical thought. His analyses of seemingly diverse phenomena such as Indian metaphysics, the Melanesian "mana," the Naturphilosophie of Schelling, modern poetry, etc., are profound without being pedantic. Introduction and translation by Susanne Langer. Index. x + 103pp. 5⅜ x 8.
T51 Paperbound **$1.25**

CATALOGUE OF DOVER BOOKS

*THE ANALYSIS OF MATTER, Bertrand Russell. A classic which has retained its importance in understanding the relation between modern physical theory and human perception. Logical analysis of physics, prerelativity physics, causality, scientific inference, Weyl's theory, tensors, invariants and physical interpretations, periodicity, and much more is treated with Russell's usual brilliance. "Masterly piece of clear thinking and clear writing," NATION AND ATHENAE-UM. "Most thorough treatment of the subject," THE NATION. Introduction. Index. 8 figures. viii + 408pp. 5⅜ x 8.　　　　　　　　　　　　　　　　　　　　　　S231 Paperbound **$1.95**

CONCEPTUAL THINKING (A LOGICAL INQUIRY), S. Körner. Discusses origin, use of general concepts on which language is based, and the light they shed on basic philosophical questions. Rigorously examines how different concepts are related; how they are linked to experience; problems in the field of contact between exact logical, mathematical, and scientific concepts, and the inexactness of everyday experience (studied at length). This work elaborates many new approaches to the traditional problems of philosophy—epistemology, value theories, metaphysics, aesthetics, morality. "Rare originality . . . brings a new rigour into philosophical argument," Philosophical Quarterly. New corrected second edition. Index. vii + 301pp. 5⅜ x 8　　　　　　　　　　　　　　　　　　　　　T516 Paperbound **$1.75**

INTRODUCTION TO SYMBOLIC LOGIC, S. Langer. No special knowledge of math required — probably the clearest book ever written on symbolic logic, suitable for the layman, general scientist, and philosopher. You start with simple symbols and advance to a knowledge of the Boole-Schroeder and Russell-Whitehead systems. Forms, logical structure, classes, the calculus of propositions, logic of the syllogism, etc., are all covered. "One of the clearest and simplest introductions," MATHEMATICS GAZETTE. Second enlarged, revised edition. 368pp. 5⅜ x 8.　　　　　　　　　　　　　　　　　　　　　　　S164 Paperbound **$1.75**

LANGUAGE, TRUTH AND LOGIC, A. J. Ayer. A clear, careful analysis of the basic ideas of Logical Positivism. Building on the work of Schlick, Russell, Carnap, and the Viennese School, Mr. Ayer develops a detailed exposition of the nature of philosophy, science, and metaphysics; the Self and the World; logic and common sense, and other philosophic concepts. An aid to clarity of thought as well as the first full-length development of Logical Positivism in English. Introduction by Bertrand Russell. Index. 160pp. 5⅜ x 8.　　　　　　　T10 Paperbound **$1.25**

ESSAYS IN EXPERIMENTAL LOGIC, J. Dewey. Based upon the theory that knowledge implies a judgment which in turn implies an inquiry, these papers consider the inquiry stage in terms of: the relationship of thought and subject matter, antecedents of thought, data and meanings. 3 papers examine Bertrand Russell's thought, while 2 others discuss pragmatism and a final essay presents a new theory of the logic of values. Index. viii + 444pp. 5⅜ x 8.　　　　　　　　　　　　　　　　　　　　　　　　　　　T73 Paperbound **$1.95**

TRAGIC SENSE OF LIFE, M. de Unamuno. The acknowledged masterpiece of one of Spain's most influential thinkers. Between the despair at the inevitable death of man and all his works and the desire for something better, Unamuno finds that "saving incertitude" that alone can console us. This dynamic appraisal of man's faith in God and in himself has been called "a masterpiece" by the ENCYCLOPAEDIA BRITANNICA. xxx + 332pp. 5⅜ x 8. 　　　　　　　　　　　　　　　　　　　　　　　　　　　　T257 Paperbound **$1.95**

HISTORY OF DOGMA, A. Harnack. Adolph Harnack, who died in 1930, was perhaps the greatest Church historian of all time. In this epoch-making history, which has never been surpassed in comprehensiveness and wealth of learning, he traces the development of the authoritative Christian doctrinal system from its first crystallization in the 4th century down through the Reformation, including also a brief survey of the later developments through the Infallibility decree of 1870. He reveals the enormous influence of Greek thought on the early Fathers, and discusses such topics as the Apologists, the great councils, Manichaeism, the historical position of Augustine, the medieval opposition to indulgences, the rise of Protestantism, the relations of Luther's doctrines with modern tendencies of thought, and much more. "Monumental work; still the most valuable history of dogma . . . luminous analysis of the problems . . . abounds in suggestion and stimulus and can be neglected by no one who desires to understand the history of thought in this most important field," Dutcher's Guide to Historical Literature. Translated by Neil Buchanan. Index. Unabridged reprint in 4 volumes. Vol I: Beginnings to the Gnostics and Marcion. Vol II & III: 2nd century to the 4th century Fathers. Vol IV & V: 4th century Councils to the Carlovingian Renaissance. Vol VI & VII: Period of Clugny (c. 1000) to the Reformation, and after. Total of cii + 2407pp. 5⅜ x 8.

T904 Vol I	Paperbound	**$2.50**
T905 Vol II & III	Paperbound	**$2.50**
T906 Vol IV & V	Paperbound	**$2.50**
T907-Vol VI & VII	Paperbound	**$2.50**
	The set	**$10.00**

THE GUIDE FOR THE PERPLEXED, Maimonides. One of the great philosophical works of all time and a necessity for everyone interested in the philosophy of the Middle Ages in the Jewish, Christian, and Moslem traditions. Maimonides develops a common meeting-point for the Old Testament and the Aristotelian thought which pervaded the medieval world. His ideas and methods predate such scholastics as Aquinas and Scotus and throw light on the entire problem of philosophy or science vs. religion. 2nd revised edition. Complete unabridged Friedländer translation. 55 page introduction to Maimonides's life, period, etc., with an important summary of the GUIDE. Index. lix + 414pp. 5⅜ x 8.　　　T351 Paperbound **$2.00**

Orientalia

ORIENTAL RELIGIONS IN ROMAN PAGANISM, F. Cumont. A study of the cultural meeting of east and west in the Early Roman Empire. It covers the most important eastern religions of the time from their first appearance in Rome, 204 B.C., when the Great Mother of the Gods was first brought over from Syria. The ecstatic cults of Syria and Phrygia — Cybele, Attis, Adonis, their orgies and mutilation rites; the mysteries of Egypt — Serapis, Isis, Osiris, the dualism of Persia, the elevation of cosmic evil to equal stature with the deity, Mithra; worship of Hermes Trismegistus; Ishtar, Astarte; the magic of the ancient Near East, etc. Introduction. 55pp. of notes; extensive bibliography. Index. xxiv + 298pp. 5⅜ x 8.
T321 Paperbound **$1.75**

THE MYSTERIES OF MITHRA, F. Cumont. The definitive coverage of a great ideological struggle between the west and the orient in the first centuries of the Christian era. The origin of Mithraism, a Persian mystery religion, and its association with the Roman army is discussed in detail. Then utilizing fragmentary monuments and texts, in one of the greatest feats of scholarly detection, Dr. Cumont reconstructs the mystery teachings and secret doctrines, the hidden organization and cult of Mithra. Mithraic art is discussed, analyzed, and depicted in 70 illustrations. 239pp. 5⅜ x 8.
T323 Paperbound **$1.85**

CHRISTIAN AND ORIENTAL PHILOSOPHY OF ART, A. K. Coomaraswamy. A unique fusion of philosopher, orientalist, art historian, and linguist, the author discusses such matters as: the true function of aesthetics in art, the importance of symbolism, intellectual and philosophic backgrounds, the role of traditional culture in enriching art, common factors in all great art, the nature of medieval art, the nature of folklore, the beauty of mathematics, and similar topics. 2 illustrations. Bibliography. 148pp. 5⅜ x 8.
T378 Paperbound **$1.25**

TRANSFORMATION OF NATURE IN ART, A. K. Coomaraswamy. Unabridged reissue of a basic work upon Asiatic religious art and philosophy of religion. The theory of religious art in Asia and Medieval Europe (exemplified by Meister Eckhart) is analyzed and developed. Detailed consideration is given to Indian medieval aesthetic manuals, symbolic language in philosophy, the origin and use of images in India, and many other fascinating and little known topics. Glossaries of Sanskrit and Chinese terms. Bibliography. 41pp. of notes. 245pp. 5⅜ x 8.
T368 Paperbound **$1.75**

BUDDHIST LOGIC, F.Th. Stcherbatsky. A study of an important part of Buddhism usually ignored by other books on the subject: the Mahayana buddhistic logic of the school of Dignaga and his followers. First vol. devoted to history of Indian logic with Central Asian continuations, detailed exposition of Dignaga system, including theory of knowledge, the sensible world (causation, perception, ultimate reality) and mental world (judgment, inference, logical fallacies, the syllogism), reality of external world, and negation (law of contradiction, universals, dialectic). Vol. II contains translation of Dharmakirti's Nyayabindu with Dharmamottara's commentary. Appendices cover translations of Tibetan treatises on logic, Hindu attacks on Buddhist logic, etc. The basic work, one of the products of the great St. Petersburg school of Indian studies. Written clearly and with an awareness of Western philosophy and logic; meant for the Asian specialist and for the general reader with only a minimum of background. Vol. I, xii + 559pp. Vol. II, viii + 468pp. 5⅜ x 8½.
T955 Vol. I Paperbound **$2.35**
T956 Vol. II Paperbound **$2.35**
The set **$4.70**

THE TEXTS OF TAOISM. The first inexpensive edition of the complete James Legge translations of the Tao Te King and the writings of Chinese mystic Chuang Tse. Also contains several shorter treatises: the T'ai Shang Tractate of Actions and Their Retributions; the King Kang King, or Classic of Purity; the Yin Fu King, or Classic of the Harmony of the Seen and Unseen; the Yu Shu King, or Classic of the Pivot of Jade; and the Hsia Yung King, or Classic of the Directory for a Day. While there are other translations of the Tao Te King, this is the only translation of Chuang Tse and much of other material. Extensive introduction discusses differences between Taoism, Buddhism, Confucianism; authenticity and arrangement of Tao Te King and writings of Chuang Tse; the meaning of the Tao and basic tenets of Taoism; historical accounts of Lao-tse and followers; other pertinent matters. Clarifying notes incorporated into text. Originally published as Volumes 39, 40 of SACRED BOOKS OF THE EAST series, this has long been recognized as an indispensible collection. Sinologists, philosophers, historians of religion will of course be interested and anyone with an elementary course in Oriental religion or philosophy will understand and profit from these writings. Index. Appendix analyzing thought of Chuang Tse. Vol. I, xxiii + 396pp. Vol. II, viii + 340pp. 5⅜ x 8½.
T990 Vol. I Paperbound **$2.00**
T991 Vol. II Paperbound **$2.00**

CATALOGUE OF DOVER BOOKS

EPOCHS OF CHINESE AND JAPANESE ART, Ernest T. Fenollosa. Although this classic of art history was written before the archeological discovery of Shang and Chou civilizations, it is still in many respects the finest detailed study of Chinese and Japanese art available in English. It is very wide in range, covering sculpture, carving, painting, metal work, ceramics, textiles, graphic arts and other areas, and it considers both religious and secular art, including the Japanese woodcut. Its greatest strength, however, lies in its extremely full, detailed, insight-laden discussion of historical and cultural background, and in its analysis of the religious and philosophical implications of art works. It is also a brilliant stylistic achievement, written with enthusiasm and verve, which can be enjoyed and read with profit by both the Orientalist and the general reader who is interested in art. Index. Glossary of proper names. 242 illustrations. Total of 704 pages. 5⅜ x 8½.

T364-5 Two vol. set, paperbound **$5.00**

THE VEDANTA SUTRAS OF BADARAYANA WITH COMMENTARY BY SANKARACHARYA. The definitive translation of the consummation, foremost interpretation of Upanishads. Originally part of SACRED BOOKS OF THE EAST, this two-volume translation includes exhaustive commentary and exegesis by Sankara; 128-page introduction by translator, Prof. Thibaut, that discusses background, scope and purpose of the sutras, value and importance of Sankara's interpretation; copious footnotes providing further explanations. Every serious student of Indian religion or thought, philosophers, historians of religion should read these clear, accurate translations of documents central to development of important thought systems in the East. Unabridged republication of Volumes 34, 38 of the Sacred Books of the East. Translated by George Thibault. General index, index of quotations and of Sanskrit. Vol. I, cxxv + 448pp. Vol. II, iv + 506pp. 5⅜ x 8½.

T994 Vol. I Paperbound **$2.00**
T995 Vol. II Paperbound **$2.00**

THE UPANISHADS. The Max Müller translation of the twelve classical Upanishads available for the first time in an inexpensive format: Chandogya, Kena, Aitareya aranyaka and upanishad, Kaushitaki, Isa, Katha, Mundaka, Taittiriyaka Brhadaranyaka, Svetarasvatara. Prasna — all of the classical Upanishads of the Vedanta school—and the Maitriyana Upanishad. Originally volumes 1, 15 of SACRED BOOKS OF THE EAST series, this is still the most scholarly translation. Prof. Müller, probably most important Sanskritologist of nineteenth century, provided invaluable introduction that acquaints readers with history of Upanishad translations, age and chronology of texts, etc. and a preface that discusses their value to Western readers. Heavily annotated. Stimulating reading for anyone with even only a basic course background in Oriental philosophy, religion, necessary to all Indologists, philosophers, religious historians. Transliteration and pronunciation guide. Vol. I, ciii + 320pp. Vol. II, liii + 350pp.

T992 Vol. I Paperbound **$2.00**
T993 Vol. II Paperbound **$2.00**
The set **$4.00**

Dover publishes books on art, music, philosophy, literature, languages, history, social sciences, psychology, handcrafts, orientalia, puzzles and entertainments, chess, pets and gardens, books explaining science, intermediate and higher mathematics mathematical physics, engineering, biological sciences, earth sciences, classics of science, etc. Write to:

Dept. catrr.
Dover Publications, Inc.
180 Varick Street, N. Y. 14, N. Y.

Purse 3 kinds of data   corresponding
                           phenomenological

1.   mere given   esthetics
2.   existence, impact   ethics
3.   relational, mediation   logic

all intrinsic values are outside of knowledge.